T0147955

SILVER DIASPORA

SILVER DIASPORA

A Journey up from
Hudson Aristocracy

CHRISTOPHER T. RAND

SILVER DIASPORA
A JOURNEY UP FROM HUDSON ARISTOCRACY

Copyright © 2014 Christopher T. Rand.

*All rights reserved. No part of this book may be used or reproduced by
any means, graphic, electronic, or mechanical, including photocopying,
recording, taping or by any information storage retrieval system
without the written permission of the publisher except in the case
of brief quotations embodied in critical articles and reviews.*

iUniverse books may be ordered through booksellers or by contacting:

iUniverse
1663 Liberty Drive
Bloomington, IN 47403
www.iuniverse.com
1-800-Authors (1-800-288-4677)

*Because of the dynamic nature of the Internet, any web addresses or
links contained in this book may have changed since publication and
may no longer be valid. The views expressed in this work are solely those
of the author and do not necessarily reflect the views of the publisher,
and the publisher hereby disclaims any responsibility for them.*

*Any people depicted in stock imagery provided by Thinkstock are
models, and such images are being used for illustrative purposes only.
Certain stock imagery © Thinkstock.*

ISBN: 978-1-4917-3994-5 (sc)
ISBN: 978-1-4917-3995-2 (e)

Library of Congress Control Number: 2014913594

Printed in the United States of America.

iUniverse rev. date: 09/12/2014

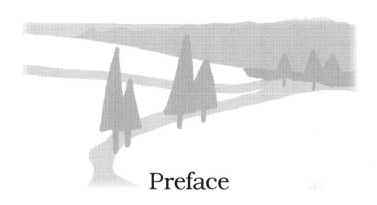

Preface

The story that unfolds here begins with the dissolution and dispersion my family and those closest to it experienced over the past century.

America's white, Anglo-Saxon elite has gradually, voluntarily and with some grace abandoned its political and economic dominance in the United States. This transformation, most unusual for any dominant ethnic group, has been fervently embraced by many members of this elite, sometimes for purely frivolous, even sexual reasons — exasperation over a stuffy culture or bad cooking, not to speak of the often extreme racism and substantial economic inequalities in the society at large. But it *has* happened, to such an extent that there is indeed no longer even any Protestant on the Supreme Court, and one will understand why after reading this story.

At the outset the members of the family, in all its length and breadth, lived in a world of great wealth. They were among the richest people in the United States. As a small child I heard my mother's mother describe her wealthy New York Gay Nineties Astor-Livingston past and her profligate siblings. In flashes I passed through a panorama of the many places at home and abroad on which the voyagers in the family focused alongside the vivid figures around them, with their adamant and often reckless acts and beliefs — a full cast in equal measure sarcastic, long-suffering, glamorous, blindly superstitious and randomly frustrated: comedians of the erratic.

They then came up against a dilemma, compelled to choose between staying on in their ancestral world or keeping up with the times in the nation around them and integrating themselves into the American mainstream. With each generation, the pressure on these individuals to choose between escape or immersion into the society — at considerable cost either way — became more and more intense. They passed through stages where their lifestyles became increasingly anomalous in the new country about them and came to see their status and relevance shaved down under the pressures they went through in this grinding mill of transformations.

The scene moved through the middle Hudson with its lavish estates, and my father's Connecticut hinterland lying behind the Hudson world, and its democratic townships contrasting sharply with my mother's Astor mansion and patroon neighbors as they radiated concentrically from the havens of frugal Congregationalist ministers, although they were affluent in their own right nonetheless.

My immediate family embarked on a voluntary diaspora in search of a better new world. My father struggled as the unyielding escapist, my mother the hypochondriac who fashioned her escape with his. In the early childhood I spent north of San Francisco in a world deeply shaken by the war in the Pacific and even the mystery of Hitler, distant as he was, my father left, assigned to China as an intelligence operative fighting the Japanese. In the aftermath of the war and its hangover, the remorseless Cold War, he resisted coming back to America but under family pressure returned grudgingly before quickly going back to the Far East as a journalist.

My mother, overburdened with responsibilities, moved us to Santa Barbara for the climate and we met a broad range of new characters. By then wholly estranged, she divorced my father and married a charismatic figure and gifted social organizer who introduced her to the glamorous Southern California world of high-level tennis. In the interim I went on to a boarding school back east, my father's alma mater. Off and on, the background rose up sharply and dominated these experiences in the old world. I saw shadows of my grandmother's earlier high times.

After school my exposure to the new times sharpened when I moved on to the University of California at Berkeley. My world at college expanded further, especially in a boarding house with students on the GI bill who had served in Germany and Korea. I became close to writers and linguists striving to preserve California Indian languages and they formed a refuge between the two worlds of fraternity life and leftish activism in the ubiquitous Cold War. Meanwhile I managed to spend time abroad with my father, one summer in Afghanistan, another at the Brussels World Fair. We traveled around and I absorbed his many theories on what was really happening in the world. My imagination inspired by travels in Afghanistan, I proceeded to study Arabic and Persian at Cal, hoping this would lead to brilliant involvement in the new world I saw dawning. I ventured on to the Middle East with fellowships for further studies, then proceeded on to New York and beyond in work related to the oil industry.

Inexorably, in the course of it all, the world of my parents and their company gave testimony that by the eighties the thirties were dead. Richard Nixon assumed the presidency and the Cold War claimed my father as one of its innumerable victims.

My mother, losing many of the closest people in her life in a very short time, including her second husband, became bereft. She lived a reclusive life for a while and then began traveling about, following the tracks of one of her uncles, who had done exploration in Africa in the late nineteenth century, pursuing an expedition fraught with disaster. In her travels she met a group of flying doctors in Kenya and joined their organization as a volunteer administrator. She stayed there almost twenty years and passed on a variety of descriptions and reminiscences.

By the nineties America had begun to squander the triumph and achievements it had struggled for half a century to attain. The Soviet Union collapsed but we all saw that this did not bring America peace after fifty years of hot and cold war. In time Nixon's eventual successor Reagan adopted his global policies and enlarged on them.

We soon mounted the preliminary invasion of Iraq under Reagan's successor, George H. W. Bush, under whom this country came more and more to resemble a giant Ponzi scheme. Nixon then died.

My mother, already alienated by our actions in Vietnam, reacted indignantly to my description of all this. As she aged, she had a couple of serious health setbacks in Kenya. She returned to America, visiting the Astors' ancient world again, now finding it physically deteriorating while paradoxically a new democracy had emerged in it. She secured a final residence for herself in a Santa Barbara retirement center and spent her declining years slowly turning demented and losing her ability to drive or even move around. I attended to her some in those days.

I share the thinking of many (perhaps most) people who have emerged from this Anglo-Saxon elite: it doesn't much matter who has political or even economic power in this country as long as its greatest values remain in place, foremost its legal, judiciary, and political systems. (Well, maybe with campaign finance and electoral college reform, the restructuring of the tax system and an end to the death penalty.) The diaspora has run its full circle.[*]

---

[*] For this insight I am indebted to an article by the Harvard law professor Noah Feldman, who states "The decline of the Protestant elite is actually its greatest triumph" (New York Times, June 20, 2010)

Contents

1
Once the Richest:
Astors and Livingstons

While we tend to assert America is a very young country, in my mother's family we had a slice, a tranche, of that new world that was ancient. It had largely arrived before the Revolution, established itself in this country over three hundred years ago and reached a peak of aristocracy. For a period after the Civil War (in which it was a major winner) it was perhaps the richest family in the nation. In ways it comported itself rather the way some families used to in Europe in the distant past. It radiated out from one of a cluster of major estates a hundred miles up the Hudson from New York City, most eminently the Vanderbilt and Mills Mansions and Hyde Park, the country estate of Franklin Delano Roosevelt.

My mother's mother, Margaret Chanler, grew up in that world as one of eight siblings descended from John Jacob Astor the tycoon. General John Armstrong established the mansion in which she grew up, Rokeby, in 1815. Armstrong had been President Madison's secretary of war and the United States' emissary to France in Napoleon's time and had a hand in the Louisiana Purchase. He also as it has been said "blotted his copybook" by letting the British burn the Capitol and White House in the War of 1812.

Napoleon gave him some merino sheep from his own farm in Corsica. Armstrong proceeded to raise those in this new estate, which he named La Bergerie, the Sheep Farm, in honor of Napoleon's gift. He actually built the house as a modest French villa in appreciation for architecture he had known in France and at the outset it had only two stories.

He then married Alida Livingston, a descendant of Robert Livingston, who in 1685 had been granted a massive area of land, Livingston Manor, running eastward from the Hudson above Poughkeepsie. Robert had helped draft the Declaration of Independence and his son and heir Philip signed it. They were aggressive landlords with an expansionist policy and a constabulary of their own. By the end of the nineteenth century their progeny with their various branches had come into possession of three-quarters of a million acres of land north of New York City in Columbia and Dutchess Counties. They owned most of the Catskills and everything in a band twenty or thirty miles wide stretching from the east bank of the Hudson to the Massachusetts and Connecticut state lines.

But General Armstrong's contemporary, Astor the tycoon, who had started out as a butcher in Waldorf, Germany, established a fortune which while perhaps not as great as the Livingstons' was far more enduring. His son, William Backhouse Astor, married General Armstrong's daughter Margaret — Peachy — "married conspicuously *up*," in the words of the chronicler Justin Kaplan. John Jacob, or William, then bought the Rokeby estate from General Armstrong for fifty thousand dollars.

Astor had come to the United States and honed his butchery skills by becoming a skinner and trader of animal pelts, which he acquired mostly from Indians in Canada. Those pelts at the time were the most valuable export commodity produced in North America. Astor's first enterprise was to ship the furs to Shanghai from a harbor he established — Astoria in Oregon — in exchange for teas, spices, and silks. This trade foundered and at that point he turned to acquire land in Wisconsin, Missouri and above all Manhattan. He moved there in 1784, discovered that New York City was expanding and sank his earnings into farmland just up from the inhabited areas of lower and central Manhattan (and Astoria, Queens), holding onto it, leasing it out to property developers but rarely selling it. He became perhaps the richest man in America in the process. Among Astor's biggest property acquisitions were the fruit of his discovery that some real estate in Manhattan was occupied by squatters who had no actual title to those lands; after thorough painstaking research Astor bought the properties and evicted the squatters, simply. He came to acquire five hundred properties in Manhattan, whose population had grown from 25,000 in 1780 to 500,000 when he died in 1848.

Astor had already given his son William Backhouse an excellent schooling, making sure he got the superb German university education he himself could only have dreamt about. This included studies in Heidelberg and Gottingen, with a hired tutor. While at Gottingen, William formed a close friendship with a man who later became a renowned philosopher, Arthur Schopenhauer.

Under William's inspiration, the old Armstrong estate was renamed Rokeby, after a similar property in a poem by Sir Walter Scott. William B. turned it into a neo-Gothic mansion and successive owners added the third story, mansard roof and tower and many of the bathrooms which now exist. With the growth in the family, it soon became necessary in any event to expand the original house, which could accommodate only two children or so, to its ultimate scale of forty-three rooms.

John Jacob's wealth became public knowledge when the *New York Herald* published his will at his death in 1848. The *Herald* had it totaling eighty million dollars, and William Astor, trained to become a partner in the business, doubled, perhaps even tripled that. (The chronicler Kaplan, however, says John Jacob died leaving just $20 to 30 million.)

Incidentally, it has been stated that while Astor and a number of other "robber barons of the Gilded Age" such as Rockefeller, Vanderbilt and Carnegie had immense fortunes — Rockefeller, Vanderbilt and Astor ranked one through three, with Jay Gould at eight — the present-day Mexican tycoon Carlos Slim, the world's richest man around the time of this writing, has ten times what they had combined, and in nineteenth century dollars to boot. (Slim, among other things, has an immense holding in *The New York Times*, exceeded only by that of the Sulzberger family.)

William and Armstrong's daughter had six children, the oldest of whom they named Emily after the heroine of *The Mysteries of Udolpho*, a bestseller of the time. Emily Astor married Sam Ward, a figure with spectacular ups and downs who remained central to family myth well into my mother's time. Grandson of a lieutenant colonel and son of the founder of the 40 Wall Street Bank, Ward drove the bank out of business, went out to California, made a fortune there, returned to New York and reopened the bank, which held on a while before collapsing again. At that Ward went to Washington, where he became a famous lobbyist of the day — the King of the Lobby, some called him.

Sam and Emily produced Margaret (also called Maddie), who married a Civil War officer and congressman named John Winthrop Chanler. They lived in a house on Thirty-fourth Street and had eight children who survived into adulthood, my grandmother Margaret and her siblings. They came to be called the Astor Orphans as Maddie and her husband John left them when they died in their forties.

Incidentally, the great composer Antonin Dvorak was also the son of a butcher in Central Europe and he too came to the United States, though unlike John Jacob Astor he stayed only for a while. But he left a magnificent legacy, perhaps a much greater one: a contribution that has lived on gloriously, beyond a flamboyant fortune.

2
Out from the Hudson: The Astor Grandmother

M y first encounter with my grandmother Margaret the Orphan came during World War Two at Miss Thomas' School in Tucson. I had been sent there at age seven from my home in Marin County north of San Francisco to recuperate from respiratory problems. By then Margaret Aldrich, as she had early in the twentieth century married Richard Aldrich, a music critic, came to visit me there. She had become a widow. She brought me a pale blue and white handkerchief showing the islands of Greece, the product of an organization she supported which backed the Greek resistance to the Nazi occupation. She went on to tell me that Uncle Ben, a close family friend in Marin, had passed away. I failed to understand what she meant and she tried to explain that he'd gone on to a better life.

She stood out like a fist in this humble western world. She was a product of the Gay Nineties, after a fashion, I came to learn over the years. Not that the Nineties were all that gay, in her case anyway, though at one point she had had hopes of becoming a concert singer. She was a great niece of Mrs. William Astor (Caroline, "Aunt Lina") and a distant cousin of Ward McAllister, a genteel native of Savannah and social climber who had gone out to San Francisco in the Gold Rush era, made a fortune there as a lawyer between 1850 and 1855 then moved on to New York, where he rose to become the major social arbiter of said Nineties and mentor to Mrs. William Astor.

In the words of the social historian Eric Homberger (Mrs. Astor's New York), "McAllister's world was to be found on the spine of Manhattan, on Fifth Avenue from Washington Square to the southern edge of Central Park." McAllister proclaimed that in those days there were "only four hundred people in fashionable New York society" and it was they who were entitled to inclusion in Mrs. Astor's annual ball. McAllister once even published a list of those four hundred. They turned out to number only 313 and consisted mostly of bankers, brokers and people of inherited wealth. They included a couple of dozen men, including McAllister himself, who called themselves the Patriarchs.

My grandmother disparaged McAllister as a "genial impresario" with "courtly manners and a great deal of social imagination" whose "famous number" was merely "a real estate detail": Mrs. Astor's ballroom had space for only four hundred, and even then she had to use the gallery beside her dining-ballroom to accommodate them. There were no musicians or actors among those 313 and no Harrimans or Rockefellers either. Their money was too new.

McAllister also maintained a mansion in Newport, Rhode Island, the great Gilded Age summer watering hole, where he would rent sheep and cows to add dimension to his soirees.

One of my grandmother's future sisters-in-law, the Italian-educated Daisy Chanler, wife of Winty Chanler, though on McAllister's list, claimed that his diagram of the New York social hierarchy was "not unlike Dante's description of Paradise" but she felt it was "flat and arid, a Sahara without lions or lion hunters."

The novelist Louis Auchincloss confirmed this, describing the difference between contemporary New York society and that earlier time. Today you had to be very rich to belong to it but also quite talented, claimed Auchincloss on Dick Cavett's television show in the 1960s: "It's very pictorial." The great spectacle of a recent era, Truman Capote's Black and White Ball for Kay Graham at the Plaza in the mid-sixties, had an invitation list of 658, including figures endowed with talents of every conceivable stripe. In the Gay Nineties, though, the top society men and women were largely stout and overweight, not very elegant, scarcely talented at all. My grandmother was reasonably trim but not stylish or light in any way. Daisy Chanler asserted that the four hundred "would have fled in a body from a poet, a painter, a musician or a clever Frenchman."

The famed soprano Marcella Sembrich, once asked if she'd sing at the ball, quoted a fee of $3,000. When Mrs. Astor agreed on the condition she not mingle with the guests Ms. Sembrich replied, "In that case, the fee will be only $1,000."

In short time, in 1886 *The Social Register* made its appearance in hardcover, edging out Mrs. Astor's four hundred "as a field guide to 'society,'" in the words of the chronicler Liz Widdicombe. Its membership included nearly two thousand of the nation's most prominent families.

Daisy Chanler also wrote that Grandmother Margaret along with her two sisters Alida and Elizabeth "danced and dressed badly" and "had no circle of familiar friends." As teenagers the sisters were sent on a two-year visit to Europe to learn European manners and customs. At one point in England, my grandmother met Lord Balfour and was invited to an audience with Queen Victoria but declined, hearing she would have to curtsy before the queen. She held that that was undemocratic — no one had to curtsy when brought into the White House and the presence of the American president.

Early in life, in 1898, my grandmother had been a heroic figure of sorts, a nursing administrator in the Spanish-American War. By the time I met her, she had stayed on at Rokeby with her son (my mother's older brother Richard) and his wife Susan and their children. On December 18, 1939, well before we entered World War Two, President Roosevelt gave her a luncheon at Hyde Park, where he awarded her a Congressional Medal for her service in the Spanish-American conflict. Her son's wife, Susan, was invited along. Susan had an uncle, Hamilton Fish, an isolationist right-winger who had been congressman from Rokeby's (and FDR's) district since 1922. Susan recalled years later that Roosevelt, who really could not stand to be alone, at the lunch as almost always kept up deliberately trivial patter which no one could break through, joking with Susan about Hamilton Fish, who had kept him in a state of outrage. In the midst of all this, someone brought El Presidente a telegram on a silver plate. FDR read it with great excitement. It announced that the German pocket battleship *Graf Spee* had just been scuttled off Montevideo, Uruguay. This was when Britain was about to be thrown alone into the struggle against Hitler on the Western Front and it was a stroke of fantastic good fortune for Britain — the Allies' first victory of the war.

Eleanor Roosevelt, suppressing the animosity she had long felt toward my grandmother, offered her a gracious reception at the luncheon and even wrote an appreciative article about her.

Rokeby was a place with a progressive side in spite of the great wealth it represented. My grandmother would repeatedly rail against the injustice she had witnessed as a six-year-old: the 1876 presidential election where the Republican Rutherford B. Hayes was declared the winner even though the Democrat Samuel J. Tilden (as others since then) had actually won the greater number of regular, and even electoral college, votes.

In her memoir, *Family Vista*, she talked of sights she had seen back at the start of the century. On a trip to China she came upon a great range of feathers on Guam, from all the birds migrating between Russia and South America, and in the Philippines the inscription "Pabst" etched on trees by a former beer salesman, then a prisoner of war, alerting his rescuers to the route on which his captors had taken him. Then, as a nurse in Cuba, she saw a pig entering a room where she was looking after a dying officer. A Puerto Rican doctor came in and she asked him if he could protect the officer. He refused sharply and charged that an army doctor had called him a "dago nurse." He had graduated from Bellevue Hospital College and would not be so mistreated. Later she told the story to a captain, who apologized to him in the name of the army, the congress, the senate, the Supreme Court, the cabinet and the president.

Susan shared her liberal spirit. Hamilton Fish the Republican had gained a lock on Rokeby's district and during the thirties would visit Germany as Hitler's guest and fly about the country in Foreign Minister von

Ribbentrop's plane (or so Susan's son Ricky rumored). Susan, though, in spite of her connection with Fish, was a deep believer in democracy, very active with her own family during the war in Bundles for Britain and other pro-British efforts against the Nazis. She used to talk about the British historian Alistair Horne, whom she'd known well when he was a child. Right after Britain went to war in 1939, Horne had been put on a boat at age thirteen and sent to the United States to study at Millbrook Academy and be bedeviled by his schoolmate Bill Buckley, who kept gleefully informing him the Nazis were going to win the war.

On her visit to Miss Thomas', my grandmother offered one further piece of information. She mentioned that the one-time opera star Natalina Cavalieri (Lina also) had been killed by a random bomb during an American air raid over Florence. She was seventy; my grandmother had outlived her. Again, I had no idea who she was talking about. Later I learned that Lina had once made a fortune in a brief marriage off her brother Bob, yet another of the Astor Orphans.

My mother did not know how my grandmother had managed to make that trip to visit me. What amazed her especially was that she herself had not known the way to my school. However, she assured me much later, my grandmother made such dramatic moves all the time. During the war it was hard for civilians to take a train. My grandmother got a return ticket to New York by prevailing on one of my mother's old Vassar college friends, Martha McGahan, then at *Time* in San Francisco, to let her borrow a press pass. With that she went right to the front of a long line and bought the ticket. "When you are old, you can get away with anything," she told my mother, to my mother's horror.

My parents got married at the church near Rokeby on a gray June day in 1934, just after they finished college. My grandmother wrote at the time that the guests at the Rokeby reception after the wedding all felt chilly "and approached their food from the piazza to their great discomfort." (A story has run through the family that the guests each found a natural pearl in the oyster they were served.) My grandmother herself was seated "with some thirty Ancients like the President's mother [Sara Roosevelt] at a safe distance in the dining room," while my mother had her company in the library in the tower, at the top of which her brother Dickie had four trombones playing Bach. Of my father the groom, my grandmother wrote that he looked "absurdly young, happy and manly."

One cause of the chill undoubtedly was my grandmother's refusal to allow alcohol at the reception. My father's brother John, Jake, recalled that when he drove over from nearby Salisbury Connecticut with other relatives for the ceremony they stopped at Stissing House in Pine Plains and there tanked up on 3.2 beer to see themselves through the day. Then at one point in the midst of the reception, as the guests were sipping on pink lemonade, one of my mother's cousins, Stuyvesant "Stuyve" Chanler, pulled a flask of real liquor from inside his coat and started passing it around to launch a serious drink to the bride and groom.

My grandmother was about to swoop down on her nephew in a froth of disciplinary wrath when Sara Roosevelt stepped forth and declared, "I'll drink to that." My grandmother had no choice but to hold her tongue then and everyone had a drink. (It must've been a very big flask.) Another relative present at the occasion, Daisy Chanler's son-in-law Lawrence White, son of the famous architect Stanford, later wrote a poem commemorating the toast. He titled it "The Duchess Outranked."

That was a time of elegance and grace, in all. I often daydreamed of being taken back by time capsule to that wedding, announcing myself and telling all the guests and hosts about the unknown devastation that loomed before them. Theirs was a realm where the Duchess would come to outlive many, most of those around her and leave a deep imprint on those who carried on, for the rest of their lives.

3
Up from the Hudson: Offbeat Times in the War

My father was an obdurate escapist. Sometimes this yielded interesting results. After the wedding he worked briefly selling life insurance in New York — a job arranged through his father, the only one he, a classics major from Yale, could get back then. He demonstrated writing ability to a prominent editor in the city, Ralph Ingersoll, who was helping to start a new publication, *Life* magazine, and Ingersoll hired him as its first official office boy just before I was born.

An old Yale friend and Fence Club colleague of his from California, Innis Bromfield, then came up with the project of founding a bright new magazine in San Francisco, *The Coast*. He had my father and another fellow Yalie, Johnnie Holmes, then Martha McGahan, my mother's friend from Vassar, come out to help get it going. My mother waited in New York to give birth to me then worked her way out by train to join them.

The market for a magazine such as *The Coast* didn't exist, though my father's crowd put out quite a good product, a modest version of *The New Yorker* though it had numerous sharp photographs and entertaining trivia quizzes on top of good articles, poems and cartoons. It even ran a full-page photo of the great composer Arnold Schoenberg standing before a UCLA building with a fly on his forehead.

It was Johnnie Holmes who kept *The Coast* going as long as it did, which was a little over two years. Holmes had been head of the glee club at Yale, was very social and turned out to be a gifted fundraiser in the old Eastern world. He even got money from my mother's cousins the Schermerhorns, from Mrs. William Astor's family. (Who were also related to some people named Jones — the direct inspiration for the birth of the expression "keeping up with the Joneses." One of the Jones children, Edith, later married a man named Wharton.)

For a time William Saroyan (from Boston himself) would contribute a short story to each issue of *The Coast*, for twenty-five dollars. Sometimes he'd come in two hours before deadline and bang the story out on an old cast-iron Royal, laughing as he did so. My father said those stories (among them "Sailing down the Chesapeake" and "The City's Night") would turn out quite well. Innis though recalled seeing Saroyan come in once just before deadline and pound out a story the editors were not happy with, so he offered to give them something else, went back to the typewriter and ran off one they did accept, which formed the inspiration for his famous play, that year's Pulitzer Prize winner <u>The Time of Your Life</u>.

By the time the war started, *The Coast* had collapsed, my father had gone on to work for the *San Francisco Chronicle* under its flamboyant editor Paul Smith, who would throw brunches with Gertrude Anderson at his Telegraph Hill flat, and Martha McGahan had moved on to the San Francisco office of *Time*.

By then my mother had given birth to other siblings, initially twins, Dicky and Mary. My grandmother, claiming there never had been twins in her family, refused to accept this and sent greetings only to Dicky (who was actually born after Mary). My mother had made her escape parallel with my father. "It's lucky I got out when I did," she'd say off and on the rest of her life, mostly about Rokeby, her childhood home along with a New York brownstone. "If I hadn't, I never would have."

In Marin, in our house in San Anselmo, she began to display the behavior of a chronic hypochondriac; I could cite infinite examples of this. She would flee the house whenever one of her children had a cold and would not let the child sit on her lap. (The child would then seek refuge with neighbors for comfort.) I remember, as a small boy, reading a little pamphlet, always around the house, titled "The Seven Warning Signs of Cancer." I can remember the relief I felt on learning that muscles (the heart included) couldn't contract cancer — unlike tissue, they could not regenerate themselves.

My mother even found wartime work as a nurse's aide in a hospital down the road from St. John's Church, where I had been baptized.

She often told grim stories of what she saw there. She recalled that one day someone fell on the hospital floor and exploded. Another time a woman gave birth to a deformed, deaf-dumb, webbed-handed baby with pointed head; no one could kill it and stay in practice, so they let it starve to death. Yet another time she saw a doctor who was universally known as a butcher start a woman through natural childbirth and decide near the very end that she would die unless he shifted to caesarean. He did not know how to go about this and had to bring in another doctor to help him. But he had waited too long. The second doctor was able to save the mother but not the baby. My mother wanted to get in touch with the husband and tell him about the first doctor's incompetence and his failure to shift procedure promptly but others in the hospital warned her off doing so. They said that if she did she would never be able to find work in a hospital again, anywhere.

One day she was on duty, a terrific explosion shook the hospital. The trees along the sidewalk out front bent over in the shock-waves from the blast, touched the sidewalk and snapped back. It turned out that was from a massive torpedo explosion in the navy munitions terminal at Port Chicago thirty miles to the east — the worst domestic disaster in wartime America.

(Of course at the time the common explanation for the blast was that it was the work of German agents. Decades later when I told this to some Germans at a dinner party, they reacted indignantly. I assured them we had not been fellow members of NATO back in those days.)

Later in the war, my mother went to work at Hamilton Field, an airbase a few miles to the north. Joe DiMaggio the great baseball player had passed through there on his way out to the Pacific, maybe briefly sick. He always carried an Indian-head nickel with him as a good luck charm. At one point by mistake he used it to pay fare on a bus in San Francisco. Word circulated about Hamilton Field that he had the entire San Francisco transit system scour its coin intake for the period during which he lost the coin and, so the story went, found it in the end.

My father, his gift for journalism notwithstanding, was left with little interesting material to work with into the early forties. Then came the war, followed by the spread of communism in Asia and our massive response to it.

His first effort to join the war effort was shot down by Paul Smith, his boss at the *Chronicle*, on grounds that a man with several children had no right to forsake his family for military adventures. My father then turned to his East Coast connections, appealing to the playwright Robert Emmet Sherwood, a distant relative and speechwriter for President Roosevelt, who put him on to a position with the Office of War Information, the OWI. At that he headed off to China and served with the OWI over much of that enormous country, joining the fight against the Japanese who were occupying it.

In our childhood, to crib from Chekhov, there was little if any childhood. But then there was little childhood in the life of anyone born around when I was. Before even emerging into thorough enough awareness to grasp what had happened, my younger siblings and I, as small children, just barely alive, had gone through almost all of life that really mattered. We woke up into Hitler, even those like me who living in West Coast America were about as far away from Hitler as one could get.

By the time we were say five or six — old enough to begin to tell what aberrant behavior really was — there Hitler was with his panzer divisions, pouncing everywhere he wished, grabbing anything he wanted and killing anyone he wanted — delivering one of the most extraordinary performances anyone has ever put on. He was possessed with such a blinding hatred of all beliefs that did not conform exactly to his own that he brought destruction on his entire nation, including all his supporters, rather than compromise on them one inch.

Even his adversary the Soviet dictator Stalin, who was as much of a mass murderer, could be flexible over values. He accepted non-Communist Cossack nationalists as vital allies during the war he ended up fighting against Hitler. He had not sought that war, either — he'd hungered for peace with Germany. Shortly before Hitler invaded the Soviet Union in 1941, the German ambassador to the Soviet Union, Friedrich Schulenberg, described Stalin and Molotov as they appeared at a Moscow railway station to bid farewell to the visiting Japanese foreign minister. In the course of this, Stalin asked for Schulenberg, threw his arm around his shoulder and exclaimed, "We must remain friends and you must now do everything to that end!" Stalin then turned to the acting German military attaché and told him "We will remain friends with you, in any event." To Schulenberg there was no doubt that this manifestation of Stalin's yearning to forestall the Nazi invasion, almost beg the friendship of German officials, was calculated to draw the maximum possible attention.

When the Russians began to stop the Germans and inflict defeat on them in 1943 all our associates in Marin County, north of San Francisco, where we lived at the time — some of them very conservative and patrician — applauded with profound relief. Then before we were eight this arch-murderer was brought to ground. We've seen autocratic figures since then, but they have all been pale in contrast to Hitler.

Gasoline tickets were among the most valuable items one could find during the war. I once met a fellow who went home toward the end of the war and received a whole eight and a half by eleven inch sheet of B gasoline coupons. Each of the coupons was worth five gallons "and you couldn't drive the girls away" he said. Is This Trip Necessary? a question — admonition, really — that we kept seeing on the back of the gas ration sticker applied to the lower left-hand corner of the windshield during and even some time after World War Two.

To get more such coupons my mother and I took the train down to San Diego at some point to join my godfather, Uncle Donald Ryan, another Yale classmate and Fence Club comrade of my father's. Donald was in the navy and was about to be shipped to the South Pacific on a destroyer. He let my mother preempt the Chevrolet he had used while living down there so she could get extra gasoline coupons by having it on her property. Years later I learned Uncle Donald was in love with her. She was fond of him too and enjoyed his company but they never established a permanent relationship: he was a very devout Catholic, which she as a hardcore agnostic found irksome.

On that trip we stayed in the Hotel Del Coronado, a venerable and massive white wooden structure fronting the water, one of perhaps five such giant hotels in California. In the late 1800s it was reputed to be the largest wooden structure in the world. One day there I stole several thick sheaves of stationery from a hall writing table. Some woman caught me, grabbed me by the wrist and took me off by elevator, presumably to haul me before the manager for a draconian hiding. I still remember the time the elevator door opened to an intermediary floor and I managed to break free and run for it. The culture of war had by then become deeply embedded in the society. Another time my mother saw me digging holes in the beach and asked me what I was doing. "Making depth charges," I informed her.

After seeing Uncle Donald off, the two of us drove all the way back north by way of US 101, which in those days was a two-lane back road. One stretch we went through, the steep sandstone cliffs near the El Capitan oilfield just west of Santa Barbara, gained notoriety shortly after that as the one place in the continental United States the Japanese managed to shell during the war. Later it was largely assumed the shelling was a mere distraction, to divert the attention of civil defense forces from a submarine which was purportedly picking up an agent off the main pier in Santa Barbara itself.

Shoe tickets were also very valuable: during the war, one could have one shoe ticket per month per child. My mother had a maid then, Elvira, who dealt in those coupons on the black market. At one point she stole some of my mother's tickets and when my mother asked her if she knew what had happened to them, she turned around and accused my mother of stealing hers. My mother was able to appear before the Rationing Board and clear herself. She then fired Elvira, who begged her to keep her on till the end of the month so she would have time to find another job.

A sister-in-law of my father's, Charlotte, Jake's wife, also came to live next door to us while Jake was out in the Far East at war. Her home was not much bigger than a garage — a guest house, a cottage up Sturdevant Road. With Donald Ryan's Chevrolet in the garage my mother could get an extra gas coupon for three gallons a week. Lottie with a huge Buick could procure enough gas to manage one trip a week to San Francisco and one to the beach.

For a time I would go to the local hospital to heal my lungs and sometimes my mother would minister to me in the course of her nursing work. I remember once occupying a bed in an alcove of the respiratory ward, looking out over a long chamber with perhaps twenty beds ranged around it. A nurse would go about holding a spittoon before each young man in bed in turn. Later

I learned that they all had tuberculosis, which they had contracted under combat in the South Pacific. I also heard that the military maintained a hospital somewhere in the remote deserts of western Utah for malaria cases, too distant from any other habitation for flies or other insects to pass that alien disease on to the rest of the country. That was when I was sent to Miss Thomas', the school where my grandmother had tracked me down.

4
The Great Astor Mansion

I had my first glimpse of the serfdom and despair that infused life in Rokeby one summer when my mother sent my brother Dicky and me on our first trip to her childhood mansion.

The train ride up the Hudson to Rokeby was an unexpectedly drab entree to the place, in spite of the brilliant summer sun — depraved, even in the early days. Coal heaps, cement slag, endless cement mills and power plants, really. A Lone Star mill then one old hulk with Germanic crossed wood-beam facade. Nabisco packaging, Hudson Wire Company, Sanitas/Wellclad. Sing Sing Prison. The deep gorge — chasm almost — of the Rhinecliff railway station and the narrow rickety iron bridge overhead, spanning the Hudson.

Rokeby was unlike any property I'd ever seen. Especially coming as I had from California, where any woods one can find are so sparse one can see through them. Rokeby, one of a number of grand old estates holding down the east bank of the Hudson for a stretch of about thirty miles north of the Rhinecliff railway station, was well ensconced behind a stone wall and an almost impenetrable spread of deep green darkness. Among other things, it was a dairy farm raising its own hay. It had a large barn with milk cows and a silo that smelled like burning tar.

The mansion dominating the grounds stood at the round dead-end of a long gravel road in from a roadhouse now punctuated by a state historical marker. It was a structure three stories high, perhaps eight thousand square feet in area, crowned by a slate mansard roof and, to the left at the rear, a five-story tower topped by a flagpole. A veranda the width of the mansion, which they called the piazza, rose up from the gravel past enormous potted century cactuses and curved round stone steps and high white wood columns supported the roof above that. A spacious veranda, that piazza. Chaise longues, cushioned armchairs and metal tables lay scattered about it. One could hold two or three parties at a time out there.

Through the immense front door beyond the piazza, you would pass into a main floor with a very lofty ceiling, twelve feet high, and walls of Catskill stone two feet thick. Cavernous and refreshing, twenty degrees cooler than the outside in summer. Doors beside marble busts on column-pedestals led to two reception rooms on each side of the broad hallway, each with its own fireplace. In one of these two rooms the walls were covered with hanging but unattached wallpaper. Beyond those were a dining room to the right and a parlor to the left, with a pair of grand pianos and a whole long wall of French doors looking out over a series of fields and slips of dirt road and arbors that rolled down to the Hudson, then, beyond that, rising up quite formidably at that angle, the

Catskills. A magnificent setting for a ball, or a formal dinner, or a combination of several different kinds of evenings all at once.

There was a massive skylight over the main floor, then a smaller one toward the rear, over a lesser rear upper staircase. On my first visit I wandered about the attic and failed to understand that light came down through a skylight but rarely up from it, especially when it was covered with dust. So I did not take note of it, stepped onto it and fell straight through — plummeted to the staircase below.

Somehow, though, I missed the stairs. I swung wide and dropped to the third floor beside it instead and landed on my rump. This took me by shock and gave me a terrible pain in the back, but oddly I survived it. The pain lasted only about a day. Had I hit the staircase with its sharp-edged steps, my fate would have been worse.

From this summer I came to see that the rich are different from the rest of us in one way: they can afford to be irrational for much longer periods of time than can the less rich. Still, unchecked, they can shake themselves to pieces. The Orphans, thanks to William Astor's avaricious snobbery, inherited a very large share of the Astor fortune in time. As we have seen they came to play a dominant role in the social life of New York and Europe from around 1890 to 1925. From my earliest childhood, I remember hearing that several of these Astor offspring did squander the fortunes they eventually got and I came to see instances of this with the passage of time.

This was not true of my grandmother, and there is a strong written record underlining this. In 1886, one of her older brothers, Winthrop ("Winty"), married Margaret "Daisy" Terry, as we have seen, and in time Daisy wrote a book of memoirs, *Roman Spring*, which provides a vivid portrait of the other world in which some of the people around my grandmother had immersed themselves as early as then.

As a youngster in Italy, Daisy had been exposed to some extraordinary people — Eleanora Duse the famed actress, Franz Liszt, Donna Maria who became the wife of Gabriele D'Annunzio (who later had an affair with Duse), then a scholar who would read Dante to her and her step-siblings twice a week for three years, with two to three lessons for each of a hundred cantos. (Later Daisy deprecated him rather as a "one-book man.")

In time she converted to Catholicism, which she followed most arduously. She also devoted herself to writing. At least when one gets away from the theology, *Roman Spring* is a cultivated and interesting book. It's the only eyewitness account of the late 1880s Rokeby-Chanler world I've been sad to finish. I really didn't want it to end.

After Daisy's marriage to Winty, a gifted hunter and fine fox hunter — a "charming idler" she labeled him — they went to live a while in Rokeby. She found the atmosphere around Rokeby hard. Before the marriage she said that Winty's family had rained anti-Catholic books and pamphlets down on her. Once at Rokeby she felt as if she was watched and criticized in enforced silence as a Catholic and even packed her bags and tried to leave after one argument of obscure substance.

The hardest person for her to deal with was my grandmother and nowhere in her book did Daisy refer to her by name. Only once did she even call her "M" (a designation which does not so much as appear in the index). She did write that shortly after she moved in, my grandmother and her two sisters went up north to Lake George for a summer trip. In their absence, Daisy went about trying to liven up Rokeby's appearance. She put a piano in the drawing-room and added drapes and bright colors — only to find that when the three orphan-sisters returned "they were shocked beyond measure by the liberties I had taken with the drawing-room. One of the sisters [my grandmother obviously, by context] refused to set foot in it; if we sat there after dinner she retired to the religious gloom of the home parlor to mark her disapproval. One or other of the children would join her and sit with her for a while, as with one bereft."

That September Daisy gave birth to her first child, Laura, at Rokeby. Laura was baptized by the village priest. "This same sister-in-law suffered even more acutely from this than from the desecration of the funereal drawing-room," Daisy went on. "I heard she told one of her brothers that the kindest thing one could do to the infant would be to kill it in its innocence." Whenever the "rosy child" was brought into the room, "her pious aunt would solemnly leave the family circle, so as not to lend the approval of her presence to the disgrace. One afternoon we were having tea by the tennis court, watching a game. Cecilia [Laura's Italian governess] wheeled up the baby carriage in which Laura sat, all fair and fluffy. M. [sic] rose and fled, as at the approach of a leper. She once sent me word, through one of her sisters, that she loved the child better than anything on earth, had even gone into the nursery one night to kiss it in its sleep, but that she could not acknowledge it in the presence of others."

Finally Daisy and Winty got out. They moved on to New York then Washington, where Winty and his old friend Cabot Lodge would go out to Rock Creek Park with another old friend, Teddy Roosevelt (by then president), and experiment with the latest craze to hit the country — skis imported from Norway. By around the turn of the century, my grandmother had bought out all her other siblings' shares in Rokeby. Four of her five brothers already had homes. One, Willie ("Blue Willie"), had sold his Rokeby share to a sister, Elizabeth, and moved to New York City. He won election as a Democrat to Congress but only for a term; his district was gerrymandered to the Republicans at the time of the inauguration of McKinley and Theodore Roosevelt.

Elizabeth then married far and away the most important progressive figure in that world, John Jay "Jack" Chapman, a major essayist of his day. He had previously been married to a fiery Italian-American with long black hair, Minna. Before they married he took her to a dance at Harvard and thought he heard another young man make a derogatory remark about her. This so angered him that he attacked the man and knocked him out. Then reappeared with his left arm missing from about the elbow on down — having thought he had killed the man, he thrust his left hand into a coal fire in an access of deep remorse and held it there until it burned and had to be amputated.

When in time Minna died, Chapman married Elizabeth and they lived in a mansion they had built, Sylvania, just to the north of Rokeby. Sylvania was the work of Charles Platt, the architect who designed the Freer Art Gallery in Washington, around 1903. In the words of the literary historian Edmund Wilson, in his notebooks The Thirties, the Chapmans told him "Sylvania was well proportioned and fine in detail, but not so practical as it should have been — high French windows let in the cold in winter." Prominent were a screen and decoration by my grandmother's brother Robert, a "big bad bust of one of the Chanlers in the library, old allegorical engravings, and Italian eighteenth-century water colors. Fine view past the sundial through the space between the trees to the Hudson. Old barn with pigeons in eaves, hay presser that was turned by a horse...." Mrs. Chapman's sister, concluded Wilson, considered Rokeby "the real big house, the Chapmans' merely a villa."

Chapman wrote and saw published a book of around 135 pages on the man he asserted was the strongest figure in the nation back in the high-water mark of slavery, up to the eve of the Civil War: William Lloyd Garrison. Chapman called the slave trade "probably the most brutal organized crime in history" (certainly one could list it among the top five) and said that Garrison, almost alone in the entire nation, demanded against crippling odds through his newspaper *The Liberator* that the crime of slavery be addressed at once and abolished. Virtually no one else in the country dared make a public issue of it, not even such progressive-minded writers as Ralph Waldo Emerson (until well on in life, in his fifties). Chapman claimed the American people were staying off that subject because they "were not given to historic speculation and were mentally enfeebled by success." They were paralyzed by "a sort of subtle freemasonry, a secret belief that nothing must be disturbed."

Chapman also quoted Garrison writing about the "inoffensive" vices of the Pharisees, among them the tendency to sit in the front pew in church. Showing where one sat in church was a vital matter to Chapman, who insisted on occupying a rear pew at the church in Barrytown, down the road from Sylvania.

(Daisy Chanler further stated that Jack Chapman turned out also to have done excellent translations of Dante.)

After the Chapmans had built Sylvania, my grandmother persuaded Elizabeth and their sister Alida also to relinquish their shares in the estate to her, on grounds that she, unlike them, would never marry. Even though Elizabeth and Jack Chapman lived in their own mansion, my grandmother's coming into full possession of Rokeby and over time turning it into a little principality for her ideas and prejudices gave Jack Chapman a nervous breakdown and it took him a year to recuperate from it. The woman had outlasted all the others, after all. They called her "the last of the Manchus," after the Chinese dynasty which was also expiring at that time.

Another figure connected with the family was one of the preeminent architects of the day, Stanford White. He remodeled Rokeby in 1895 at my grandmother's request. His original ideas included circular radiators in the library, which took the edge off the frightful winter cold. He blasted out the basement so he could have a furnace installed in it and he put in bathrooms upstairs. (Electricity came later — my mother remembered a woman in the mansion, Augusta, whose sole task was to keep kerosene lanterns filled and clean their wicks.) Plainly my grandmother had much to thank White for. She had a plaque set in the wall of the main hall at Rokeby commemorating the reconstruction work he did on the place.

In that era, White had had an affair with a beautiful young musical star, Evelyn Nesbit. One could hardly call it an affair, really. In *The Architect of Desire* Lawrence White's granddaughter Suzannah Lessard makes it clear that he raped and deflowered her when she was sixteen. Later Harry Thaw, another figure in New York society and a psychopath in his own right, married her then in belated rage at his conduct shot and killed White at a rooftop theater in Madison Square Garden (originally designed by White). My grandmother, devoted as she was to Stanford, was one of two relatives who appeared at his funeral, showing that she could be conned. Years later Thaw, after judged insane and serving time in a mental institution, went out to California and on a tour of Santa Barbara and the works of George Washington Smith declared "I shot the wrong architect."

(Lately one major architecture critic, Paul Goldberger of *The New Yorker,* commenting with others on the execrable Xanadu Mall just outside New York in the New Jersey Meadowlands, wrote, "In really big projects in this region, there's been nothing as horrible as that. I would put Madison Square Garden on the same scale, but it's not recent.")

Suzannah Lessard has Evelyn Nesbit ending up in her midseventies running a sculpture studio just under the Hollywood Freeway.

5
Arizona and California Backwaters; Sedgwick Interlude

I had found Miss Thomas', the wartime school, a strange place. We were served Spanish rice almost every supper and almost every meal I remember seeing one child or another rush out, hands to mouth, to go vomit.

For some time I lived in the balcony next to the room of another student in a higher grade. She was named Felicia Spira and had just come from Belgium. She showed me that in Belgium the numeral one looked like our seven and they put a dash through their sevens. In those days I had no idea why she'd come over so suddenly from Belgium and she didn't tell me. Perhaps she didn't know either. I did hear that her family had been in the diamond business. Another student, a boy slightly older than me, good at reading the Old Testament, turned out years later to have come from Hamburg. His parents had changed their name; one of his grandparents had been a rabbi. I picked up some European perspective through exposure to these children from the old continent. At one point, toward the end of the war, I wrote my mother, "Churchill will give Poland to Russia if America agrees." I had no idea what I was writing about — just echoing the statement I'd heard from them. But they turned out to be correct.

I had trouble adjusting in one area. I had come dimly to understand that to a person who has lived almost all his life in fear of entrapment, ill health is the ultimate form of entrapment — it is nature, the forces of the universe, fate, what you will, slowly closing you in and up. Erecting walls around you, so that ultimately you end up in a corner from which you cannot escape. A lot of people, maybe most people, don't mind the walls as long as they seem benign, abandon themselves to them almost, just as they were happy to be in bed sick when younger. I felt terror having to go to the infirmary with the flu and remember how I'd sit by the open window, sucking in the cool air through my mouth in an effort (partly successful) to lower the temperature of my mouth to the point where it'd show up normal on a thermometer and I could get discharged. Then another time I saw a classmate lying back in his bed exulting that he didn't have to do anything till it was time to get up and out to the bus home for vacation.

I also felt some pride later to have gone to that school when I came to realize that the most important story of the rest of the century was unfolding right then, just a little more than three hundred miles away from me: the development of the atomic bomb in Los Alamos, New Mexico. Of course, in the decades to come, I became repeatedly exposed to arguments that that was nothing to be proud of, the bomb was a curse, and our country was going to use it again at almost any time on innocent civilian populations (blonde blue-eyed ones excepted), the way we did on my first summer vacation home from Miss Thomas'.

Among the many famous figures residing and working in Los Alamos during the war were Klaus Fuchs the German-born British physicist and Edward Teller, who later helped develop the hydrogen bomb. At one point, I heard decades later from Teller's wife Mici, she received permission once when her husband was off on business to leave the base and drive off for a week's vacation in Mexico with Fuchs and another couple, in Fuchs' car. The car broke down in Marfa, Texas and they had to wait there two days, not spending all their time there together, till Fuchs had it repaired and they could move on.

After the war it turned out Fuchs had been spying all along for the Soviet Union. When the FBI learned of the layover in Marfa, Mrs. Teller recalled further, its agents grilled her and the others about it relentlessly for weeks, in an effort to learn how they had spent every minute there. Plainly Fuchs had rigged the layover to enable him to contact his Soviet control and pass all he knew about the nascent bomb on to him. In the end the British sentenced Fuchs to eight years in prison for his treachery.

Incidentally, when I gossiped at a meal on what I'd heard from my grandmother about our Astor forebears, a teacher told me that the tycoon's great-grandson John Jacob IV (son of Aunt Lina and a first cousin once removed of my grandmother's) grew up rich and was considered a shiftless dissolute libertine. He suffered through a miserable marriage, engaged in a messy affair, went through a divorce then married a nineteen-year-old beauty, to public scorn. Then when he and his pregnant bride took the maiden voyage of the *Titanic* and it became torpedoed by the iceberg, he put her on a lifeboat and stayed on board the sinking vessel, where he met his death. Other men on board, including the captain, had leapt onto lifeboats and the public came to regard the dissolute John Jacob IV as a heroic figure after all.

One day that April, an old black woman who worked in Miss Thomas' school came across the courtyard in tears. She told me that President Roosevelt had just died. Somehow, perhaps irrationally, I felt that meant the war had ended and we could all, finally, go home.

The war did end. Back in Marin, on V-J Day, my family and friends took me onto the streets, church bells tolling all around. A woman handed me a cracker with Roquefort cheese on it. We were across from Old Baldy, the knob-hill across from our house with nothing on top but dry grass. I'd see fires on it at night every now and then.

My father, however, did not want to come home. My mother saw someone from the OWI passing through and asked him to have my father ordered back, but he gave her the brush-off. When my brother Dicky came on a visit to San Francisco almost forty years later, we went by the old house in San Anselmo. He pointed to a little stone wall where he would sit every afternoon for months waiting for our father to return. Finally my mother had Ben, the older figure in the community, send my father a telegram before he died, telling him to come back. He returned in the end, a few weeks after Christmas. Our mother had to drive him around all evening until he could face going into the house with the four children inside. Our father never forgave her for having him ordered back. My mother had been desperate for a baby and eight months later gave birth to her fifth, Diana (brought on a month early by induced labor). My father repeatedly scoffed at the timing and the idea that one could induce labor. He soon went back to New York to look for a job and found work as a reporter with the old New York *Herald Tribune*, which sent him back to China.

Less than a year after the war, we moved from Marin to a warmer, drier place — Santa Barbara, a small city near Los Angeles. My mother chose that destination because her sister-in-law Lottie knew it and recommended it. Lottie's mother lived there and knew Dan Nugent, a man who'd made a fortune early in life in St. Louis and who now with his wife Adelaide owned a magnificent beach property ultimately graced with a view of eight offshore oil rigs. A few children I came to know there even lived in houses with towers that contained bells, though we rarely heard them tintinnabulating.

Besides the Nugents, another resident of the area was a gentleman rancher, Francis Sedgwick, who had gone to the same prep school in Massachusetts as my father, Groton, then Harvard, and became a major figure in our lives.

I went up to Santa Barbara from Arizona at the end of the school year. Life about me went on adequately, if not very well, given the absurdity of the world the war had created, although my mother, considering me a nuisance, quickly put me in another boarding school, La Loma Feliz, in the hills behind our new home.

Its name was Spanish for "the happy hill," but we all called it "the home of the fleas." There we had the main school then up on the side hill a separate school for the very young, known as Igliff. A couple of tough, humorless women, Ina Richter and Mrs. Lee, ran the school. They had a station wagon that everyone called Carry passing back and forth between the two branches. One of the students there claimed to be Sigmund Freud's grandson. I assume he really *was* Freud's grandson, because I find it hard to imagine a ten-year-old inventing such a distinctive claim. He was caught at the bottom of the hill between the two branches very early one morning, in a desperate attempt to run away.

That fall the Arizona Desert School down near the one I'd attended in Tucson folded. La Loma Feliz became swamped with students, largely from Hollywood, who had been at that school and suddenly found themselves with no place to go — no flamboyant place, anyway.

One of these students was a fat youth named Bob Manning who got me down in the basement of the main building once and drew out a pen-knife, which he pushed against my belly at excruciating length. I remember screaming without letup. He didn't actually cut into my skin, though there was a little scratch. Later when I complained about it, one of the teachers, a fortyish man who'd come over from the Arizona Desert School, chewed me out as much as Manning for letting that happen. His attitude became even less sympathetic once it was discovered that I'd stolen most of the syringes in the dispensary, all the rocks in the classroom of another teacher, Mr. Dietrich, and a few other objects — not to mention the eighty dollars my mother found in my bureau drawer. I was ordered to return everything to its original owner in person. My only rough moment came after I wrote a note to Mr. Dietrich; I'd misspelled his name and he erupted at that, not the theft.

I also recall my mother sitting talking to a math teacher named Mr. Carpenter, who wore jeans, a Levi shirt and a cowboy hat and smoked cigarettes that he rolled himself. She was trying, with no success, to persuade him that he was not effectively managing to convey the essential concepts of his subject to me. Decades later, hearing my older daughter Leila do her times tables, I realized that I had had a ridiculous schooling. I was still doing the tables late in the sixth grade and here she was doing them almost as well late in the fourth — and she couldn't even abide math.

After that summer my mother told me she was going out to China to see my father. That was just before the Communist revolution whose triumph many people were not foreseeing and there were quite a few Westerners in Beijing then. The day she arrived, a colleague of my father's named Barbara Stevens disappeared. This rough-and-tumble reporter had against all warnings taken a domestic flight to the far western province of Xinjiang. In those days of propellor craft, Chinese pilots tended not to warm up their planes — would take off cold as soon as they turned over the engines — and those would often fail once the plane was airborne. A few days later word came that her plane had crashed. Both my father and his friend Graham Peck, author of a classic of the era, *Two Kinds of Time,* had been chasing after her and when my mother mentioned her at a banquet in Beijing my father kicked her under the table to silence her. My mother returned to California in a month, resolving not to go live in China, but then changed her mind and wrote my father as much. He turned her down — told her it was too late.

In Santa Barbara we saw one flash of brightness from my mother's Vassar times, Elizabeth "Bis" Lorentz, nee Meyer, my godmother and wife of the celebrated documentary filmmaker Pare Lorentz. She was related to offspring of the Bavarian immigrant Levi Strauss the outfitter, who had set up his business in San Francisco in

1853 in the wake of the Gold Rush, and her father ran the *Washington Post*.

Knowing Bis had been one of my mother's interesting undergraduate experiences at Vassar. There she knew characters like Mary McCarthy and later would talk about her puritan background, her skill as a writer then the literary colony they had in New York after my father finished Yale, a Shakespeare club, my mother at first just tolerated but then gradually respected for what she called her "histrionic talents."

Bis was younger than my mother but they graduated together as my mother took a year abroad to study in France. While there, on May 6, 1932, she went to meet the famous author Colette at a big book fair with an elegant gathering and was told she had come early enough to see the president of France, Paul Doumer, preside over the opening of the fair. At Colette's booth she heard a *bang-bang-bang-bang* very clearly. The president had been shot. The fair was closed, the president fell swimming in blood and died and the meeting degenerated into chaos. He had been killed by a Russian emigre, Paul Gorguloff.

Bis was a good violinist and after college she hung around George Gershwin and his friends a certain amount.

She was with the composer when he contracted a brain tumor at thirty-nine. In a July 15, 1937 letter to my mother, Bis stated that when Gershwin first got sick he was taken to hospital in Los Angeles and examined thoroughly for three days, especially to see if he had a brain tumor. They found nothing wrong, said it was all mental and put him in the hands of a psychiatrist. That man was the one who finally made the right diagnosis. Even in a semistupor, George responded to every one of his tests. He even got up and tried to play the piano at the doctor's request (it had taken the doctor two hours by that time to get through to Gershwin's consciousness). Though Gershwin did respond and exert a great effort, he couldn't make his fingers coordinate at all, and that convinced the psychiatrist that the pressure of a tumor was the cause of his suffering. They took him to the hospital and by that time the pressure was increasing rapidly. It took them quite a while to locate the tumor even then. They had thought it was a cyst, not a tumor, and sent for a Johns Hopkins specialist but they had to operate before he could arrive. When they cut out the cyst, they found the real tumor in back of it right inside his brain where it must have been growing for months, maybe years. Bis and six or seven others were with Gershwin's brother Ira all night at the hospital while they operated. At six thirty in the morning when they left they were celebrating. Three hours later he was dead.

In the letter Bis concluded "They say that even if they had found what it was earlier, it would not have made any difference. There was no chance for him to live, and if there had been, at the most it would have meant paralysis. So it's better this way."

Bis knew Oscar Levant better; he was a prodigy whose poor parents in Pittsburgh sent him to New York, where he spent his time playing for Gershwin. She also hung out with Harpo Marx and remembered listening to Levant teaching Marx harp chords over the phone. Both Oscar and Harpo, she said, "liked to take out babes" but they'd often ask her along on their dates just to have someone they could talk to.

Then the playwright Sam Behrman found Bis jobs, first in England, where she went to work for Alexander Korda in the movies, and then on to Los Angeles where she shared a room in a studio as a junior writer with Ring

Lardner Jr. and Budd Schulberg. In the winter when it was cold the three of them would stand about a heater in the center of the room and Lardner and Schulberg would have long political arguments. Ring was the communist and Budd, who argued against him, always lost. Years later Bis learned Schulberg had been a communist too and it turned out they had staged these debates to win her over to the cause by attempting to prove to her that no argument could prevail against Lardner's irrefutable Marxist logic. They failed — their machinations had left her furious.

Schulberg quit the party in 1940, then, called by the House Un-American Activities Committee to testify in 1951, named eight other Hollywood figures as members, including Lardner, who went to prison for a year for refusing to talk to the committee.[*]

Francis Sedgwick was like my parents from Boston and New York. We called him "Fuzzy," an old family nickname; others called him Duke. After working a while and doing a year of graduate study in finance, Sedgwick had become an investment banker with Dillon, Read. He had a nervous breakdown and was advised to go west and get out of banking and the then rather anti-Semitic investment business. So in the thirties he came to Southern California with his wife Alice, a railroad heiress, and many children, buying a large, elegant house with tennis court and swimming pool on Cathedral Oaks Drive near Santa Barbara as well as a large ranch in rugged territory over a range of mountains to the north, in the Santa Ynez Valley.

Virtually unknown then, Santa Ynez has, with the sharp improvement in roads, become famous as the home

---

* 2008 obituary by Timothy Weiner, New York <u>Times</u>.

of some excellent wineries, as well as Michael Jackson and the tennis star Jimmy Connors, among other celebrities, but in those days it was Country and Westernland. At a gas station near the ranch, I saw a young woman in black lipstick wearing cheap silvery rings on most fingers, a Bogart-type felt hat and a jacket that read "Wild Horse Race Pro Tour." Of the towns the jacket listed on this tour, more were in this area than anywhere else in America. Sedgwick used to talk of driving home at night from Cathedral Oaks to his ranch over a twisty road up the San Marcos Pass during the war with his lights out at fifteen miles an hour, following the dotted line.

Sedgwick's ranch was on Foxen Canyon Road, named after a rancher from the previous century, Benjamin Foxen, who informed General Fremont in his invasion of California that Mexican forces had secretly taken position to ambush him near Gaviota Pass, a short distance to the southwest. Fremont was able to catch the forces by surprise and Mexico ceded California to the United States just after that in January 1847. A century later, oil was discovered on Sedgwick's ranch, sulfurous and heavy but commercial.

They named the field Zaca and in time it produced about fifteen million barrels.

La Loma Feliz failed six months after the Arizona Desert School collapsed. The trustees of the school brought Francis Sedgwick in to preside over its dissolution. I was sent to another school, a day school on the other side of town, where we had a teacher, Mrs. Inglis, who claimed her father had worked in the stables of the czar of Imperial Russia. When my mother returned from China, Sedgwick started coming over to our house for dinner, by himself. On some occasions I'd hear him down in the kitchen very loudly singing

You are my sunshine, my only sunshine
You make me happy when skies are gray

At other times I'd see him and my mother listening to records in the living room; I remember once seeing the two of them lying side by side as Ezio Pinza sang "Some Enchanted Evening" from *South Pacific*, the hit musical which had just come out. (Years later I remember the mother of a schoolmate telling me she listened to "Some Enchanted Evening" nine hundred times in a row when it first came out that year.)

Yet other times my mother would take us up to the Sedgwick ranch visiting. Sedgwick would get up around dawn and exercise frantically to loud hopped-up Mozart on special mattresses in his studio. He would preside over lavish lunches, prepared by Nancy, a cook from Marseille, and expatiate on subjects like capping the T at the battle of Jutland or stoating rabbits. He talked about his old school, and my father's, Groton in Massachusetts. To emphasize its superior schooling he described a couple of fellow students who went on a tour of the world after graduating. In every country they visited they learned the local sport or athletic contest and invariably won the second time they engaged in it. Sedgwick's father, Babbo by nickname, already well in his eighties, came to stay with him then. In those days I was called Temple (a middle name used to avoid confusion with my father, the original Christopher) and Babbo would call me Temple of Baal.

In the afternoons Sedgwick would insist on going for horseback rides — magnificent country for that, one had to admit. Once at the tail end of a string of people plunging through high shrubbery in a dry arroyo bed I was almost torn off the back of the horse I was riding by the limbs of the shrubs and had to scream for help.

Sedgwick in those days became a sort of authority figure, at least in my mother's eyes. Once I scratched a (misspelled) Bad Word on a door of her four-door Ford convertible and after she found out that I knew what it meant said she'd report me to Fuzzy if I ever used it again.

For a time then Sedgwick also maintained a school on his ranch, run by a fellow named Bryant. At the same time one of Sedgwick's younger daughters, Kate, cut her lower lip to get out of playing clarinet in Mr. Bryant's music class. I could empathize: by then I was smearing poison oak on my arms at La Loma Feliz in an attempt, futile as it turned out, to get out of riding classes there. I had learned in Arizona that I was poor at dealing with horses, perhaps because I didn't know how to push other living things around (ones bigger than me, anyway). I'd woken up in a hospital down there once after being thrown from a horse in a stampede and developed a fear of horses — came even to develop a fear of the sight and smell of horse manure. When I refused to keep riding, everyone around me called me a quitter but the school allowed me to become one anyway.

I became good friends with Francis' second son Minty, Francis Minturn Junior, and went back to the ranch repeatedly to visit him. He collected beautiful automobile photographs of Cords, Duesenbergs, Pierce-Arrows and Hispano-Suizas out of the twenties and thirties — extraordinary custom vehicles, some with sixteen cylinders. There was even a shot of a Bugatti. The prime interior designer of the time had the scarcely decipherable name of Muehlemeister. The Hispano-Suizas from the 1920s had Geiger clocks in them. From 1921 to 1923, the clocks had the name Geiger above the center; after that, below. (Minty once saw a 1921 Hispano Suiza where the clock had the name below the center. When he pointed that out to the owner, the man became quite distressed.) His father also subscribed to *The Illustrated London News*, which had dazzling advertisements for Rolls Royces and Bentleys.

Francis Sedgwick would claim bluntly to my mother that he had had his eight children to perpetuate the proud, superior genes of his race, keep them dominant in the America of which he knew little and cared even less. But he lived out his life in a high pitch of frustration, while grabbing at everything he wanted in his immediate vicinity. I remember him chasing me with a tennis racquet when I was around ten for walking behind him while he was about to serve in a game. Later he told me he'd had to do that because my father was gone and I needed adult male supervision. Telling me this, he referred to me as "old ear."

There were a few other incidents. Another time Minty's older brother Bobby grabbed my brother Peter by the ankles, turned him upside down and started "wheelbarrowing" him around the parking lot, making him walk around on the gravel on his hands. Francis was there, watching it, egging Bobby on. We had to leave for the day, so that episode ended quickly, but another time, in the pool, when they ducked Peter, forced his head under the water, and he complained, the old man snapped, "Don't be fresh."

Fuzzy slapped Mary once in front of my mother. After that we ceased going to the Sedgwicks'.

You'll never know how much I love you
O please don't take my sunshine away

Long afterward, reading a bestseller that had just come out about one of Minty's younger sisters, Edie —-famous for a brief time, a discovery and disciple of the artist Andy Warhol's — I got the impression his father Francis stayed perhaps not in line but anyway within a narrow range of controlled frenzy as long as his father Babbo stayed alive (though when Babbo married a young woman toward the end of his very long life his son renounced him). We resumed seeing the Sedgwicks at times my father came by and later, when I could exercise a modicum of independence, having learned to drive, I continued to see Minty anyway because he ceased attending school at the ranch and went on to other places I frequented in the future.

6
Cold War Hangover

A round then in 1946 I saw my father in our living room, on his way back to China, working the short wave in an attempt to get a broadcast of an early atomic test, in Bikini Atoll.

As time went on after that, I became repeatedly exposed to arguments that the development of the nuclear bomb was nothing to be proud of, as I have said. I found it hard to respond to those charges back then. When I complained about them to my mother she replied "Well, what do you expect? If enough people accuse us of being about to use it, a lot of others will overhear them and believe them, or half-believe them." Which gave us perhaps not exactly a free ride in the competition among nations, but certainly an easy one, for the rest of the century.

Moreover, till then a fear had prevailed among many scientists that the world was slowly depleting all its energy-bearing resources, wood as well as fossil fuels, and slowly turning uninhabitable. Now a group of supremely gifted lockpickers had come along and gleaned Nobel prizes by manipulating invisible neutrons and isotopes and giving devastating proof that that was not so.

All my contemporaries collected atomic bomb rings you could find in cereal boxes, little plastic red bombs with a window at one end, through which you could look into little sparks flying around in the inside. Every boy had to have one of those.

To me now, that era was largely memorable for specific sights and sounds. In our house there was a dial phone, number 2464 (later WOodland 9-2464, finally 969-2464). I attempted to make a call from it but failed and found Dicky and Mary laughing at me. When I demanded to know what they thought was so funny they informed me I had to lift the receiver before I could start dialing. A fine point one did not learn in boarding school.

We had moved up to more complex forms of competition. We spent much of our time attempting to redeem slightly offbeat brand cola bottles, the three of us, but being rebuffed by store after store where the brand was not sold. We also engaged in a competition of looking under Coke bottles for their city of origin, to see whose bottle had traveled the farthest.

Other times we'd go to Hendry's Beach. On our return we always had to swab our feet with kerosene by the back door then rinse them off with water from the tap because there always was tar on the beach. I never learned whether that was from the ballast in tankers passing along the channel or from the seeps of heavy oil that ran all the way along the coast, from Rincon to Point Conception.

My mother had a succession of governesses, including an old German woman, Kati, in Marin. Kati would cry out "Ellenbogen!" whenever any of us put an elbow on the table. I'd hear her whispering a word at the end of every month. What's that? I asked. "German for 'rabbit,'" she explained. One had to mention that word then to get through the next month without crisis. I remember once pouring Worcestershire sauce on a piece of meat at the kitchen table right by the back door to the garden in Marin and flooding the plate as the (probably primitive, in those days) bottle-stopper was missing. To keep Kati from seeing what I had done, I slurped up the sauce in those days before additives; it tasted marvelous. Among its ingredients was something called "eschalots," a word I'd never seen before or since. (The early computer entrepreneur Norbert Bushnell once stated that the human memory was far superior to that of the computer in that anyone could recall instantly what the back door of the house where he lived at eleven looked like. Or at eight, in the case of this Marin back door.)

Among the governesses who followed Kati, the young warm ones did not stay long: they went off to get married. One of them, Judy, took drugs and got into knife fights down on Haley Street, a stretch of slum then — the police prevailed on my mother to keep her longer than she would have liked so they would know where she was and could keep an eye on her.

Finally an older woman from Scotland who called herself Nan and had worked for the Sedgwicks came and stayed with my mother for well over twelve years.

She was extremely strict. On a year we took off in Cambridge, she made us all take two-hour naps in the afternoon when not at school. I did not dare read during them for fear the book would be found, did not dare listen to the radio through earphones for fear of being burst in on and exposed. My mother in any event used to tell me, "We're not going to become slaves of the radio." Hence I spent naptime sucking Life Savers; that source of pleasure vanished with time, leaving only a small wrapper that did not offer much diversion. Moreover, one had to space out the Life Savers to make them last out the nap period; the allowance put a limit on the number one could buy. It was all right as long as I had a watch, but one day it broke down so I tiptoed out onto the porch to see if I could peer around at a neighborhood clock tower and when Nan came in to announce the end of nap-time the first thing she spotted was my bare footprint in the dust and she screamed at me for having gotten out of bed prematurely. It was a treat to be able to go to bed later than 7:30.

More intense than this was the Cambridge School Leggings Trauma. One did not wear leggings, snow pants, to the Cambridge School. Period. No matter how cold it was. If one did, one got what happened to Carole Greenberg in the fifth grade — shrieked and sneered down into hysterics. I was with my siblings made to wear leggings in the winter. I never dared show up with them at school. What I'd do was duck behind bushes in front of the Littauer Center on the way, take them off and stuff them into my green Harvardian book bag. An older, physically mature classmate who always refused to say whether or not he'd had sex yet, and sometimes took days off from class to make spare money shoveling snow, once saw my bulging bag and said a bit tauntingly "Leggings, Temple?" (Again, my name in those days.) But I survived. My siblings did as I did, though more out of respect for my seniority than conviction. I remember Peter once expressing some wistfulness about going against Nan's orders.

Then finally one day the reckoning came. Someone — maybe Florence, the wife of the maintenance man in our house — had seen us stashing the leggings behind the bushes and the day I came down with a bad cold Nan came in and just let me have it. "I have friends," she declared with contemptuous finality. "And they let me know when there are things going on behind my back." I fought back, screaming that I wouldn't be able to survive the jeering if I showed up wearing those pants. "You mean what people say about you is more important than your health?" she lashed back. I managed to mumble a half-coherent response to that too and a compromise was worked out: somehow my mother found a pair of brown long johns for me, and I wore those awhile, under my trousers.

Later Mary claimed the maintenance man used to go up to her bedroom at night and fondle her. When she complained about this our mother said "Oh that's bushwa."

Around election time I can remember once we'd returned to Santa Barbara from Cambridge asking my mother if I could see the polling place down on Toyon Road, where she'd been working on election day. This was toward evening. She told me I could go if I promised not to engage in any discussion with Nan afterward on how I'd conned her into letting me see how the voting process worked. We went down to Toyon Road and I saw the booths and the matrons in the clear, early dusk — light coming through massive arched Spanish windows and falling on big ochre-tile squares — and sure enough, returned to see Nan in anger demanding to know why I'd made my mother take me down there. I did exactly what my mother asked me not to do, which was to talk back, read off my rights as a citizen of a democracy. The outcome of the argument was that my mother broke out crying, hard. Over the years it occurred to me that that was because she was torn. She couldn't stand having me be right at Nan's expense. She was extremely dependent on Nan, after all.

Once, when Martha McGahan was staying at our house, Peter got into an argument along with everyone else and was sent up to his room. Our mother went by shortly, stating coolly, "I'm going into the bathroom to kill myself." Then Nan burst into Peter's room, brought her arm back, announced "I'll give y' this!" and let him have it across the face.

A favorite axiom of Nan's was "The truth always hurts."

Nan did have her redeeming qualities. She liked to gamble, on the horses and everything else, and she drank and smoked, so she was mortal.

As soon as we'd moved to Santa Barbara, with its benign climate, where one could play tennis about 355 days a year, my mother enrolled me then my two brothers in lessons for the sport. At first we took practice with an old hand, Hal Gorham, so devoted to the game it was said his wife allowed no mention of it around the house. My faint enthusiasm for that game, as well as any other, more or less vanished when, after I had been taking lessons for two years, my sister Mary in her second week on the courts had no trouble beating me 6-0, not quite blindfolded.

We soon also began taking lessons from a gifted younger pro, Byron DeMott, originally from Los Angeles. He had gone to Hollywood High (home of the Sheiks) with the comedy team of Gallagher and Sheehan, had served in the army and had had a cancerous larynx removed after years of heavy smoking, so had a very hoarse voice. He was more diplomatic than Hal, essentially a matchmaker, and focused on getting up games and developing young players.

My mother had really seemed to withdraw by then. Once I remember her picking me up in her car after I'd gone shopping downtown. I kept trying to talk to her but she would respond only curtly. Finally she wouldn't talk at all. Then, another time, as she was working in her room, I sat around and tried to make conversation, but she wouldn't talk, so I began whining and then she snapped that if I wasn't going to be quiet I'd better leave. It took me twenty years to cease taking these manifestations of withdrawal personally.

In any event, new figures did emerge in the world around her. She became involved as a volunteer with Americans for Democratic Action, the ADA, which in those days was headed by an upcoming young liberal senator, Hubert Humphrey of Minnesota. One of her fast friends was Harry Girvetz, a professor of political science at UC Santa Barbara, author of *From Wealth to Welfare* and at one point head of the local ADA chapter. He used to take me with his son John and one of my brothers to Class C California League baseball games between the Santa Barbara Dodgers and the Visalia Cubs. In 1950, on another trip up north, we passed through Sacramento for a Democratic convention and heard the keynote speaker, FDR's son Jimmy Roosevelt, who was about to run (unsuccessfully) for governor against Earl Warren.

That year my mother poured most of her energy into Helen Gahagan Douglas' senate campaign. I once saw this candidate at a picnic at Tucker's Grove not far from our home. Another volunteer and friend of my mother's, John O'Gorman, an alcoholic liberal Irish chemist, raffled off lemons to help raise funds. A Republican won the raffle. "Well, lemons to the Republicans, I always say," John cracked. He once saved my brother Peter, catching him as he slipped and fell off a cliff twenty-five feet above Hendry's Beach, where we'd been spending an afternoon, and he lost his teaching job at UC Santa Barbara because — unlike Harry Girvetz — he would not sign the loyalty oath the university regents demanded all their teaching personnel sign if they wanted to keep their jobs at that point near the start of the Cold War.

Over a dinner sometime around then he described how with the ADA he gave the *Washington Post's* famed political cartoonist Herbert Block (Herblock) an award and said his organization had found Herblock's cartoons exciting. It turned out Herblock was a self-effacing person. "Oh gee, didja?" he told O'Gorman in a squeaky little voice, genuinely moved by this modest honor.

At her fundraiser Helen Douglas gave a very emotional, almost hysterical speech. In the end she lost to her vicious opponent (R. Milhouse N., for those who don't like to see that man's name in print).

In those days Richard Nixon reminded many people of a two-bit grifter. "Would you buy a used car from this man?" they'd ask. He made his political fortune as a congressman at the apex of the anti-Red scare in the nation, leading the investigation into the accused one-time communist Alger Hiss (for alleged actions a decade and more before the Cold War, when the Soviet Union was a friendly state), ultimately getting Hiss convicted and jailed. But in the forty years that followed, by the way he took over and supervised management of the Cold War, Nixon came to have a greater impact on the broader world I moved around in than perhaps anyone else.

Of all the political events I witnessed in those days, however, the most gripping occurred on March 1, 1954, when four Puerto Rican nationalists fired gunshots down onto the floor of the House of Representatives from the spectator's gallery, wounding five congressmen in a violent demand for total independence for what had just become a commonwealth. Of course this was an outrageous act and the perpetrators served sentences of a quarter century for it, before Jimmy Carter, a later president, granted them clemency. One of the assailants, Lolita Lebron, said the assault was committed "for political expediency and not because of a concern for human rights." Whatever one might say about the rights or wrongs of this crime, it had an impact on me that a less forceful act would not have. It vividly showed me something I never lost sight of: that Puerto Ricans — and indeed Latins in general — often had a deep grievance against the United States government if not people. Ms. Lebron later became an advocate of nonviolent civil disobedience, but her point had long been made.*

In that era I came to spend days of free time at the Santa Barbara Public Library and the magazine rack at Leiter's Drugs. I went on to read everything I could get my hands on about World War Two in a hunger to make sense of it and I branched out to anything else that fell before my gaze. (I also began spending God knows how many hours reading Ripley's Believe It Or Not. There was the medieval German printer who walking home while he glanced over a text he'd just printed up saw a typographical error and died of a heart attack on the spot. Also Dick Tracy with his panorama of criminals, from No Dice Lipelli on out. And world maps everywhere: it kept irking me to see that most of the expanses on them were blue — the power of the British Empire — though that blight soon came to fade away.)

One book I will never forget though I can't remember its title was the work of a young American fighting with

---

* The New York Times, August 3, 2010

the Finns in their war against the Soviet Union just before World War Two. This author wrote of snow troops going out on patrol at night looking for fires. It was normally twenty below zero there in the winter and everywhere Soviet troops were emplaced they would set up a bonfire, so whenever the Finnish snow troops spotted flames in the dark they would pull a murderous raid on all around them. The author devoted much space to a reindeer they used as a pack animal, whose name I do remember: Kerttu. One statement he made especially mystified me: Finns boasting that they shot down one Soviet plane for every forty-four anti-aircraft shells they fired. In those days I thought it amazing that it would take as many as forty-four shells to bring a plane down. A great waste of artillery, it seemed to me.

There was Eddie Rickenbacker, whose plane went down in the south Pacific near the pork chop–shaped atoll of Canton Island (near where Amelia Earhart had disappeared right around my birth), languishing thirty-four days at sea without water; he later founded the now-defunct Eastern Airlines. One pilot's radio message "Sighted sub, sank same" became a household phrase. Another pilot meantime flew his airplane down the smokestack of a Japanese aircraft carrier.

American troops in some unit down in the South Pacific used the password "lollapalooza." If someone when challenged started to say "rara" they'd blast him away.

My godfather Donald Ryan had left a valise in our old workshop on his return from the south Pacific and I used to go through it. I'd come up with old bottles of salmon eggs, fishing flies, notes he took in a navy course and K-rations with their crumbly stiff blocks of chocolate. The chocolate smelled of old, mildewed *National Geographics*. I'd unwrap it, lick it, put it back and explore other objects, the button-sized compass, the ampoules of ammonia, the gauze roll. The chocolate looked like the creamy, pink-brown earth of northeastern Arizona desert, of Canyon de Chelly. Finally one day I devoured it. It was dry but delicious.

A person I came upon as I walked about the neighborhood was a boy roughly my age, Charles, walking his dog. We played for a while with his dog till his mother called him in for lunch. After dropping by a few Sundays more I met Charles' older sister Julia as well. Julia already knew everything about the human body and claimed she was going to become a doctor. She befriended me and would sit on the sofa between Charles and me, explaining drawings in anatomy books. She talked some about sexual functions in a detached, clinical way which made the subject seem hardly different from any other process, like breathing or eating.

At one point she told me Julia wasn't her original name and she came from Ukraine, as did her parents. Her father had come first, out of Ukraine on foot. He was Jewish and had been in a Nazi labor brigade during the war, going up through Ukraine with a Nazi division then returning once it was driven back. He survived because he was tough. As was his cousin. On hearing footsteps outside his house, that cousin got under his bed, gripped the bottom of the springs, hugged them from below. When the police came in they glanced under the bed but found no trace of him.

"I'm not Charles' sister either" Julia told me another time very quietly, when we were alone. "They sent for me later."

In fact it turned out Charles' parents had not wanted him. Another time, though Charles was about, he wasn't interested in joining us. His face was red and he sniffled and shambled in and out of rooms. "His father forgot his birthday," Julia explained.

The next time I saw Charles sulking about I asked what had happened and Julia told me about Mrs. Whitman, over whom Charles had developed a crush at school. His father had a caseful of mementos from the war, including a German first aid kit and some maps and obscure medals. I told him about Uncle Donald's valise which I'd found in the workshop and that emboldened him to break into the case. He wrapped some of the medals up and sent them to Mrs. Whitman, labeling them only "From Santa Claus." Mrs. Whitman came upon him in the hall and said nothing about them, just dryly addressed him "Santa Claus."

Unlike Charles, I could get out of this setting. The world back east had a powerful pull not only on my parents but also on me. I grew up feeling it necessary to get out of California perhaps once a year. Normally that meant crossing the United States. Decades later to be sure I came to see that as a casual matter, jet travel where the only inconveniences were local, the often deliberately difficult and expensive forays in and out of airports. Once on the plane one could take a window seat and, after the first dramatic spectacles of the Sierra, the Nevada desert then the Rockies, just count the sections in the farmland below as they passed by, one 160-acre square after the other.

My first unsheltered trip across America was different. My father had gone on his way to New York, to check in for an assignment to cover the war in Korea for the old *New York Herald Tribune*. I went east to start boarding school, at his old alma mater in Massachusetts.

To qualify for that school I had had to spend the summer being tutored in Latin, by my father. At the end of the summer we drove by a mission near Santa Barbara named La Purisima Concepcion. I had no idea what that meant and when I asked him he scolded me sharply. Had I wasted the whole summer? he demanded. I argued back that I had learned there had to be two "s"s in "Purisima," as there were in Latin.

7

To the New England Roots

My trip back was by train, in the company of Henry Francis, another boy starting out at the school, and his mother. Henry also lived in Santa Barbara. His parents had known the Nugents while they were living in Massachusetts, would rent their house on the beach in the summer and finally moved out West for good. (Another Santa Barbaran who went to Groton was John Belmont, a descendant of August Belmont, who as a figure in the Gay Nineties, after a fashion, had played a major role in financing the Union's operations in the Civil War and later established Manhattan's IRT subway system.)

Our trip covered the land slowly but strikingly, in the daylight hours. At some point while the train clacked through Kansas, I rubbed the soft part of my throat just below the right ear and felt a sore slowly growing lump. At first alerted by literature my mother had kept on the subject at home I thought it was cancer but could feel a similar lump on the left side as well that was just as sore and growing just as fast. Perhaps mumps, an ailment common enough to dwell in the memory bank of experiences kids my age shared. I discovered I could keep going on the trip, even after the change of trains in Chicago and the inevitable visit to the Museum of Science and Industry, as long as I said nothing to Henry's mother about my condition. When finally we reached Grand Central in New York my father met me and immediately said I looked as if someone had punched me hard on both cheeks and put me up at his residence of the moment, the Algonquin Hotel, to recover.

Henry's mother went on to Europe and in short order contracted a terrible case from me, which kept her bedridden in Copenhagen for two weeks.

The hotel room looked out across an airshaft at dark gray bricks and my mother's mother, who came to visit, brought — and ordered me to consume in volume — neet's foot oil, consommé and a thermos of tea so concentrated it kept me awake all the following night. As a result I heard my father talking over beers all night long with Graham Peck, the old friend from days in China. He stated at length that he was "growing disenchanted with Maddie," and on seeing that I'd been following this conversation told me to go brush my teeth, though I hadn't yet had breakfast.

In partial consolation for all this, another old China hand, Preston Schoyer, a writer who had lived a long time in Hong Kong and had a Chinese wife, would come over and tell me his Chinese stories about a person who grew a tumor that eventually outgrew the man and dominated his life.

Then my grandmother did elaborate on Aunt Lina, Mrs. Astor — the mistress of the ball, the one whose maiden name was Schermerhorn — and her grandmother Emily. Emily had a brother, William Waldorf Astor, who moved to England when his wife was outdone socially by Lina. In the Spanish American War the one-time libertine John Jacob IV lent his yacht, the *Nourmahal*, to the navy and even offered it the use of two of his railroads. After he died on the *Titanic*, his funeral was held in Rhinebeck and he left $150 million (perhaps $2.4 billion now). William had a son, Vincent, who married Brooke Astor. Years later Brooke was brought to Rokeby by helicopter to participate in the hundredth anniversary of Vincent's birth. The helicopter parked on the lawn before the piazza.

As with any tycoon and his legacy, Astor inspired all sorts of fantastic stories. My father, overhearing my grandmother, commented some on these. The least spectacular story was Longfellow's question to William Waldorf, who visited him at his home on Brattle Street in Cambridge, on whether or not he felt guilt at evicting people for not making payments on their mortgages (he didn't). There was the fantastic story of Captain Kidd's treasure buried in Penobscot, Maine (or perhaps Manhattan) and acquired by John Jacob from an Indian chief who knew where it was, in exchange for some whiskey. The trunk contained an incredible treasure in jewels and coins. This was totally apocryphal, but much of the public found it convincing, for how else could a man legitimately amass a fortune as rapidly as Astor had? Then there was the other side of the portrait — William trying fruitlessly to establish that his ancestry went far back before the humble crass butcher from Baden to a medieval crusader, Count Pedro d'Astorga of Seville. Also apocryphal — some serious genealogists from London determined that John Jacob's father was named Jacob Ashdor.

I didn't see my father again for three years.

In spirit, my father's alma mater and my new school Groton was an extension of the realm Rokeby belonged to, largely from the world of the English Channel. Almost all the ancestors of the people there had been Protestants from England, the Netherlands or Normandy — a group of gifted accountants and whalers transparently trying to rise above themselves.

The school motto was "Cui servire est regnare." It became clear to us early in our Latin studies that this meant "To serve Him is to rule." That is, serve Him (Christ) and rule Them — whoever "They" may be. (I thought in later years of the British expression "Divide et impera" — divide, of course, and rule even more.) In our time though they didn't translate the motto that way — they said it meant "To serve Him is perfect freedom."

In general, academically, Groton was an exceptional school.

Our time marked an interregnum between two long eras. In its earliest decades, the school had been rather conventional, as we have seen. For over half a century it was under the stewardship of its founder Endicott Peabody, an Episcopal minister and overpowering figure. One point my father repeatedly made about Peabody was that whenever a boy was ordered to leave the school, or left of his own volition, he felt he had failed as a headmaster. Conversely he stayed close to alumni. One such, Richard Whitney, an investment banker and president of the New York Stock Exchange, embezzled well over a million dollars from friends, relatives and the New York Yacht Club, inter alia, during the thirties. For this he was sentenced to Sing Sing. At one point Peabody asked him if he wanted anything; Whitney said he needed a left-handed catcher's mitt as the ones in the prison gym were all for the right handed. Peabody sent him one.

In the more recent past Groton became largely a product of the liberal current running through the richly multiethnic society as a whole, with its emphasis on coeducation, broad ethnic diversity, equal rights and a concurrent libertine spirit — "Beverly Hills," as people often label it in its current manifestation. Robert Moss, a theologian and faculty member in my time, who moved on shortly after I graduated, told me years later "I am amazed at Groton's ability to survive. When I came back on visits in the sixties I didn't believe it would. I thought it was falling apart." There had been disciplinary problems all around. One student successfully slipped a tape recorder into faculty meetings, recorded sessions of highly sensitive material on his fellow students and was caught in the end only because he had played his tape back to one of them and that student, badly shaken, complained to the authorities. Long hair proliferated and the headmaster banned it but could not make his ban stick. Years later, after the school straightened out, relatives sent their two sons there and found that the school's academic performance had slipped: it was deliberately recruiting slow-witted athletes and some people on the faculty were insensitive. The place now allowed students free rein to flash their wealth around, if they had it, which most did since tuition had risen to $29,000 a year.

In the interregnum, though, under headmaster John Crocker, conventional as he often was, we had strict standards. For instance, in 2010 the school invited Republican presidential hopeful Mitt Romney to give the Prize Day address — Crocker would never have allowed that.

Being a church school, it was devoted to religious studies and sacred music. It had a choir and music director Edward Gammons, who played Bach and other masters on the chapel organ (but not the likes of Brahms, who did not believe in God). We also had extraordinary teachers. Many of them, while talented, had matured during the Depression and had had little bargaining strength in their search for university positions; several of them for instance could not afford to complete work on their PhDs, at Harvard even. As an example, those of us who took Greek and had to keep with it for three years once choosing it as an elective had a different teacher each of those years — Norris Getty, Melvin Mansur and Frank Groten, each one exceptionally versed in classical literature. One of my fellow students in these classes — the son of a Harvard professor himself — continued briefly with Greek when he went on to Harvard but told me that he found the professors' approach there stilted and academic — dry, in contrast with the much richer courses we had taken at Groton.

These gentlemen also taught Latin. Though an imposed language, one we were compelled to take even before our teens — unlike Greek — and thus one toward which I for one never came to feel warmth, it had its wry moments. Once going through a Latin vocabulary for homework I came upon the word for "in vain," frustra (with a long mark over the *a*) and laughed for about an hour on seeing that. And the rhythm of the deponent verbs utor, fruor, fungor, potior and vescor remains with me to this day.

One teacher of German and French was Ernst Loewenberg, who came to the United States as a refugee from Hamburg. He would engage us in lengthy conversations in French class. I remember once his criticizing a movie we'd just been shown for having no poetry. From him I learned that one could have poetry

Christopher T. Rand

in poverty. He was once shocked on seeing me read *Mein Kampf* for a paper and swore he thought he'd never see the day it was allowed in coursework. He went on to tell me one couldn't tell, in translation, how execrable the original German was.

Another French teacher, Roger Moore, was very good, as was Mr. Loewenberg, in getting us to converse in French. He also was capable of exposing us to paradox. In one examination he threw a curve ball past most of us. He had a passage for us to translate: Jean-Paul Sartre saying, "We never were freer than under the Nazi occupation." We couldn't get that — aren't you less free under an occupation, after all? Moore laughed, explained that that was the sort of paradox Sartre just loved. Then after another quiz, when none of us could figure out how to translate "Mediterranean" into French, he grinned at a big map over his blackboard showing in big letters "La Mer Mediterranee."

The English program was superb too. One of my teachers, James Satterthwaite, showed me I could write. Third form year, ninth grade, was crucial as we had English under James "Ace" Waugh, who was largely responsible for showing me a Third Way. Till then, since getting to Groton anyway, I'd believed you either had superior athletic ability or got very good grades; otherwise, you were pathetic, simply. I would wonder how pathetic I was, especially in the face of superior academic performances from others. I sought refuge in the memory of Charles down the street from the Sunday school on the North Side in Santa Barbara and decided he was pathetic — certainly there was no point to his life that I could see. But largely thanks to Ace through the materials he gave us to read and discuss, another key element of life manifested itself: irony (and beyond that, anarchism, nihilism, the random bizarre). Incidentally, I learned (again years later) that some other teachers asserted that Ace was a communist and complained of this to Crocker. "He does his job," Crocker retorted, and dismissed the objection.

Yet another teacher was Richard Irons, a protégé of the famed British philosopher of history Arnold Toynbee. Irons was a masterful teacher of European history and had us writing long papers our tenth grade year on such subjects as Yalta, the Battle of Jutland and Chamberlain's capitulation at Munich. He even offered seniors (sixth formers) a tutorial on Toynbee's *Study of History*. In those days Toynbee was viewed as one of the seminal thinkers of the West. He kept writing into the sixties and everything he wrote — largely travel pieces, toward the end — met with very broad public reception. The moment he stopped writing though people stopped reading him. Again, Irons was a teacher of exceptional quality; again, few of the professors we later encountered at the university level were of his caliber. One of my classmates went on to study in the Netherlands at the elite University of Utrecht but said that none of his teachers there, even, were as good as Irons.

8
Grandmother's High Times and Decline

One feature of life at a Massachusetts boarding school was that I would spend vacation time at family places, primarily Rokeby, though I visited Providence Rhode Island as well.

My mother's father, Richard Aldrich, came from there, from a modestly prosperous family, prominent whalers. His brother John was still alive then and when I visited him he took me to see his art class, complete with genuine nude model, then to meet an aged relative, Mrs. Burleigh. Her house was a fixture of central Providence in those days. Surrounded by buildings belonging to Brown University (whose motto, <u>Dum spes spero</u>, I had become able to understand ("Where there is hope, I have hope")), it had a window made of old beer bottle bottoms and was not for sale. Brown tried to get it for decades, and finally did, when she died at 103.

My grandfather Richard had originally hoped to get involved in politics, but he had a terrible stutter that stayed with him all his life, possibly a manifestation of deeply suppressed anger. He would struggle and stutter through an elaborate sentence phrase by phrase, gulp and gesture by gulp and gesture — finally reach the end of it, climb up over the edge and establish himself on it as if pulling himself out of a maelstrom into balmy sunlight. One of his nephews, David, was afraid to be around him — feared that the momentum of the stutter would end up in an explosion. This stutter always existed, but did it get worse after he married Margaret Chanler? No one of course can tell anymore — could tell for over a decade. The Harvard philosopher William James, a distant relative, tried to cure the condition while Richard was a Harvard undergraduate but as my grandmother said he was "too strong a character to be affected by James' psychological waves."

After completing his studies at Harvard in the mid-1880s Richard turned to music instead. At first he wanted to be a pianist and studied a while in Austria, but his hands were too small even after he cut the tendons between his fingers, so he turned to writing. He went to work for the *Providence Journal* as a reporter, editorial writer then critic and after that passed on down to Washington for two years as secretary to his senator, Nathan Dixon. He then went on to New York, to the *Tribune* then the *Times*.

He was the music critic for the *Times* from 1902 to 1924, when he became critic emeritus and assumed an administrative role on the paper.

He met my grandmother Margaret at a dance for one of her nieces. As she described it in *Family Vista*,

We danced together, and met again before long. He spent Easter with the Chapmans and we were soon friends. A year or more went by before either of us realized that the crystallization of unmarried ways was invaded. A man of forty-one and a woman of thirty-five are beyond the easy romance of early years. They have to feel that they are becoming necessary to each other, that their established lives belong together. The drive of their rising emotion must reach the point of union for what each one is in oneself.

They married when he was forty-three. Had he not met her he probably would never have married at all. In a photograph from the era he was already short, bald and moustachioed, rather like a Hashemite king, and his wife frowned angrily at the ceiling. He had brought her into a world she had disparaged and shunned in her earlier years, brought her out of the deliberately colorless even grim domain Daisy Chanler had lamented.

The Bethlehem Steel magnate Julius Schwab, who owned the mansion across from her West Seventy-fourth Street house, was a patron of the arts. It was through the renowned soprano Marcella Sembrich that my grandparents met Schwab. My grandmother (as well as Johannes Brahms) was a passionate admirer of Ms. Sembrich, who, she said, had grown up in absolute poverty in Poland — her father was a musician and she learned the violin as a child. Later she attributed her success as a singer to her violin training.

Many times Schwab would invite my grandparents over for little impromptu concerts in his spacious drawing room and my mother often reminisced about such evenings.

During the war my grandmother, drawing on experience from her dramatic career as a nurse's aide, borrowed the use of the Schwab Mansion bowling alley and billiard room for packing Red Cross garments, dressings and wool. Another time in 1920 she saw Warren Harding play cards at Schwab's, just before he became the Republican presidential nominee.

All sorts of extraordinary people ended up in the company of my grandparents at the New York house — even the famous philosopher Bertrand Russell and his wife, at one point. Mostly, though, the entertainment swirled around the rich music world of the day.

My mother often referred to her mother and her Aunt Amey, Richard's spinster sister, as "bluestockings," an expression prevalent in the early twentieth century for women who made a great show of devotion to artistic and intellectual matters they weren't talented enough to understand. Still, the rich world of music Richard brought created a powerful bond between him and my grandmother.

My grandfather was friends as well with the great composer Gustav Mahler and the Romanian George Enesco, whom many of the day considered a great conductor and legendary violinist. (Eventually the name of a town in Romania was changed to Enesco in his honor.) A niece, Hester LaFarge, once recalled an evening in the brownstone with Enesco. When they got talking at dinner about Beethoven's *Ninth Symphony*, which Enesco had conducted and indeed performed in many times, he arose, went to the piano and played an improvised adaptation of the symphony from beginning to end. Another time Enesco arranged to play an entire, unpublished opera for them, from a tragedy by Sophocles. Mrs. LaFarge recalled yet another luncheon when she and my grandmother were alone with Dame Myra Hess, a great pianist of the day who was scheduled to give a concert that evening. As it happened my grandmother could not go to that concert, so Dame Myra played most of the concert works for them right then on the piano. She would play for my grandfather whenever she was in New York, after thrombosis confined him to a couch in his living room. My grandmother also stated that the famous pianist Harold Samuel rehearsed his Bach concerts for a week at her home during his concert tour in New York. A lady named Coolidge held a festival of chamber music in Tanglewood every autumn and after it my grandparents would invite a few of the performers down to Rokeby.

My mother remembered attending another piano concert with her father, the famous pianist Gabrilovitch and a violinist colleague. It was a hot summer night and Gabrilovitch started sweating in the middle of it and wiping his brow. He said, "It's a hot night, isn't it," and his colleague replied "Not for violinists."

My mother recalled as a child going to Carnegie Hall to the first concert of Yehudi Menuhin, a child prodigy of perhaps eleven. After the performance and the standing ovation it earned Menuhin thanked the audience for its exuberant response, for that meant that his father would reward him by letting him have an ice cream soda after he retired from the hall.

Richard Aldrich's position was one of considerable influence — as of course it remains to this day. Only four cities in America had a music critic then (the others being Philadelphia, Boston and Chicago).

He was in particular a major early voice in affirmation of the works of Brahms, Debussy and Richard Strauss. He was less enthusiastic about Camille Saint-Saens and downright derogatory about Hector Berlioz. He stated that the latter's music, though "presented as the fairest product of the modern impulse of its time in art," somehow "turns to ashes like Dead Sea fruit, as you try to lay hold of it." Berlioz' life was "a perpetual paroxysm of love, hate, grief, hyperbolic and unmeasurable emotion" and Berlioz' musical thought was "almost always superficial. His musical invention is terribly, wearisomely commonplace. How few of the themes in any of his most important compositions are expressive or beautiful, or find their way to the heart! The pomp and glitter and the wealth of color with which he sets them forth can only hide their poverty."* He also told my mother that Beethoven did not know how to compose for the human voice and cited the grueling ranges in his *Ninth Symphony* as an example. He also spoke disparagingly of Beethoven's imitation of bird songs in the *Pastoral Symphony* – a purist, he contended music was the ultimate art form and should not be used to advance other forms of natural expression.

As a teenager living in the city, my mother was devoted to the theater and captivated by the storied actress Helen Hayes. She went to a couple of her plays in 1928, especially *Coquette*, and hung out to see her by the stage door afterward. Once, after a hasty dinner at her place, she and her close friend Jane Wyatt, later a famous actress too, went "dressed to kill" to a performance at the Maxine Elliott Theater and waited outside afterward till Ms. Hayes came out with Charles McArthur, her eventual husband, and whisked off in a "touring car".

Finally, on April 13, my mother screwed up her courage and decided to try visiting Ms. Hayes after a matinee performance of *Coquette*. Dressed in black patent leather shoes, a polka-dot velvet dress, white coral beads,

---

* These observations come from his collected pieces, <u>Musical Discourse</u>.

a black velvet hat, gray fur coat and a blue leather bag, she went to the play with a friend, Louisa Munroe. (By then she had seen Ms. Hayes' performance twice and her mother and Uncle Chester had already met her on social occasions.) She wrote the actress a note on her card asking if she could meet after the performance. She was squeamish about passing on the card but she recalled that her mother had told Ms. Hayes she'd seen the play twice, and Ms. Hayes replied "She must like to cry, then." At that her friend Louisa insisted she press the card on an usher. The usher soon told them Hayes would see them.

After the final act, a man took them to a massive iron door, which a maid opened to a dainty little room. Ms. Hayes came in, still made up. My mother wrote a description of the meeting. She said that Ms. Hayes' eyes were what she noticed most, "a beautiful greenish gray."

Her friend Louisa asked, "Do you feel very much what you act?"

"No," Ms. Hayes replied. "If we did that, we would fall to pieces. After the first few times we get a way of doing it."

"Just like musicians, isn't it?" Louisa replied. "I was told by one that they mustn't feel too much what they are playing."

"Oh, I didn't know that," Ms. Hayes replied, "interested".

When my mother replied that she'd seen *Coquette* three times, the actress said she didn't believe *she* could and Louisa stated she'd seen *What Every Woman Knows* four times. That, the actress replied, she thought she could do; she loved to act in it. By the time her career wound down decades later Ms. Hayes had won a total of three Tonys, two Oscars and an Emmy.

My Groton English teacher Jim Satterthwaite once told me about a friend named Freiday who had taught briefly at Groton during the war and later went to live in a residence-hotel in San Francisco. Freiday had a record of Queen Victoria speaking German which he had picked up in a used-record store and Helen Hayes, who once assumed the role of Queen Victoria, had him play it for her when she learned of it.

My mother saw her father break out in tears twice. The first occasion was when the violinist Albert Spalding gave him a surprise concert at Rokeby. The other was when the great Polish pianist Ignatz Paderewski embraced him at a party on his last trip to the United States. My grandmother had arranged a luncheon between Paderewski and Mr. and Mrs. Adolph Ochs, the owners of the *Times*; soon afterward an editorial appeared in the *Times* supporting Poland's claim to recognition as a free nation.

Richard had brought an openhearted, liberal spirit to that world. For one thing, as Jack Chapman wrote in a letter to Daisy Chanler, he "of course believes that religion of *any* sort is an obscene sort of subject, that ought not to be mentioned; and that no honest or educated man can have anything to do with it." Another side of this liberal spirit revealed itself when his brother-in-law Winty died in 1926. A furious argument arose in the family after this — whether or not Winty, a Catholic, should be allowed burial in the family vault in New York's Episcopalian Trinity Cemetery or whether he should even be allowed to have last rites there administered by a priest. There was no compromising on this bitter argument. Even Richard was forced to take sides. He wrote Winty's widow Daisy that he was "heartsick" to announce that he could not attend his funeral. Finally Winty was buried in Geneseo, where he had lived for decades on a farm.

After Richard died, just before I was born, the rich world he had formed about the great music of his day slowly, quietly slipped from grasp. Viewing my grandmother's world from a modern perspective one could say there was virtually no wiring in it, for one thing; though they weren't ever at the heart of her life, the absence of phonographs or gramophones (other than the cumbersome Victrola with its records a quarter-inch thick) left her deprived in a way. More important of course was the end of the musical evenings, social swirls and soirees themselves. On top of that, she gradually turned totally deaf. Her world became one of large empty silent halls and chambers, all the more confining in the cold half of the year, when all present saved on fuel by heating only the rear half of the mansion.

When I returned to Santa Barbara on one of my school vacations I heard my mother announce to us that she was getting a divorce from our father and marrying Byron the tennis professional from whom we had been taking lessons.

I for my part went into a state of remorse at the thought of losing my father, but could not articulate my feelings or lash out effectively with them. "But you will always have your father," my mother told me. "He will *always* be your father." I never really believed her.

Up at the Sedgwicks' ranch one eyewitness heard Francis ask "Did you hear what happened to Maddie?"

"Yes," replied one of his lady guests. "Isn't that terrible?"

My grandmother unlike me could articulate her feelings and simply refused to accept the remarriage. She would have no part of "a woman married to two husbands" — somewhat paradoxically as she was also vehemently anti-Catholic. From then on she would address my mother, by mail, as "the Rand children's mother."

9
Divorce and Remarriage:
A New, High-Powered World

Somewhere in here, maybe a bit earlier, my mother came to develop a real resentment of my sister Mary. She harbored this resentment for decades and it came to border on the pathological. I never definitively grasped the reason for it, though I heard some grim attempts to explain it. Maybe, I speculated in time, it was because she'd had too many children. I wondered with the others why she'd had all the children she had. One theory was that she liked to be pregnant — felt constructive, useful, by forming the child. "I don't see why Roman Catholics are the only ones who should have children," she once told Lottie.

The actual job of looking after the child, once born, though, brought her distress. She gave up coping with raising the five children alone, unabetted by her husband, and in effect signed the child-rearing task over to a hired manager, or heavy.

Years later I also learned that Mary had had trouble with her periods. She said that she got her first period at age thirteen or so and went to our mother with the news; she claimed that our mother put her down so hard, or perhaps insulted her so badly for her apprehensiveness, that she did not have another one for five years. Diana, whose bedroom was next to hers, used to hear her moaning and thrashing almost every night, then would get up in the morning to see her bedclothes wrapped and twisted all over the floor.

Just about then, when I was back at Groton, I received word that my siblings, still in Santa Barbara, had contracted polio. Mary's attack was the worst — she stopped being able to breathe and they had to put her in an iron lung. Peter had some paralysis in his legs for a time. Diana didn't have any obvious symptoms but came down with a terrible case of what seemed to be the flu — perhaps a mild polio attack. Dicky wasn't affected. Maybe he had developed some immunity from spinal meningitis up in Marin ten years earlier, where a renowned Doctor Faber saved him by giving him a big sulfa dosage. Reverend Crocker had me into the headmaster's study and got me to kneel down and pray with him over this.

Peter went back to walking normally and in time Mary got out of the lung, though she never totally recovered from a crick in her throat and always had to tilt her head to swallow. But that had been a horrendous experience nonetheless. Then by the end of the decade the miracle of the Salk vaccine. I whipped down to the Santa Barbara courthouse to get my shot the moment the shipment came in, in deep gratitude. It was the first time in history that man had become wholly liberated from plague. (AIDS came a generation later, but if you got that it was usually your own fault, not like playing touch football on some rain-soaked lawn — and anyway they came up with a treatment of sorts for that.)

Diana, being the youngest, came to spend more time around our mother and Byron than the rest of us. To this day that era stood out to her for the powerful stench of the Liederkranz cheese, popular in those days, which our mother and Byron would bring out with crackers every evening at the start of the drinking hour. My mother had continued to be very dependent on Nan. She and Byron had had a symbiotic relationship with her, almost a ménage à trois. The three of them would play cards by the fireplace — Byron and Nan would spend much of their time trying to cheat each other.

When I asked Diana many years later why our mother had kept Nan on so long after we had grown up, she surprised me by saying not because she was dependent on her, not because she couldn't cope without (or with) her, or not even because she was in some way attracted to her, but because Nan kept an eye on Byron. Byron had to be watched, literally all the time; you'd let him out to go to the store on an errand and he'd pick up some woman — or even worse a bottle of wine — and you wouldn't see him till the next day.

Byron had seen combat out in the South Pacific, first shipping out to help ward the Japanese away from the strategically located pork chop-shaped Canton Island atoll about midway between Hawaii and Australia, then fanning out to other nearby islands such as Tarawa for combat. Diana used to ask him what it had been like in the war. He repeatedly refused to talk about it. Finally he did, briefly: "I will tell you just one thing about it, and never mention it again" he said. "It's absolutely terrible when you're driving along with your buddy in a Jeep and suddenly there he is, blown to smithereens."

We spent much of our time then in a second home, a beach house southeast of Santa Barbara. Our neighbor in the next house over, Larry Johnson, who'd been a radio operator on a bomber, didn't want to talk at all about the war either. Larry was a union glazier making $2.70 an hour then, plus 5 cents in vacation pay and 7.5 cents toward a hospital plan.

When we lived down there, Byron had a couple of large black poodles to which he was devoted. One of the poodles really did stand on the tracks behind the beach house and get transfixed by an oncoming train.

Byron had been a very gifted tennis player, but he was a contemporary of Bobby Riggs and could never defeat him; Riggs after all once won Wimbledon, in the late thirties. Byron would point to Riggs as an example of a player who should never have been good at tennis but used his wits to maximum effect. The odds against him winning in Wimbledon in the men's singles, men's doubles and mixed doubles, all together, had been 120 to 1. Riggs bet on himself in all three (obviously strictly against the rules, if not the law) and won.

Byron also said that whenever there was a dance after a tournament in which they had played, Riggs would busily go about dancing with almost every girl in the place. Time after time a girl would slap him in the face and walk off before the dance ended. However, Riggs always left the place with a girl under his arm.

Byron needed to make a living in any event, so turned professional shortly after high school, thereby excluding himself from eligibility for any more tournaments, which were open only to people labeled amateurs in that era.

Byron worked for Robert O'Dell, who ran, perhaps owned, Santa Barbara's Biltmore Hotel and Coral Casino as well and the Clift Hotel up in San Francisco, where my mother and Byron often stayed when they went up north. O'Dell was a tough old bird. He wouldn't let any man with long hair into the Biltmore. Once an employee of O'Dell's was having dinner with a friend in a restaurant downtown Santa Barbara and unburdened herself of a long tirade against her boss. O'Dell happened to be sitting in the next booth and fired her on the spot. O'Dell tried to fire Byron once, too, but the players' committee, then headed by Haley Fiske, a devoted player, came to his rescue.

Byron had an insatiable appetite for social activity. He and my mother went to parties at the house of Lou Soles and his wife Dawn, who came from a somewhat eccentric Canadian family and was about the age of Soles' children. The Soles had a dramatic beach house on Fernald Point right next to the Nugents. Dawn used to worry about the breakfast, luncheon and dinner parties Lou made her throw all the time — virtually her only chore in life. At one of the parties she threw everyone, male and female, had to show up as Groucho Marx. A friend of my mother's named Eleanora who did public relations work with Conde Nast in Los Angeles talked of going to another Soles party where none of the guests wore more than transparent tights and big green fig leaves over the relevant areas. At one point they all formed a conga line and Eleanora remembered one big figure from the local social whirl standing behind her "making a nuisance of himself." (Others would hear this fellow go about singing "Footprints upside down on the dashboard.")

My mother and Byron took players a number of places for group matches with players in other clubs out of town. The most dramatic setting they visited was the court an old friend of Byron's had built up by Zaca Lake expressly so he could bring groups for matches there. The lake was in the dead center of Santa Barbara County, surrounded by primitive mountains. One reached it down Foxen Canyon Road, past the Sedgwicks' old ranch Corral de Quati, on a rough road past huge jack beams pumping on a Texaco lease, unpaved for about four miles, with five stretches where one had to cross deep gravel-lined streams. The lake itself was extraordinary, one of two in the state that were fed by springs rather than runoff or streams, an oblong body of water up to sixty-five feet deep in a bowl of mountains, those to the north dry but the one to the south heavily forested. In fact Jacques-Yves Cousteau almost brought an underwater vessel up to film the bottom of this lake. Sitting before the windows over the lake, framed by enormous tormented sycamore branches, one looked out at little glistening waves in a high breeze over the dark water. There were a few cabins around the corner from the lodge, then a dock with a few canoes and an area roped off with floats for swimming. Years later during a major forest fire about five hundred firefighters descended on this lodge and helicopters came and dipped buckets in the lake. One couldn't see flames from the lake though, just an expanding ferocious glow over the ridge. The ridge to the south, on top of the lush mountain, must have been fifteen hundred feet above the lake.

Another time Byron took his team to play a club in La Jolla. On that visit my mother and a fellow player, Dora Bradley, the sister of Innis Bromfield from Yale and *The Coast*, went to Sea World, where they really did see a duck get up on a stool before a piano and hit the keys with its wings — "Not very accurately, but it played," my mother stated in amazement.

Dora told us that a gold inlay once popped out of one of her husband Joe's teeth when he was at the dentist and slipped down into his lung. A feverish campaign arose to get it out. One doctor said it would have to be removed surgically but Joe refused to go through with such an operation. Finally they heard of a doctor down at San Diego Medical School who had a cord with small TV-eye that one could insert into the lung — like the instrument used many years later for an angioplasty or a bladder examination — and with the aid of that they had the inlay out in ten minutes.

Another sister club of Byron's was the Palm Springs Racquet Club. The great Hollywood star Dinah Shore was a tennis enthusiast who frequented that club, even at one point married a player there who worked as a summertime building-plasterer (in days when they still plastered walls). On one team visit there Byron brought along a lovely young student of his, among others. Harpo Marx came up to her in the bar in the evening after the matches and said someone elsewhere at the bar would like to talk to her. That person turned out to be Kirk Douglas. He invited her out for dinner with another couple then walking her back to her room asked if she'd care to spend the night with him. She declined.

Another time we went to a pro-celebrity exhibition at the Beverly Wilshire Hotel courts, attended actually by very few people. Present was the brilliant baseball entrepreneur Bill Veeck as in Wreck, playing with complete abandon in very short shorts exhibiting his plastic leg, telling us that Grover Cleveland Alexander in the twenties was a better pitcher drunk than sober. Also present was James Mason, the famed actor. Mason would press the elbow of his racquet-arm to his waist, race at the ball with his arm fixed and propel the ball forward (usually into the net) by the momentum of his body. He never swung his arm at all. Later we had lunch at booths in the adjacent restaurant and Mason talked quietly through the whole meal with one of the other players about opportunities in West Los Angeles real estate.

Another of Byron's clients — certainly no student — was Johnnie Rosselli the gangster. That was down in Los Angeles, before Byron met my mother. Byron would see a gunman at each end of the court, loaded .45 in shoulder holster, whenever Rosselli came for lessons.

(My mother recalled a story from my father's mother, Bay, however, which topped that. Bay once took a trip with a friend to New York, down a new turnpike in Connecticut, in the friend's chauffeur-driven limousine. On the way, they spotted another chauffeur-driven limousine stalled on the side of the road and stopped to offer assistance. Their chauffeur managed to get the disabled car running again. The passenger in the other car, grateful for their intercession, told them that if they ever needed help down in New York they should give him a call. He handed them his card, on which was inscribed a telephone number and the name Al Capone. Neither my grandmother nor my friend had ever heard of him, as his principal theater of operations then was Chicago. He did however also have a strong presence in New York, as it turned out. They proceeded on their way. Some months later burglars broke into the Park Avenue apartment of my grandmother's friend and stripped it of its valuables. The friend remembered Al Capone's offer and called him in distress. In a few days a man came to her apartment bearing a large suitcase, which he opened to reveal an enormous collection of jewelry, silverware and other objects. He had brought instructions from Capone that if she saw anything in there that was hers, she could reclaim it. She saw quite a few things that were, and did.)

There were a number of horrendous driving catastrophes in Santa Barbara in the fifties. I recalled the worst of them all in the aftermath of a drunken afternoon party at Lou Soles' on Fernald Point, right by the railroad tracks. A guest named Nagle — a diabetic — drove off with his whole family, which was annihilated by a train as he tried to get across the tracks. Soles stopped his big parties after that.

At one point in those years, a friend of Byron's arranged for him to go to Paris and teach at a club there, while the French pro at that club took his place in Santa Barbara. Byron went there for half a year with my mother, Peter and Diana. My mother prevailed on my father's brother Bill, who was then running the United States Lines, to get them a first-class stateroom on the *America* for second-class rates, moving the barrier one door down the deck. Afterward Bill told her the favor had caused him deep embarrassment and she was never to ask that favor of him again.

Another brilliant player of whom Byron talked often was Herb Flam, who made a big splash for a while. (He, with Art Larson in 1950, played the last all-American men's final in US Nationals/Open history.) "You ought to study business like Flam," Byron kept telling me. "That way you too can end up on *The Sixty-Four Thousand Dollar Question* and make a fortune by getting all the right answers." Herb became a compulsive gambler, though, losing up to $100,000 in backgammon at the LA Tennis Club, then someone saw him in Spain, endlessly riding an elevator, shortly before he committed suicide on putting all his remaining money on himself at a European grand-slam tournament.

Byron continued to maintain contact with many other top players. One of them was Richard "Pancho"

Gonzalez, whom he brought up once in the fifties to Santa Barbara to play in an exhibition. Gonzalez started out as a brilliant teenager player in Los Angeles. The squeaky-voiced Perry Jones, the dominant figure in Los Angeles tennis in those days, first barred him from an Eastern tournament because of poor performance in school, but soon relented. Gonzalez won the 1949 US title in a five-set final versus Ted Schroeder, then signed a contract for $75,000 (brokered by Bobby Riggs) to challenge the champion Jack Kramer on a pro tour. He lost ninety-six matches to twenty-seven, then struggled in round robin matches in the early fifties, then routed another star player, Tony Trabert, in a 1956 tour, seventy-four to twenty-seven. Then beat the younger champions Ken Rosewall and Lew Hoad and retired to a lavish club in the Bahamas till 1964. Kramer had refused to play him since his first tour as he had become more experienced. Then Gonzalez went on a tour with the Australian star Frank Sedgman, whom he beat, though he got no recognition for that, and sat around Los Angeles from then on out, playing here and there in pro tournaments.

Gonzalez was a tough man with a scar down one cheek who claimed he knew a man who'd spent twelve years in jail, mastering the trick of picking twenty-six cards off a deck. My mother had got to know Gonzalez and studied him, considering him the greatest player in the world. She said he was sold short by all the other pros because he had a poor mind and turned pro at nineteen out of stupidity. The Mexican Davis Cup squad offered him almost everything to come down to Mexico and remain an amateur. When Kramer offered him $15,000 for the later tour (while offering Trabert $80,000) Gonzalez was infuriated and worked him up to $30,000. My mother was in Los Angeles watching a tournament at the time the haggling went on and heard Gonzalez talk a lot about the matter. He was very cocky, knew he could whale Trabert but was very honest and said so in all simplicity and Trabert had no chance to do more than argue back since he refused to play in pro tournaments at the time. Gonzalez ended up against yet another top player, Francisco "Pancho" Segura, in the climactic finals of this tournament. There, Gonzalez proved himself magnificently. He tired out Segura, thirty-four, by keeping him on the string in the first set, throwing away sixteen set points with a sharp backhand about three inches below the net, until the score was twenty-one to nineteen, and then taking the next two sets, six-three six-two.

One players' hangout was Arzy's, somewhere around Beverly Hills, where many players went to get their racquets strung. Once on a visit there I met a girlfriend of Gonzalez's and listened to her harangue at length on how he was blowing all his great chances in life.

In the days before the war Byron would go out to Catalina Island off Los Angeles and give lessons to Paulette Goddard and Charlie Chaplin, who kept losing bets that Byron couldn't hit dimes on the service line.

Now in the Santa Barbara exhibition Gonzalez toyed around with another good Los Angeles pro, Carl Earn, who played respectably till the end, when Pancho got bored and dispatched him with three stunning drop shots — three slice shots in a row which cleared the net and bounced back onto Gonzalez's side before poor Earn could get to them.

Later at the Beach House, Byron just marveled over the match. "Have you ever seen anything like those three drop shots?" he exclaimed, shaking up martinis. Of course I hadn't. I asked him if Gonzalez was the best player ever, and he said, "Close; but the great master Bill Tilden would have beaten him. Gonzalez could serve the ball anywhere he wanted — but Tilden would always know where the serve was coming, and he'd be right there for it."

Three decades later Gonzalez came back to Santa Barbara to play in a seniors' tournament. By then he was living in a van and had contracted cancer.

Once Byron had Tilden scheduled to play an exhibition match at the Biltmore but Tilden had served time earlier for pedophilia and when O'Dell found out about that made Byron cancel the appearance.

In those days the biggest tennis event in the area was September's Pacific Southwest tournament at the LA Tennis Club. Byron recalled one of his oldest friends, Jack Tidball, ending up in the Pacific Southwest finals one year in the thirties against — Ellsworth Vines, then one of the highest ranked players in the world and, like Riggs, one-time Wimbledon champion. Hal Gorham was there at the match, but it dragged on and on, Vines taking the first two sets and leading in the third, and Hal decided to get started on the long hot drive back to Santa Barbara on the narrow 101-ribbon with its hectic traffic. The next morning Hal read that Tidball had pulled the match out in five sets.

Years later, when I showed my mother the New York *Times* obituary of another brilliant player from those days, who should remain nameless here, she read it and said "It doesn't comment on his stealing money and jewels in the LA Tennis Club locker room, for which they put him in jail."

One of Byron's tennis students was David Crosby, son of Floyd, a cameraman who had done magnificent documentary work with Pare Lorentz then participated in the filming of *High Noon*, a movie which, while brilliant and highly successful, presented a left-wing message. Those who worked on it were largely blacklisted by the industry for years afterward. Floyd Crosby lived about Santa Barbara for some years, unable to find film work in Los Angeles. The man who wrote the script for *High Noon*, Carl Foreman, was also denied work and went off to England, where he spent the rest of his active life. David Crosby went on to make a living as a performer with such people as Stephen Stills, Graham Nash and Neil Young. Another celebrity Byron taught was Walter Pidgeon; he would come up to the Biltmore often but only rally, never play. A beautiful teenage contemporary of mine who took lessons from Byron was warned by her mother to stay away from Pidgeon.

Byron had had one great pupil of his own, Pauline Betz. He met her as a teenager working at a Thrifty Drug fountain in Los Angeles, took her out on the courts and introduced her to the game, taught her how to play from scratch, from the fundamentals on up, and saw her through the junior girls' championships. Then she left him for another coach and never gave him any credit, which embittered him. Ms. Betz went on to become a five-time Grand Slam singles champion, winning once at Wimbledon and four times in the Forest Hills nationals. Her career was foreshortened when the USLTA forbade her from playing in further amateur tournaments on hearing that she was seeking to turn professional, even before she did so. Jack Kramer labeled this "a crime" but Ms. Betz declined to complain about it and kept grinding out wins anyway, defeating Althea Gibson in 1959 when five months pregnant with her fifth child.

Another of Byron's best teenage girl players, though not as talented as Ms. Betz, was Natalie Wentworth.

Good as she was, Byron knew she was not championship material. He kept saying the game was for dumb athletes, foolhardy spirits who laughed at risk and slugged their way up out of disaster — for the most part drab-looking girls who needed some device to get boys to take notice of them lest they remain mere wallflowers. My sister Mary, while not drab or dumb, was a natural athlete and Byron also devoted quite a bit of attention to her; she even in time acquired a ranking among the top twenty Southern California girl players, though she was badly beaten in a match by Darlene Hard, who went on to become one of the best woman players in the world.

Yet another talented young local was Betsy Lester. She had started her life out in the Channel on San Miguel Island, where her father had kept a herd of sheep. Right after Pearl Harbor the navy commandeered the island for a gunnery range. The story I kept hearing from Betsy was that the navy gave her father thirty days to get himself and the sheep off the island. I don't remember the fate of the sheep, but she always said her father committed suicide. Members of a family named Warner who actually owned the island were also ordered off at once and when they dragged their feet the navy mounted a bombing raid on their house.

My grandmother would not let my mother into Rokeby after her marriage to Byron. She had to dominate everyone in her presence. If she could not run someone she would banish him, or her, generally on obscure but very strongly-held pretexts. Foremost among those were people who had divorced and remarried and those who had converted to Catholicism. She had become even more repressive than she was in the past, in general — "got more and more sour as things went on," declared one nephew of hers, Willie Chanler, in an oral history decades later. For instance she would not allow her eminent neighbor Gore Vidal onto the premises and banished Dwight McDonald for taking off his shirt while playing on the estate's tennis court.

Her sister-in-law Aunt Amey insisted she keep seeing my mother, though. Once a year the two would meet for tea at the Stanhope Hotel near Amey's Upper East Side apartment. Their last meeting, my mother had Byron come pick her up at the hotel, but she knew her mother would want to sneak a look at him, so had him fetch her at the rear. After their meeting she said she was going out front and her mother followed along, keeping to the background but peering. Unsuccessfully.

Once when Peter was staying at Rokeby he heard Uncle Dick finally talk back to our grandmother — yell back at her. They were near the top of the main staircase, between the two halves of the building at the landing by the two opera-box alcoves with their velvet curtains, and he was excoriating her for not talking to my mother anymore or letting her in the house. Chanler backed him up and Byron was allowed to come to Rokeby for one visit and go about on a tour, accompanied by Uncle Dick, while my cousin Winty kept an eye on our grandmother and moved her around, making sure she did not set eyes on the visitor.

My mother and all the other Chanler women used to scoff at the Chanler men and state that they had little backbone and the strongest people in the family were all women. My mother frequently pointed out that while Archie, Bob, Winthrop, Lewis and Willie were the only ones who could have passed the name along, Bob, who became an important painter of vivid screens and murals, had only girls, and Archie, an eccentric loner, never had children though he was married for a while to the preeminent "chick lit" (or maybe even "broad lit") writer of his day, Amelie Rives — who abandoned him for Prince Pierre Troubetskoy. Archie then founded and devoted his life to overseeing a couple of industrial enterprises in Virginia. He had Stanford White, a close friend, design the factory buildings for these companies, but as Suzannah Lessard has pointed out White had no experience with industrial design and the enterprises failed. Still, the five Chanler boys did produce five Chanler boys who lived on and produced heirs of their own.

I recalled my grandmother dragging people, the young in particular, to museums, historic houses and old churches most people of my generation found boring and compelling them to listen to her descriptions of those then hear out her lengthy readings from interminable nineteenth-century novels. I remember once when my grandmother dragged me around New York City to look at all the historic sites she took me for lunch to Fraunces Tavern, a revolutionary-era tourist restaurant near Wall Street, where all the staff were dressed like Ben Franklin and Gouverneur Morris. They didn't talk like them though — it shocked me to hear a headwaiter crassly complaining about something in a thick Brooklyn accent. If one listened to my grandmother, however (and few of my generation did), one could learn something. For instance I remember her taking me to see Carl Schurz's statue when I was staying with her at The Brownstone on Seventy-fourth Street; I would probably never really have gained a sense of this major figure's importance otherwise. Many intellectuals would pay her court, among them the literary scholar Fred Dupee from Bard College up the road and Alan Nevins the major Columbia University historian from whose text I studied American history as a teenager. I can remember meeting Nevins once and to my surprise hearing him state proudly that he'd got two hours of her recollections on tape for Columbia's American oral history project.

My mother did claim that Chanler Chapman was one person who could be rough on her mother. When his mother Elizabeth was dying he yelled at her to go over and pray by her bedside, though she was unconscious by then anyway.

Incidentally Chanler did assume some significance in the literary world of his time: he became Henderson, Saul Bellow's Rain King. Bellow as a young man taught at Bard College and lived in a small flat above the garage on Chanler's grounds. Bellow and Chanler fought. Bellow said Chapman drove his tractor over his huge hay fields "like a real king, knocking over fences, breaking stone walls and pulling up boundary-markers." He also kept dogs in the garage, the dogs made ferocious noise at night and Bellow complained: a writer needs peace and quiet. (Conversely we have Germaine Greer years later denouncing Salman Rushdie, under a death sentence for *The Satanic Verses*, which was critical of his Islamic heritage, as "a megalomaniac, an Englishman with dark skin," then going on to point out "Jail is a good place for writers; they write." There are few barking dogs in jails, though.)

Bellow bought a decaying mansion after that and had the black chronicler Ralph Ellison, then also at Bard, come in as a tenant. Ellison among other things mixed the martinis, but he also had a Labrador that befouled Bellow's herb garden.

In the end, Bellow fashioned Chanler into about the only character he ever described in vivid terms, aside from his own self. Bellow once recalled "Alfred Kazin asked what Jews could possibly know about American

millionaires. For my purposes, I felt that I knew enough."
He called Chanler "the tragic or near-tragic comedian
and the buffoon heir of a great name. I can't imagine what
I saw in him or why it was that I was so goofily drawn to
him." But, going through tormented times, after losing
family and a small legacy, "For the tenth time I went back
to page 1, beginning yet another version of Henderson."*

---

* <u>The New Yorker</u>, April 25, 2005

10

The 1956 Shocks: Interesting Times, Harsh Conflicts

When I first arrived at Groton, a week late, I went through a mandatory rough initiation. A boy a year ahead of me, waiting on table, kept punching me on the back of my head as he passed by my chair at dinner. I didn't dare complain about this -- and then, for no reason that I could see, he stopped. I suspect someone saw him and told him he would be expelled if he kept that up. Years later I heard the claim, from a class spy, that there was a secret spy in every class. Perhaps one in mine, or his, had passed word of this bullying on to the authorities.

I moved on, became acquainted with high-powered nonviolent talented peers. One somewhat older student with whom I frequently got into arguments, or at least discussions, was Joseph Francis "Joe" Fletcher IV, a talented writer and editor in chief of the literary magazine, *The Grotonian*. Joe had strong, thoroughly reasoned theories on almost everything and in those days was rather a leftist. He was the son of a major figure at Harvard, a groundbreaking Divinity School professor also named Joseph — articulator of one of the earliest, and most carefully worked out, arguments in favor of euthanasia.

Minty Sedgwick was another of my schoolmates, though I didn't have much to do with him because he was a class below me. I did resume visiting him at his ranch from time to time — his family had moved down the road to a six-thousand-acre spread they named Rancho La Laguna. Sedgwick had a real live gasoline pump at that ranch.

One of my classmates, Paul Ditzen, would argue with me endlessly. One meal when he sat to my left he kept dumping knives, forks and spoons into my left coat pocket in protest against a point I was making. I removed all the ones I could but still found myself leaving the dining room with several on me. Paul, the son of a minister in Bronxville, New York, became gripped with what Mr. Crocker called devotion to "evangelical poverty," decided it was immoral for him to stay on in this affluent environment and walked away one evening fourth form year. He killed himself two years after that.

Another figure I hung around was George Gund III, oldest son of the richest and most powerful banker in Cleveland. He was a rebellious soul. In the later words of one classmate "As George frequently broke rules, blackmarks were a constant danger and I remember getting some just for being near him."

As a benchmate of George's in Charlie Rimmer's 3C Math I learnt as much as I needed to know about Cleveland, from Moe Dalitz to the Majestic Tie Shop and Mayor Halle. He was the one student in our dormitory who had a phonograph and we used to listen to hit records of his such as Frankie Laine favorites and Earl Bostic's *Night Train*. At the same time his rebelliousness extended to politics. He was even more informed — and informative — on the Los Angeles Zoot Suit Riots of the 1940s than those of us from Santa Barbara, a near-suburb of that metropolis. He was a talented athlete, especially in such cold-weather sports as hockey. While I in time was yanked up to B division he did not rise and was asked to leave after tenth grade (fourth form). Over the years though we came to see him as a figure larger than life.

Another of my classmates, and a close friend, was the fellow who went on to the University of Utrecht, Jan Van Roijen, son of the Dutch ambassador and later himself an ambassador to Israel, Indonesia and the UK. Jan went to Groton because Dean Acheson, secretary of state in those days, told his father to send him there. Acheson said the school was tough but good for the soul. Jan, while praising the caliber of the education there, suffered from extreme boredom.

I got to know his father moderately well. A striking individual. He couldn't stand Acheson's successor John Foster Dulles — partly I suspect because Dulles had once received him in shirtsleeves — and admitted that the Netherlands was totally subordinate to the United States in its foreign policy, but he also warned against underestimating the Soviets. Incidentally, in those days the Netherlands had two foreign ministers, a Protestant and a Catholic, to maintain domestic peace. (Joseph Luns, one of those ministers and later secretary general of NATO, once told Dulles they had to have two foreign ministers because the Netherlands was very small and had more foreign territory to cover than anyplace else.) Jan's father served many years in Washington but never became the dean of the diplomatic corps there because the ambassador from Nicaragua — uncle of another of our classmates — had come earlier and stayed longer. Jan's father had been arrested three times in World War Two, where he served in the resistance. The third time it looked as if he was going to be kept in prison but then a Finnish doctor who used to minister to the Nazi secret police chief Heinrich Himmler had him released — all the Finn had to do was lay a hand on Himmler's belly and the Gestapo chief's severe abdominal pains would be assuaged. Once the Finn would not minister to him unless he promised to have a group of people released, Van Roijen among them.

On occasion we did have exposure to the world beyond the school. Once we were taken to Boston to a theater where Tyrone Power gave a full-length reading of Steven Vincent Benet's *John Brown's Body.*

My sixth form (senior) year Dean Acheson came up to Groton. This distinguished alumnus of the school was one of what are now considered to be the five grand men who built our postwar foreign policy, along with Harriman, Kennan, Bohlen and Chester Bowles. We the sixth formers were granted a special audience with him, meeting in the library, where he addressed us. At one point he compared international relations to herds of elephants going at one another in the jungle "in a state of dynamic equilibrium." He pointed out that there was nothing that could be done to set up an anti-Soviet alliance on the southern flank of the USSR because Afghanistan adamantly refused to go in on any such alliance. To some question routinely posed by someone, he complained about "Foster" Dulles, stating that he was a person of little warmth — he'd taken train rides with Dulles a number of times and found the man had no desire to converse with him.

Some of the students, it turned out much later, were gay. In the atmosphere of the time, though, with pervasive hostility toward any features of the gay life style — from an endless torrent of bad jokes on out, most perhaps even then focussed on the flamboyant entertainer Liberace — none of those students dared allow any suggestion of their instincts to manifest itself. Some of those students were among the most tense and argumentative around.

Returning twenty-five years later, I realized the one enduring beautiful element in the place was the sound of a bird cawing in the early morning, no matter how dark or grim it was outside. By then I no longer felt alienated from Groton, resumed contact with several classmates and have gone back for reunions, keeping up with those incidental fellow voyagers ever since.

By then as I've said the school had long gone coeducational. I met a woman who'd visited the place once, in the thought of nesting her daughter there, and was amazed how small it was. One reason its stewards kept it small, I learned later, was the size of the chapel: that would not accommodate more than about 350 students all told and since attendance at services remains mandatory (more or less) that was where the size of the student body had to remain.

Where does one go after Groton, if not to Harvard (or Yale)? My choice was the University of California at Berkeley, which was just beginning to turn into what one could call an interesting arena of ideas in harsh conflict.

After my mother and Byron returned from their half-year in Paris, then attended my graduation at Groton, we proceeded to New York, where we were to pick up a new Ford at a dealership on Broadway, following a purchase that had been arranged the previous fall, then drive the car back West. No car was there. The salesman on duty hemmed and hedged about getting another car from out of town in a day or so. Byron just said "Well let's forget about it then." He turned and started to walk out of the showroom. They had a car for him in half an hour.

It was hard to find housing at UC Berkeley even then and I spent my freshman year there in a boarding house with other students, mostly from small cities cast about the state, many on the GI Bill. We'd get into endless bull sessions, often prompted by talk about venereal diseases in the army, where one fellow-student, Dave, had served, and the drastic remedies the medical authorities resorted to to cure those. Dave sang, to the tune of "Stranger in Paradise," the unofficial army anthem of service in Germany — "Take my schwantz, I'm a stranger in Heidelberg."

Another tenant, Ralph, had fought in Korea. He did not feel he had been serving for a cause though — "I was fighting to save my ass" he kept saying. He had a friend on campus who used to hang out of a plane window photographing North Korea. Then later, in Japan, Ralph tried to get close to a girl from a department store, even took her to the movies — though her mother sat behind them tapping him on the shoulder whenever he tried to hold her hand. Finally his father forbade the marriage and when his tour was over he returned to the States — still single.

I'd argue with one of my fellow younger students, Mike, about Hemingway and the Bible. Conversation would drift from some of the seamier details of sex to the hereafter. Mike was the one who came up with all the examples of incest in bull sessions. He got no closer to sex by freshman year than trying to lay a virgin who was so tight he couldn't get in. Then we had an argument with Phil from Minnesota on whether his state was superior to California. He bragged how cold it got on Lake Superior and on one point of contention someone rushed down to get an atlas and "creamed" him on some minor forgotten point. Mike told Stan to wear a Cal jacket on vacation so he could look collegiate and seduce all his sister's friends. "They're all brats" Stan retorted. Mike said his own sister did have the brains to appreciate the Four Freshmen. And the father of them all, Stan Kenton and City of Glass.

The conversation would move on to folkloric speculations, apocrypha, secret information Roosevelt had received that the Japanese were about to unleash their attack on Pearl Harbor and his refusal to take steps to head it off, then a story that had circulated in America for a decade — that the Ford Motor Company was offering a car to anyone who gave it a 1943 copper penny. Then much speculation on what would happen if hydrogen bombs were dropped on LA or the Bay Area. It'd take a ring of them to cripple Los Angeles, said Dave, but one that hit the center here in the Bay Area would be sufficient to its task, and they'd need just one on Manhattan (source for the name of the project that had produced it in the first place). We would speculate almost without end on what would happen if the Soviets invaded California. Or what would happen if a civil war broke out again in this country. "Immediately invade the Soviet Union," counseled Jerry, another housemate.

At Cal in 1955 the registration fee was three dollars a semester. When three years later that was raised to twelve to help finance the new student union, everyone around me screamed like hell. Lots of left-wing rhetoric got into that act. To get into Cal then all one needed was a B average from a recognized state high school. That didn't mean one had to know how to write. Everyone (except those who'd passed their college boards) had to take an English exam on admission, and if (like many if not most) he or she failed had to pungle up twenty dollars and enroll in Subject A, "bonehead English." That was another intense subject of indignant discourse in my boarding house: most of my fellow residents were in a state of permanent outrage over this, claiming the program was just a device for extorting money. One Subject A teacher I got to know at meetings of the literary magazine *Occidental* (who also complained about having to have sex at odd hours because her husband moonlighted) merely retorted that all her students said that but none of them could write a decent English paragraph, let alone sentence.

At some point though several of the fellows in the boarding house wandered in and out, accusing one another "you laugh like an irresponsible foetus." "*Oe*, get it?" They were after all gradually becoming liberated by the likes of T. S. Eliot and Ezra Pound.

We underwent some indoctrination in ROTC, Reserve Officers' Training Corps, which was a mandatory course in those days: in classes they were constantly lecturing us about nationalism, self-determination, irredentism and the virtues of NATO. In one movie on an attempted communist takeover of the United States the agitators all looked like economics graduate students. It was very easy to get a perfect score on the air force ROTC tests: you had only to exaggerate the power of the USSR. Army ROTC showed a movie where people were controlling elections with machine guns.

In time my social network expanded slowly and I met several fellows with whom I came to share an apartment. Then Minty Sedgwick, who'd also taken on the nickname Duke (inherited from his father with the natural passage of time), was not accepted to Harvard and followed me to Cal, still a year below me. He dropped behind almost as soon as he enrolled in the university. One evening just after the semester started he called and invited me to go over to San Francisco with him and drink and listen to music at the home of a friend of his father's. I said I thought that would be an excellent idea and went off to line up one mutual friend, Eric, whom I'd met on the literary magazine.

Conversation was not at the start very animated and didn't pick up until Minty got going with Eric on the subject of anthropology review — he was in a cold sweat because he had been skipping lectures and didn't think he had the time or the energy to catch up. They got talking of Eric taking exams for him.

Early that school year I began listening to the radio. Combat had exploded in two areas of the world, Egypt and Hungary, and threatened full-scale war. In Egypt, Britain and France attempted to take control of the area around the Suez Canal, which Egypt's President Gamal Abdel Nasser had nationalized that summer, and there already was aerial warfare. Both America and the Soviet Union denounced the Anglo-French aggression. The Soviets darkly threatened to use nuclear weapons on the British if they did not pull back from Suez. In time the British and French did pull back. (This was the third of perhaps four major flashes over a forty-year period that could have led us to war with the Soviet Union, the others being the Berlin Blockade of 1948, the 1950 invasion of South Korea and the 1961 Cuban missile crisis.) The Israelis, who had crossed Sinai to join up with the British and French, pulled back too but they unlike their allies achieved a diplomatic gain in the form of international military protection: Nasser had to agree to let United Nations forces hold strategic points on the Egyptian side of the border with Israel, to prevent either nation from invading the other in the future.

William Faulkner sent a letter to *Time*, which the magazine published in early December, excoriating critics of the Anglo-French invasion. He declared that we had little right to criticize England's actions in Suez because England's motives often lay outside her own country and she had always borne the weight of the fight for the West, even now that none of us could afford not to fight.

In Hungary the Soviets were totally unprepared for the popular uprising against their satellite regime, which crested on October 23. There had been little sign of impending trouble beyond a massive outpouring of support a few months earlier in memory of the late justice minister, Laszlo Rajk, when his remains from a 1948 execution were reinterred in a Budapest cemetery. Now a former communist leader and political prisoner, Imre Nagy, formed a nationalist government and moved to expel the Soviet presence from his country and withdraw from the Warsaw Pact, the Soviet military alliance. The student rebels who rose up behind him with the Hungarian military quickly had the Soviets to the wall. Pal Maleter, a general, commanded the breakaway forces and senior officers in the Hungarian Air Force said they would join the rebels if the Soviets didn't leave Budapest by three o'clock the following afternoon.

An announcement cropped up on the radio that plans were being made to lower the draft age to 19, spreading panic (in me anyway).

One of my professors, of Hungarian descent, explained to us how the names of Nagy and others should be pronounced. I became fascinated by Hungarian names, went about learning as many as I possibly could as fast as I could. (I also learned that Hungarians who'd made it to America tended to call the supermarket chain *Saa fe vigh*.) I went to the library almost too excited to study, wondering when I would be drafted, when we would all be at war and compelled to learn Hungarian, when the Third World War would flare out, literally. After I finished work, on my way home I stopped to see Minty, who had taken a room at the Durant Hotel so he could study better for the big anthropology midterm the next day, at a cost of seven dollars per night, and I stayed about an hour discussing the Hungarian uprising in amazement.

Right after that, the Soviets arranged a meeting with the leaders of the insurrection. Yuri Andropov, then Soviet ambassador to Hungary (and later first secretary of the Communist Party — that is, head of the Soviet Union), intervened, had Nagy and Maleter arrested and swept out of the country. They would not disavow their loyalty to the uprising and were executed two years later. At the time I was taking a history course from Raymond Sontag, an eminent older scholar of Central European diplomacy. He would lace his lectures with such observations on human nature as "No one in this room thinks for himself more than one percent of the time — we're all highly influenced by what everyone around us thinks." He also insisted that history was largely the study of individuals who brought on great movements and the guiding concept in his own study of history was the title of a best-selling novel in those days, *What Makes Sammy Run?* This philosopher of the nature and use of power put the failure of the Hungarian uprising in historic perspective: the players had changed, he said, but the ground rules were very much the same as they'd been a century before, when Czarist Russia had sent troops in to suppress a Hungarian uprising against the Hapsburg Empire.

On a summer day in the mid-1960s one of my old Groton classmates saw a boy at a beach in Maine walk by with an adult and out of the blue asked him if he was any relation to General Pal Maleter. The boy, surprised, said he was Maleter's son. My classmate had remembered Maleter's striking face. For a week in 1956 that military leader had been perhaps the most important person in the world, certainly for those of us of draft age.

Minty was sitting out on my patio by then and I conversed with him briefly. He had just got a C on his anthropology midterm. He was feeling very depressed and talked about going into the army. I prepared salad for dinner while he consulted with one of my roommates on the various military requirements he could get around by choosing different dodges. Now he was sure he would join the army though another roommate convinced him that if he ended up with a C average that would keep him out. It wasn't that his marks were poor but, as he said several times, he didn't feel he was accomplishing a thing and believed the army would instill some sense of purpose in him. I wondered what would become of him. He planned to call his parents that night; they would be sure to try to stop him from going in.

He went back to his place. Later I heard that he had phoned his parents and found that they thought he should go join the army, and that was the signal for party time, so we all blasted. I eventually went to sleep, feeling that this was one of those days I could tell that I had gained a little wisdom — I was a little less naive, a little less idealistic now. Minty Sedgwick, the prime idealist who thought he could get an education from college, was going into the army.

The next weekend we dressed up, Minty in his tuxedo, I in casual garb, the others in suits, and for a long time we had cocktails to music and talked about this and that, then ordered pizza and champagne. Then Minty went on his way.

11

Bright Opinions
and Landscapes:
Father's Work Abroad

I n 1948, almost ten years earlier, my father had received one of twelve fellowships Harvard University's distinguished Nieman Foundation awarded annually to journalists. We went on to spend the academic year 1948-49 in Cambridge. The fellowship was in recognition for his work covering postwar China, the story he had received by good fortune, being thirty on the West Coast in wartime. The Nieman entitled him to spend an academic year studying anything he wished at Harvard. Another award winner with my father was Charles Willis of Fort Worth, who had lost a leg in the Pacific during the war, after which he spent three years in army hospitals. Yet another journalist winning the award that year was CBS' man in Greece, George Polk. However, a month before the awards were announced, Polk was murdered, presumably through the machinations of a Greek politician who, he had discovered, had received a bribe of $30,000. It was of course this correspondent after whom the major Polk Award for journalism was named.

That year in Cambridge, while still living under the same roof as us, my father kept a small room in the attic where he slept until five in the morning then rose to spend the rest of the day writing, studying and attending Harvard seminars.

He would talk about one person he got to know as a Nieman, the famous semanticist Ivor Richards. One day he brought back a question: how does one pronounce the word "ghoti?" Richards had asked him. "Fish," it turned out. (Enough, women and action.)

We then returned to Santa Barbara. While my father was passing through on his way back to the Far East, Mary and Dicky came up the driveway, walking their bicycles, with some local vandals and hoodlums, Pat Davis and so on in their wake. Pat had an older brother Bill who was reputedly in the marines. These hoods had stopped Mary and Dickie on the road down the hill and the twins had been able to secure passage for themselves only with the promise of comics and Cokes up at the house. Being stupid bullies, the hoods had followed Mary and Dicky home. When they arrived Nan the Scottish governess came out and gave them a terrific tonguelashing, marched them back down to their home and had it out with Pat's mother. Our father had been working in the toolshed the whole time. About fifteen years later he recalled the incident and admitted to me "I elected to let Nan handle that." The hoods never bothered us again.

After the year in Cambridge our father could not return to mainland China, which by then had become the People's Republic, so he went on to Hong Kong.

He did pass by Santa Barbara on a visit early in the summer of 1950 on his way back from his extended tour in Hong Kong. One Sunday morning I brought the paper up to my parents in the breakfast room. It was a sunny morning, June 25, and the paper in stark headlines declared that North Korea had just invaded the south. I remember telling my father that that was where his next job was going to be, and that was indeed where he went. Back to war, with no real respite.

One story he brought out of that war years later was of a man standing guard at night in Korea only to feel a hand grazing his throat in the pitch black and stroking his dog-tag. That was a Turkish scout with the UN forces, swiftly stabbing anyone who lacked such a tag in the heart. One Turkish officer, Guney, talked of assigning a soldier, during the retreat from the Chinese, to hold down a position and shoot anything that came across his path. The soldier desperately repeatedly kissed his hand and kept pressing his hand to his forehead, almost in rapture at being called a good soldier and given a key assignment.

An associate of my father's kept up with Guney after he returned to Turkey. Guney would talk of fighting Kurdish guerrillas in Diyarbekir and Dersim. They'd call the commanding officer "Mister" because if they referred to him as colonel the insurgents would realize there was a regiment in the area: twelve thousand men. Sometimes the Kurds would have five thousand men, right there, under arms. Guney's troops would chase them up into the hills, where they'd have to fight it out; hard combat in rocks as they would leave no traces behind them. Classic guerrilla warfare — it took the government forces two and a half years to pacify one zone.

Another time my father got into a big argument with Dan Nugent, the wealthy man with the magnificent beach house and luxuriant thick Korean moss lawn. My father used to call Nugent a "communistic plutocrat." Nugent had maintained he'd rather live under a communist system than endure a nuclear war and my father had replied "I'd rather just disappear than have to live under a system anything like that."

In 1952, after the Republican convention and the nomination of Nixon as Ike's running mate, Dan Nugent stated "The Republicans are going to hisssssss their way into the White House" (as indeed they did). During the 1956 presidential campaign, he spread about another press release:

Gettysburg — Death, as it must to all men, came last night to Dwight D. Eisenhower. Press Secretary James Hagerty announced this made no change in plans for November, but rather enhanced the spiritual nature of the administration. National Chairman Leonard Hall pointed out that there was no constitutional provision that the President must be alive during his term of office. Major General Howard Snyder, after performing an autopsy, declared the President was in better organic condition than any other previous candidate for the presidency.

Another time Adelaide Nugent threw a dinner and on assigning places said "You sit there, Joe; Evelyn, take that place over there; and you, you half-man, why don't you go sit over there."

Dan Nugent, for all his power to put himself where he wanted and find the ideal system of life, had no sense of spontaneity. He had honey and cottage cheese for lunch every day at twelve, took a nap until three and had tea at four.

Later, in 1956, he informed us that the perennial candidate Harold Stassen tried to get Christian Herter to replace Nixon in 1956.

Dan Nugent railed against economic and social injustice in this country then, I learned later, had worked very hard to seduce my mother, even if that would have meant marrying her.

After the outbreak of the Korean War, I did not see my father again until late spring 1953. He came to take my brother Dicky and me across the United States after Groton and we camped out in sleeping bags except once visiting a cousin in Ohio. Driving along, at one point Dicky and I looked out to see a pair of dogs having sex and giggled. Our father got furious at that and slammed his hand on the steering wheel so hard a segment of it snapped off — maybe ninety degrees' worth. (Later I thought that must have been some formula they used on that plastic — till then I had never known of anyone to break one of those wheels.) We then went up to Michigan, crossed over to Milwaukee on the *Milwaukee Clipper*, stayed one night at a park in Wisconsin (and got lectured by our father for making sarcastic remarks about Senator Joe McCarthy to the ranger), crossed southern Minnesota, visited Devil's Tower (where our father walked out into the prairie, exclaiming "darling babies" to prairie dogs which promptly ducked into their burrows), went through Cody and Yellowstone (taunting our father about his slow driving and thus getting him to explode again, telling us to be "objective" and "detached"), cut across southeastern Idaho and down Nevada to home.

While I was still at Groton, I spent the summer of 1954 with him as he traveled about Pakistan — West

Pakistan in those days — and Afghanistan. This included a trip into impenetrable Pashtun country, setting out from Urgun very near the border of the two countries, to visit a venerable guerrilla leader, the Fakir of Ipi. On the way out I remember sitting at the Basra airport next to an old Britisher on his way to Dacca who declared flatly that there was going to be nuclear war between America and the Soviet Union, because there never had been an arms race where the arms weren't eventually used. I was sixteen then and of course could not come up with any argument to challenge this assertion.

The next I saw my father after that was in April 1956, when I was at Cal. He had come to New York and my mother had got a phone call from him. A pro-communist party had won in elections in Sri Lanka, his latest assignment, and he had left the country, fearing persecution. Now he was running out of money, didn't have enough to give Peter a trip to visit him that summer, was "dissatisfied over the arrangements they had made over Peter" and by returning to the States felt he had the opportunity to stay with people, especially at the beach house, and see us all. I was elated he was coming out and rushed through thoughts of what we could do, what I could show him, how surprised he would be at the change within me.

When he came up to the Bay Area later in the spring we swung by his old place of employment, the *Chronicle*. He disparaged the spirit there, said the paper was highly stratified; people went into newswriting for the glamor, soon found themselves trapped. Then a couple of Cal professors invited him to come meet Indonesia's visiting president, Ahmed Soekarno, at the Faculty Club and he brought me along. Soekarno was a charismatic figure, one of the leaders of the Third World movement, and sat on a sofa running his fingers through the hair of some professor's small daughter.

Then, in 1958, my father found a job as editor at the American pavilion in the 1958 Brussels World Fair through a trade fair executive he'd known in India, Bob Warner. Warner offered him a thousand a month for the job, he said Nonsense, asked for double that sum — and got it.

One of his projects was to take the Circarama — a 360-degree film projection chamber Walt Disney had developed, erected in Disneyland then had replicated in the pavilion — and get its programmers to portray vivid sights of real mainstream American life, not just dramatic scenery like the Grand Canyon or Pike's Peak. He half-succeeded at that.

I joined him as a volunteer guide in the pavilion. During the fair Disney himself came by on a visit and I showed him the voting machines I was presenting to the public. Later Bob Warner asked me if I as a Californian would like to join another guide from California, Penny, for dinner with Disney, but I elected to go out drinking with friends at a nearby complex of pubs instead. In those days people from my background considered Disney just a mickey mouse guy, his work culturally beneath us.

Of course, in perspective, his role was far more profound and complicated than that. He has had an almost unmatched impact on popular culture all over the world ever since that time. I can think among many things of an acquaintance who, at auctions, acquired a couple of paintings from a set of six Salvador Dali once did for Disney. Disney's plan was to make a brief animated film around the six paintings but both he and Dali died before they could press the project through. But then again McDonald's and Colonel Sanders and many other purveyors to the global mass consumer market have had major impacts as well; I would have dined with an icon, at best.

I stayed with my father in a cheap but congenial basement studio till he went off to what was then known as the Belgian Congo and moved me to a room in a lady's apartment. In the lobby of her building was a *minutiere*, a switch which would turn on the lights up to the top of the stairs but then shut off after a couple of minutes. I was terrified of being stuck in the elevator that went up inside the stairwell once the lights went off so I'd dash up the four flights of stairs to the apartment rather than take it. Then one night someone came in at the same time I did and took the elevator — beating me to my floor though I'd run up as fast as I possibly could.

Once while my father was still in Brussels he chartered a canal boat which we took to Ghent and Bruges then up to Antwerp, where we attended a cocktail party at the American Consulate. Other times we'd walk around the streets of the city and talk. One time we got going on sharks. He remarked that they were the oldest living animal, or very nearly so, because nothing could kill them (unless they invited it to). They controlled the deep.

"What about dry land?" I asked. "We don't have anything like sharks up here, do we?"

"Well," replied my father, "man is the shark of dry land."

On another occasion, he claimed that man ruled the planet because he was the only animal who had learned how to collect royalties.

At another point in the summer the subject of Private Girard came up. He was an American soldier serving in Japan who'd just caused an international scandal by shooting and killing a peasant woman near a military base on Okinawa for riffling through a heap of discarded ammunition-casings, though that base observed an unwritten law that local peasants could do so. My father flatly declared that Girard had been spared the death penalty because of "American momism and bleeding hearts." When I protested he snapped "They should've shot Girard." (He was not deeply attached to the military world. "I'm against handouts to veterans on principle" was a statement I often heard him make.)

Often when I expressed a sharp opinion about someone he would state, "Judge not, that ye be not judged." I would complain that I myself was judged all the time. "It is the fate of the young to be judged," he would reply.

Another point he made repeatedly on passing judgment, from his journalistic background: "Get the other side first."

He was a true anglophile. He'd met many Britishers of course during his travels across the East, India and Malaysia especially. He had picked up many of their jokes and songs (mostly filthy, but in an imaginative vein) and would sing those from time to time.

He had an old theory that he kept coming back to — that England indeed was not part of Europe, an obsessively warring world. It was not an exotic, distant land, he asserted, where they spoke a language different from what we understood in Amarillo Texas. True, the Channel was just a broad moat, but you had to go back to Hastings actually to find a battleground in Britain. There was no evidence of any such combat, beyond the odd carcass of a Messerschmidt. There hadn't been a foreign soldier firing a shot in anger in that country since 1050 (except for William of Orange's men). Compare that with Meuse-Argonne where the Americans fought in 1918, just forty or fifty miles from the Ardennes and Bastogne — and where they went back and fought again in 1944. Nor had the British seen much in the way of bloody revolution. Sure, they lost millions in the World Wars, but there wasn't any blood shed on their territory (and they always managed to bring in the Yanks when they had to).

That was where the British genius lay, right there, he said: keeping itself out of Europe.

On the other hand there were the Irish, long occupied by the British, and those he did consider European. He talked about his own Irish nationalist ancestry. Over the past two hundred years the Irish had staged five uprisings against the English and one of his ancestors, the Anglo-Irish figure Thomas Emmet, with his brother Robert "Robeaird" Emmet, was central in the first two of them, 1798 and 1803.

Thomas Emmet and his fellow leader Wolf Tone wanted to drive for independence carefully and gradually and castigated Robert for his violent approach. As it was, Thomas was incarcerated for about six months in Kilmainham — a grim place but not much more so than Alcatraz or San Quentin, except for the colder weather — then taken to Fort George in Inverness, Scotland from April 1799 to sometime in 1802. Robert, instigator of the 1803 uprising, was tried in the Green Street Courthouse and his death mask is now on exhibit in the Collins Barracks — beneath inscriptions on the wall, one a quote from Milan Kundera, the exiled Czech novelist: "The struggle for power is the struggle of memory against forgetting."

One can understand why it took the Irish so long to shake off the oppressive British presence. In general the British had the various Irish resistance movements penetrated and suborned and could always tell when a planned event was to unfold then contain it or quash it if need be. However, a spontaneous movement was harder for them to control. This is true of insurgencies against occupation in general — again one could recall the 1956 revolt in Hungary. The 1803 Wicklow rebellion Robert Emmet spearheaded was analogous. The British suppressed the uprising, captured him, hanged him, drew him and quartered him, but they had to live over another hundred years and more with the memory of it. Robert probably didn't understand the serious nature of the antagonist facing him. He was only twenty-four at the time and many of the people closest to him were traitors and informants — as it turned out.

The diplomat and historian George Kennan once stated "members of the literary-philosophical opposition" in Eastern Europe held the belief that they "were unique in their suffering and that they derive from it a species of superior wisdom," something common to the "victims of oppression everywhere." To that I would add that these people may be subject to a form of "intellectual snobbery," as he also stated, but more likely they suffer from isolation, alienation — loneliness in their plight, really. In other words, they are unable to be totally open about their plight, share it with others, let others know all the details about it. The police apparatus won't let them — nor will the natural skepticism of the people around them. Much of their suffering is incredible, so who will accept it as genuine?

At the same time, oppression compels the ordinary individual to view a central experience in life with uncommon sophistication. On the wall of the Collins Barracks are the subtly crafted words of one Irish chronicler: "It is not in the poorest but the richest parts of thinking man that sedition and a revolutionary spirit prevailed and first raised their heads. An extreme degree of poverty and distress will sink the mind of man, divest him even of the courage to complain and bring silence to himself and his suffering."

When the British finally released Thomas, he went on to America. My father claimed that the Emmets, with their Irish gift of gab, were as great at talking as the Chanlers and much more so than the New England-repressed Aldriches. Thomas had wanted to go off and farm in Ohio but became the attorney general of New York four years after he got off the boat. When I related this to an Irish activist, he replied, "The British knew what they were doing. They knew he knew how to talk."

12
The Gold Rush Resurgence

All Americans are lucky now in one sense: no matter where their ancestors came from, or what they did, they were all born after the Civil War, with its miserable seemingly endless bloodletting.

However, there was a small portion of the American public for whom this war was almost irrelevant. Some observers have even claimed that it was the Gold Rush, not the Civil War or even the agony of the slavery issue, that was the driving force of the nation in the mid-1800s. It sharply jolted the American world view of the day, which had been pursuit of an orderly, prosperous, boring and unadventuresome style of living. This sudden bonanza brought individuals the chance to have a different experience — make an audacious move and have a shot at much more, great affluence, after only a brief stretch of struggle and deprivation.

It also afforded an escape from the unresolved struggle over slavery. This national outrage represented an ordeal which has many parallels throughout history. One striking example was the experience of living through Nazi Germany. The German writer Guenter Grass in his December 1999 Nobel Prize lecture stated that by the time he started "writing consciously" a little less than ten years after the war, German literature "was having a hard time with German, which had been corrupted by the Nazi regime." In addition, serious German writers, older or younger, "were stymied to a certain extent by a prohibition that came from Theodor Adorno [the refugee Jewish philosopher]: 'It is barbaric to write a poem after Auschwitz, and that is why it has become impossible to write poetry today.'" Grass and others continued to write anyway, by realizing that "Auschwitz marks a rift, an unbridgeable gap in the history of civilization. It was the only way we could get round the prohibition. Even so, Adorno's writing on the wall has retained its power to this day. All the writers of my generation did public battle with it."

So it was with open-minded liberal-spirited Americans growing up in the approaching showdown over slavery. How could one continue to lead a decent life in this setting? The Gold Rush offered a powerful form of escape that did not even require exile from America. One had to take a year passing around the Horn — somewhat less if one could afford to slip across Panama, or God knew how long crossing an unknown number of mountain ranges by land. As we have seen, Ward McAllister was one man who took this bold step; another was my grandmother Margaret's grandfather Sam Ward, after his years as a lobbyist.

Yet another was one of Thomas' grandchildren, my father's grandfather, Christopher Emmet. He also escaped to California. When forty-eight he married a woman twenty-eight years his junior, Ellen Temple (also cousin of Henry James the celebrated novelist). He went out to San Francisco to try his hand in the ebullient economy there and fathered children while in his sixties. One, a daughter, Ellen (in time my father's mother), became a gifted portrait painter. James, a prissy bachelor, didn't approve of this marriage, but that merely reminds one of the joke Earl Butz the onetime agriculture secretary once told about the Pope (for which he was obliged to resign): "You no playa da game, you no makea da rules." The story came down over the generations that old Emmet did win (and lose) the Santa Ynez Valley in a weekend-long poker game. On a train trip home from a visit east, he died of a heart attack near Green River Wyoming and was returned to San Francisco packed in ice.

The Civil War was indeed a side of life back East one hardly saw in California. One boy I knew back East even castigated me once for coming from California because it had not taken part in the Civil War. Indeed one of its senators, William Gwin, was arrested by Lincoln just after Lincoln had suspended habeas corpus. But New York turned out the greatest winner of all in that struggle. Its stock market exploded in the decades to follow and even sanitation and public health made immense strides after the Civil War, as Eric Homberger reports. In the late 1800s, the value of a square foot of land in Manhattan doubled every year. The city, in its huge blocks of stone and concrete, its armories and statues, passed through the stage of commemorating the Civil War in majestic glorified form. There are the looming presences of Sheridan, Greely, Farragut, Carl Schurz and of course Ulysses S. Grant. (Sheridan was later condemned by left-wing critics for developing a strategy for massively exterminating Indians.) In the Grand Army Plaza by the southeast corner of Central Park there is St. Gaudens' statue of Sherman with the angel of victory and then at Eighty-ninth and Riverside the Soldiers' and Sailors' Monument for Union veterans.

John Jacob Astor and his descendants of course left a great legacy in the city. Among John Jacob's vast holdings were the Park Hotel on Broadway, which he turned into the Astor House; much leased property in Richmond Hill near Varick; the city's leading theater at the time, the Park, which he allowed to run down; and a palatial residence near Astor Place. He also established the New York Public Library.

In 1921 the New York Yankees actually bought their stadium's twelve-acre plot from the Astor estate for $675,000, but John Jacob was long gone by then. The first Waldorf-Astoria Hotel came into being in 1897, built by John Jacob's great-grandsons William Waldorf Astor and John Jacob IV, who up to then had been bitter rivals. Then followed the Astor Hotel in 1904, near Times Square; the second Waldorf-Astoria opened in 1931 after the first one was razed to cede place to the Empire State Building.

By then, starting in October 1904, a group of massive subway systems had been constructed in New York. Each station had its own symbol for the sake of the many passengers who could not read the signs in it as they were illiterate immigrants. In the Astor Place station on the Lexington Avenue Line the symbol was a little ceramic beaver, in commemoration of John Jacob's career as a fur trader. By the 1980s, while almost all the stations I saw had deteriorated in one way or another, I noted that the Astor Place subway station was virtually unique in being nicely refurbished, largely from an Astor fund or even foundation, down to the beavers set in among the wall tiles. Now you see the polyethnic hordes passing before those stones and monuments they are no longer compelled to notice and wonder how deeply they pulsate to the vibrations the Civil War victory set off.

Maybe if the war had ended in stalemate it wouldn't have been worth their ancestors' while to come here and New York and the Northeast as a whole would not have become the heartland of superpower.

13
Edie's Father: The Sequel

Once as I was driving down to Santa Barbara on vacation from college my car broke down on 101 near the Sedgwick ranch. I had old Fuzzy come give me a lift. He told me Minty was then up at Fort Ord near Monterey, eating breakfast at four thirty in the morning, having just fallen in love with a girl the day before he left. Fuzzy had me get a ride down to town with the ranch caretaker William, Nancy's husband, his face looking rather like a scotch on the rocks. William felt that Minty should have taken advantage of his great education, which was open to few people his age. I argued that a tour in the army was just what he needed on principle, since he came from a rich background, and here he was quickly exposed to the harsher aspects of life.

On proceeding to actual military service, Minty had had to answer a long questionnaire, which asked among other things if he had ever belonged to any of a long list of organizations. This provided some entertainment, including lengthy, incomprehensible names of underground groups in Italian, Japanese and German as well as some communist front names in English like the Walt Whitman School of Social Sciences and the Committee to Settle Jews in Birobidjan (one of Stalin's rare unconsummated ventures in population management).

After basic training Minty went to the Army Language School in Monterey to study Chinese. Once he matriculated they sent him up to a top-secret code center, the Two Rock Ranch on Middle Two Rock Road in Petaluma somewhat north of San Francisco. Nearby meadows were covered with powerful antennae that intercepted radio messages circulating within China and Minty helped translate those.

One evening several years later when I ran into him in the area we went out on a double date with a couple of high school seniors. In the course of it he spoke of one fellow radio monitor who'd been in Turkey with the National Security Agency and absolutely swore that three local workers at an American air base in Turkey had put a bomb on Francis Gary Powers' U-2, and it was that bomb — and not Soviet missiles — that brought down the spy plane on its flight over the USSR a short time later.

Minty also said that in the course of monitoring the Chinese he had begun to become emotionally involved with them. Their numerous problems, especially in the air, gave them a depth and complexity they had been denied by the propaganda we had been hearing about them — the ordinary people among them anyway. Minty's superiors ordered him and his colleagues not to let the emotional complexities of their task affect them. "It's necessary to keep this all secret and confidential, because if the American people find out about it all, it'll just confuse them," one supervisor told him. A major task in cold war, after all — keeping those on your side from turning ambivalent about the half-comprehensible struggle they were waging.

We had little contact with Sedgwick the elder in those days. At one point Diana was bitten by a dog on Sedgwick's property and Sedgwick claimed she had been trespassing, though she had not, since she was a guest of Nancy the cook's. Later Sedgwick sent an insurance man around unctuously to dissuade my mother from initiating a lawsuit against him for this. My mother always regretted that she never sued Sedgwick but realized that Nancy would probably have been fired if she had.

Another time after that furor had died down we went up to the Sedgwick ranch for dinner sometime in 1957 and heard everyone present worrying about Edie, the nascent superstar.

One Tuesday afternoon, back from another vacation, I returned to find a letter on my desk from New York. I opened it and saw by the letterhead that it was from Groton. On reading it, I was astounded to learn that Groton, in keeping with its high sense of Christian duty, was announcing its intention to take no less than one-fourth of its total enrollment in blacks, as an example to inspire the progress of the movement toward desegregation, which was just starting to gain momentum then. (The school by that time had taken in three blacks.) I was surprised but didn't see that this was exceptionable; my first reaction was to think of going to see some black minister or another and tell him to inform Groton of any outstanding boys he might know.

I showed the letter to one roommate and he was very impressed. Groton had been playing more and more on his imagination then and he was still concerned with the novelty of behaving like a Grottie. I then showed the letter to another roommate, who was not the least impressed. He found the setting of firm arbitrary limits — "one-fourth to one-third" — offensive. I kept telling myself that the issue wasn't desegregation or the furtherance of the fortunes of blacks at all; it was a testing point of Groton's status among schools. Groton had to remain a leader both in education and in the maintenance of its Christian obligations to the larger society. To be silent would be to acknowledge, implicitly, forfeiture of that leadership. Therefore Groton had to take initiative, had to press the matter, had to accept blacks when the issue was to decide whether or not it would remain segregated for a long time, and in this sense the end justified the means regardless of "firm arbitrary limits."

Not long after that I learned that the Groton letter was a bitter hoax. Moreover, old Duke Sedgwick was the author of it. The Groton authorities learned this through investigations by a handwriting analyst. Once exposed, Sedgwick admitted forthright that he had written the letter. He kept on writing letters to alumni and the trustees, haranguing John Crocker the headmaster. In one lengthy letter dated April 8, 1957, he declared that he was "not close enough to the scene to see the reaction at Groton to the suggestion of a twenty percent negro population at the school, but he gathers the reaction was rewardingly violent on *both* sides of the issue. Good."

In a rather stilted open letter to the trustees dated January 21, 1959, Sedgwick drew a ferocious, invidious comparison between Crocker and his predecessor Endicott Peabody. Inter alia he demanded "Can those of you who knew him imagine Endicott Peabody, in an era when Exeter is perplexing Harvard by annually presenting nearly one hundred *qualified* candidates, not making every effort to raise Groton's to at least matching standards?" In the course of the correspondence, he even charged that Harvard's failure to admit Minty had been Groton's fault. By then, I learned in time, Minty had gone on to McLain's, an institute outside of Boston. One Groton classmate of mine absolutely swore that working in San Francisco after business school he'd run into Minty in that city, squiring Lauren Bacall about town.

All in all this struggle went on for seven years. Sedgwick continued to bedevil Crocker till the late sixties. Then he offered to make peace, and they did. Years after that the school invited Robert Moss, the old teacher, to write a life of Crocker, who admitted to him that dealing with this long struggle had been the toughest experience of his life. After Crocker died, though, almost twenty years later, when I told his widow Mary that I appreciated the job he had done running the school, she wryly replied, "Yes, but there were some real problems." She could only have been talking about the hoax and its aftermath.

14
UC Berkeley: Refuge in Ideas

M y father considered Egypt's capital Cairo one of the greatest cities in the world — the world's only indisputably great desert city, he claimed. By then he had drifted away from the Far East, visiting and writing about the old Indochina, then India. He was in the Middle East in the winter of 1958–59, spent a couple of months in Cairo, proceeded to Israel for a couple of months, then moved on to Jordan, spent some time there (writing fiction and *Christmas in Bethlehem*), finally ventured to Greece.

Cairo, he had seen, was also the only desert city in the world which had more water than it really needed. (With the less fascinating exception of Baghdad, which was also great until devastated by a thirteenth-century Mongol invasion that fell short of Cairo.) That great city was fed by the Nile, which carried more than four times as much water as the Colorado (100,000 cubic feet per second, contrasted with 22,500). In the great desert expanses of the globe, there were also parched and dusty old towns such as Urumqi, Kerman, Yazd and Riyadh, as well as a few ersatz communities living on borrowed water like Phoenix and Las Vegas. In fact my father described Cairo, with its desert lushness and deep history, as the only type of great city whose likes one could not find in North America. And indeed, if it had some of the ochre and red of Kerman or Phoenix, it would also be one of the most beautiful cities on earth. It has off and on been a great multifaceted center of attraction well beyond its homeland, serving as a hub of Arabic learning, the Middle East and the whole realm of Islam — a haven of refuge for intellectuals, from Ottoman tyranny on out.

The trip I had taken with my father several years before to Pakistan and Afghanistan had made a very deep impression on me. It had convinced me that the future story of the world — over the rest of my life anyway — lay out there, and that it was vital to learn as much about that part of the world as possible, starting with the languages. So at Cal I studied Persian and Arabic.

At Cal then, political life was lived on two levels. In the context of the college newspaper, *The Daily Californian*, the big issue was male students' behavior around females, especially at football games. For a long time male and female rooting sections were segregated. Then males would blow up condoms and float them over the female section. So the sections were combined — then when the USC Trojans came to play and their band marched out onto the field at halftime the males yelled, "Hey! Rubber Band!" At that, women demanded the sections be segregated again. A student leader was suspended for yelling, "Kick the broads out of the rooting section." And so on.

On a more sophisticated, ruthless level, we had *Slate* and the evolving left lashing out at the mores of the society as a whole. Looking back now I sometimes feel the only intellectual life we had then was the product of a group of left-wing thinkers and commentators, based in New York mostly, who hated the country. Again, while there was a majority who felt rather differently, they were silent — or, like Mary McCarthy, underground rather. At one point in there I had dinner over at the home of an old family friend in San Francisco, where the guest of honor was the famed anthropologist Margaret Mead. The rather bland White Anglo-Saxon Protestant guests (myself included, among the stockbrokers and lawyers) protested that our nuclear weapons might never be used and, if they were, that our military would restrict itself to "clean" versions. The chain-smoking Ms. Mead just scoffed, dismissed this claim out of hand contemptuously — wouldn't even discuss it. I sustained my spirits by imagining myself a benevolent despot.

Caught in the middle of these currents was the university chancellor, Clark Kerr. In late May, in what had become extreme heat, a major water fight broke out among fraternity houses just to the south of campus and this escalated into a panty raid on neighboring sororities, badly rattling Kerr's administration. The university authorities said they would proceed to assess damages on all residential units for the panty raid. Bowles Hall, a big men's dorm, was told to pay 45 percent of the total, the sum of $700; the question arose how to split it. The dorm mates held a big debate on this. They talked in terms of "firsts" (people who had stood around at the riot), "seconds" (people who had gone into sorority houses) and "thirds" (people who had gone in and actually taken things such as panties or in one case even dumped a typewriter with a page from a term paper in it into a wastebasketful of water). One "first" said the sightseers shouldn't be penalized, mentioning one student journalist who had gone in to cover it for the *Daily Cal* then another whose fiancée was in one of the dormitories. A "second" said only those who stole should pay, then a "third" pointed out that most of the stolen articles had been returned. One man ended the discussion by saying he hadn't even been at the riot, but he felt guilty in part for not going down to help stop it — bringing down the house. The authorities even tried to assess each person in my boarding house three dollars, but eventually decided against it.

Some years after I graduated, with the war in Vietnam, Kerr came to face full-scale insurrection from Slate and a broader force for opposition to the war, the Free Speech Movement. Kerr, though a seasoned labor arbitrator, wasn't able to handle these dissident, disruptive elements effectively and dismissed the FSM's campaign against his administration as "a ritual of hackneyed complaints." He resigned in near-disgrace (I remember one professor calling him a nun). Forty years later it came out, though, that Kerr had also been subjected to heavy surveillance by the FBI the whole time.

There were good courses too. One was a high-powered class on the history of the Industrial Revolution taught by the eminent economic historian David Landes. Over the years I had paid no attention to Nan's endless monologues down in Santa Barbara about her brother's rug empire in Lanark, Scotland. Then there was Landes extolling Lanark as a sort of holy city, the home of said Revolution.

At one point I thought seriously of leaving this scene altogether, transferring to the University of Chicago, yet another new world. I even sent for application forms and was invited by a Chicago alumnus to hear his praises of the institution. But then while studying the

Near Eastern languages I found refuge from the harsh, combative intellectual world and the football culture of the university among linguists and writers and stayed on.

I hung around the literary magazine, *Occident*, where I worked to pick up advertising for the paper, and I would do homework in the evenings, my burdens alleviated by one writer, Gene Higgins, who would come and read aloud from *Moby Dick*, Shakespearean deck-scenes then some jokes and intricate details on whaling.

One fellow student I came to know was of Italian extraction and studied his ancestors' language. At one point he showed his grandmother some rules on proper Italian speech and she retorted, "E tutto bullscitto, io parlo della mia maniera." In 1906, she had told him, it cost thirty-five lire to get to the United States.

I became especially familiar with the people in the linguistics department. My introduction was while still in the boarding house, where one veteran, Tom, told me he had gone to hear the distinguished professor Murray Emeneau lecture on the Toda tribesmen, having read about their free sexual conduct in *True*, the man's magazine.

The linguistics grad students were among the most interesting people I knew in the place, once one got past their Germanic expressions, "weltanschauung," "that was part of the gestalt," "weltschmerz," and their focus was far more remote and exotic than mine.

It turned out that northern and central California had been one of the more densely populated areas in the Western Hemisphere before colonization at the hands of Europeans. Eight languages and many dialects were spoken by Indians just between the Spanish administrative centers of San Francisco and Monterey and there had once been 106 Indian languages in the state as a whole, many as different from one another as English from Chinese. They were dying out now, if not already dead, and these graduate students took on the task of writing grammars of those languages that still were accessible. Their mentor was a long-standing professor of Thai, Mary "Chief Crazy" Haas. One of her scholars, Bill Shipley, worked on Maidu, up in the Sacramento Valley around Roseville. Another, Harvey Pitkin, was busy on Wintu in Redding farther up the valley; a third, east of the Sierra, Sid Lamb, studied Mono, which he insisted really should have been called Monache. Then there were Karl Teeter working on Yurok and Bill Jacobsen with Washo just south of Lake Tahoe, then Phillip Muhammad Abd-al-Rahman Barker pursuing Klamath. An eminent older professor, Madison Beeler, studied the Santa Barbara language Chumash. Yet another graduate student had picked a language which had only one surviving speaker, an old woman whose fluency as a source was limited as she was ill in hospital up in Eureka most of the time. Someone had even done work on Natchez down in Mississippi. For a long time Shipley entertained the notion of having a brilliant young Maidu kid stay with him and get a superior education, but he eventually gave that idea up, telling me "He'll work in a sawmill the rest of his life, wondering why he has such interesting thoughts."

Barker showed me some brilliant scrolls he had made, one of a manuscript in the language of an imaginary people, one of a map of his people's city, a descriptive map, with a man in armor holding a jagged sword astride a rampart to illustrate the arsenal and an obsequious, fat richly-clothed Babylonian "type" fingering coins, seated on a castle, to illustrate the merchants' quarter. He had a novel in the language he had made up for the community, a grammar and vocabulary of the language, several short stories and historical documents, and illustrations to the novel.

One weekend I went up to visit Philip in the midst of his labors in Chiloquin, Oregon. He had been allowed to do Klamath as the language slopped down into California. I went with another couple of graduate students and a Finn, whom the linguistics department had used that year as an "informant," a native speaker of an alien tongue none of the linguistics students knew anything about — someone who could teach the students his language, *in* his language, so they'd learn enough to draw up a good trial description of it, in training for their big jobs ahead. We passed through Redding and visited Harvey in 107-degree heat. Chiloquin we found a grimy little rural village just south of Crater Lake with a high rate of unemployment and alcoholism. The first person Philip had sought out as an informant told him, "Sure, I'll teach you the language — at twenty-five cents a word." He then found a gracious older lady well-versed in her mother tongue who was plainly happy to see it codified and set down for the permanent record. She was constantly correcting Phil's Klamath by the time we saw her.

In those times, a woman, even with a Cal degree, almost always ended up a secretary, a nurse or a schoolteacher or got married. But then life was limited for men back then too — virtually all of us faced the specter of the draft. That was to force people to make early career decisions — get them into graduate school, and married. In retrospect it was a very square, rigid world. There was a system, and the elders sternly discouraged one from trying to beat it or even work one's way around it. One couldn't just go hang out in India for a year if one felt like it — even if one could afford to. I came to consider it was this excessive, unwarranted intrusion in, pressure on, our personal lives that we were rebelling against, I and most other restless-minded people. Maybe in retrospect that was what the rebellions of the sixties were about, in essence: the control society and family had imposed on young people's lives.

Another experience in the Cal years was looking up friends my parents had made in the small Bay Area world who had come from their background, or ones parallel and similar to it. They included Tommy Church, the gifted and famed Harvard-educated landscape architect, his wife Betsy, nee Roberts, who'd lived in Paris typing manuscripts for Ernest Hemingway, and their two daughters. They lived in San Francisco.

The most prominent people we knew in Marin were the Andersons, Corona and Berrian, "Buck," and their offspring. While at Cal I heard Betsy Church describe their background at length. She claimed Corona was the daughter of the scion of a gold-rush family, the Williamses. Williams himself was a very brilliant man and in his idleness would play cards at the Pacific Union Club and do very well, but when old Mrs. Williams' money ran out, there were nothing but debts and the good times ended. Mrs. Williams died and Williams himself was put in an elders' home for the rest of his life, miserable and alone, cared for by his daughters Florence and Corona. Florence and Corona married well, Corona very beautiful, tall and with great dignity. Young Buck Anderson, her husband, was very wealthy, an only child too, and descended from one of the ten or so big families in Marin County. He was also shrewd: he played the stock market well, increased his already abundant wealth then around August 1929, when he was satisfied with his success, drew all his money out of investment and let everyone else crumble in the October 1929 crash.

Since that time old Buck never worked and lived very idly in Marin County, drinking heavily. My father held his intellect in the highest regard, though, and whenever he came to the Bay Area would pay him a visit. From time to time we would pass by the Andersons' Diamond A Ranch up in Sonoma's Valley of the Moon. Well after the war this was subdivided finally, in stages, into single-dwelling lots of an acre or so.

The children of Corona's whom my parents knew best were Mary and the youngest, Florence, Flo, who was not terribly much older than me. Mary married a bright rising young maritime attorney, Boris Lakusta, in 1942; theirs was the first wedding I attended, at St. John's.

A Doctor Tyler lived across the street from us, in a large house nestled among oaks. The hill was plagued with bees. Tyler covered the grounds with a device I have never seen anywhere else: glass jars closed at the top, open around the edge at the very bottom and in the middle, just above the edge, a flat area on which he would place poisoned meat. Every once in a while, when it ceased to be possible to see the meat for all the dead bees on it, he would replace it with a new slice.

Another time we stayed over with the Churches in San Francisco. I shared a room with Tommy, who'd sing a song that was popular then, Bing Crosby's "Mairzy Doats." I considered his home the most civilized place in California — maybe anywhere. We would sit out in the garden, under the London lamp, on the marble, in the fern-and-philodendron garden of a hundred greens, then go into the elegant living room with the marble fireplace right out of Rokeby, as my mother put it, the bookshelves packed with albums and picture books and old Hemingway works (but not the one Hemingway dedicated to Betsy Roberts, with a smartass remark about her poor typing), the pair of gilt and gray columns leading to the dining area, the framed remnants of Betsy's balloon fetish of decades past.

Another time I visited the Churches they had just bought a new car, a Buick, getting a good bargain just before the appearance of the 1956 models. It was ample inside with a gadget-laden dashboard, rich upholstery, full lighting and a very smooth carriage. In those days, I noted, you could get a used 1953 Ford for $940. Yet another time, invited to a formal dance in San Francisco, I got permission from Betsy Church to go to her house to change into my tuxedo, embarrassed though I was to impose myself in such a way but unable to imagine taking the F train home in a tuxedo. After the dance I changed back out of my tuxedo, to return to the F train. Waiting in the terminal, I watched punching-drunkards and high-school hoods tripping all over, then rode back to Berkeley feeling empty, lonesome, as though the evening had not been a success.

(Rounding out the circle, it turned out that Ernest Hemingway's Paris benefactor and advisor, Gertrude Stein, who Betsy claimed actually helped Hemingway sharpen his work into publishable form, came from a family which had made its fortune, in Oakland, building and developing the F train system.)

Betsy talked to me more about our old neighbors the Andersons. She claimed that the matriarch, Corona, had become eccentric (it was Betsy's claim that only the rich became eccentric and they had to since they had no other way to spend their time). She'd begun developing neuroses, visiting the Swiss psychoanalyst Carl Gustav

Jung, consulting others about her husband and other relatives and letting her eccentricities consume her. On her return from one visit to Jung she told my mother she addressed a group of Marin County housewives and asked them "Are you really still sleeping with your husbands?"

I did go to see Corona. She came by my bus stop with a jarring honk. I got into her car. On to San Rafael, her massive greensward, wooden steps to a mahogany dining room, immense living room then library with a vast window looking out onto lofty pines, eucalyptuses, magnolias and locusts. She had already said she was going to watch me this weekend to see if Groton had left its scar on me, adding that my father had been very badly behaved when she saw him last, self-important and showing off. She told me she liked my mother more than my father, insisted she was much more well-rounded and kind, whereas my father was cruel, not himself. None of the people who went through Groton were themselves, she asserted. They had a superiority complex and were all scarred. My stepfather Byron, she claimed, was a fine man because he wasn't inhibited and my sister Mary was natural. Fine Jungian archetypes.

We went out on the lawn and Corona proceeded to explain all her beliefs learned from "the great Jung" — emotions were almost all that mattered, man has had them since life began, reason came only recently — and reiterate that Byron was a better person than my father because he felt, did not think, and would invariably make the right decisions in the end.

I for my part told her Byron did happen to be bitterly jealous of my mother's liberal friends and recalled a time he'd got into a furious argument with my mother after they'd had dinner with John O'Gorman, the leftist chemist my mother had worked with in the ADA. I could remember hearing their screams after that dinner. Years later, in a Safeway, Byron pointed to rolls of toilet paper on a rack and mentioned that one of those would be a great gift to send someone like O'Gorman.

(Conversely, Byron, conservative as he was, would derogate Harry Girvetz for signing the University of California loyalty oath in the late forties and my mother would come to Harry's defense. Harry, she said, had paid his dues and unlike John was still married and had children to support. Byron retorted by talking about a German he'd taught with at the Del Monte Lodge before the war who gave up an excellent job to return to Germany under Hitler. "Him I admired," Byron would say. "He stuck up for his beliefs.")

I finally got Corona to take notice of my message when I recalled one of Byron's in-laws talking about her daughter, who'd got a job teaching swimming. "One of her pupils is Jerry Lewis' daughter," she'd said, "and we're so happy for her." Corona did wince at that, but changed the subject and moved on.

We were close friends with her daughter Mary and Mary's husband, Boris Lakusta. They had my father become the godfather of their second son, Alex. My mother and I even attended their fiftieth anniversary, as well as their wedding. Mary had almost been crushed to death fifteen years before that anniversary, between a gate and a truckful of horses that had reversed after its brakes slipped. Not long after, she and Boris died within a few months of each other and were buried out in the Anderson plot at Mount Tamalpais Cemetery beyond the San Rafael Mission, about ten yards away from the gravesite of my old great-grandfather Christopher Emmet. (By then Mary's caretakers were earning over

$300,000 a year looking after her, and they angrily insisted she had committed suicide.)

At Mary's funeral an old family friend related an anecdote where they'd taken a balloon up at the old Anderson family ranch, long since dissolved into subdivisions, and it had ended up in a tree. "It was foolish of Boris to arrange that," Mary'd said, "but it was such fun."

I had a fellowship which led me to spend four years in the Middle East further studying its great venerable languages. It was a part of the world that was almost terra incognita to Americans in those days, not in general very appealing to the younger, more studious ones. Europe and Latin America, and even the Far East, seemed much more congenial.

On my way I passed by Rokeby. I called my grandmother to state that I would like to come visit, and announced myself as Chris Rand. "Oh, I don't talk to Chris Rand," she replied, and hung up. My sister Mary ordered me to swallow my pride and call her back, announcing myself as Temple (the name they had given me as a small child). When I finally grudgingly acquiesced my grandmother did agree to see me.

The mansion had a gardener, Harold Day. About all he did was tend the greenhouse for my grandmother, as she had to have flowers in the hallway all year round. (After all, while my grandfather was still alive and they'd lived down in the house in New York City during the winter the gardener of the day would have flowers sent down there every week.) The Rokeby greenhouse required a great deal of heat. Uncle Dick pointed it out to me from the tower then proceeded to start talking with agitation about it. I asked him to explain what he was saying in greater detail and he replied, "Never you mind, this is not something you have to worry yourself about."

Dick was expressing himself half-coherently by then.

Grandfather Richard had been in particular a companion for Uncle Dick, who was not well versed in arts and letters, though no one ever told him that didn't matter except perhaps Richard himself. My mother was devoted to her brother and considered that he had great political, diplomatic talent. She remembered a time he was invited to a large dinner and arrived late only to find all the places taken. He had the charm and wit to go up to the hostess with an empty chair from the next room, announce "I see all the places are taken and would love to sit next to you," and proceed to do so, to her delight. My mother believed that with his talent as a mechanic he could have opened an automobile repair shop in the nearby town of Red Hook and in time become a community figure, perhaps even make his way into politics. But of course that was not deemed permissible in a person of his high-class background. He was always under pressure, from women, to excel, to be on the Harvard track, to see all the great European sights, to be a musician and an engineer. He went on to Harvard but never graduated from engineering school.

My mother claimed he used to distill applejack even as a teenager, in an area to the back of Rokeby behind the cold room, where his mother rarely ventured. She remembered her coming-out party at the Ritz-Carlton in 1929, in the depths of Prohibition, when he arranged to place glasses that were tinted a purplish-blue before each of the guests so that they could have liquor and her parents would not notice that in the dim light. (The *New York Times* published the guest list for this event; it ran into hundreds of names and took up half a page.)

My mother and Uncle Dick would have parties in Long Island in late summer before the New York social rounds began and she remembered times she had to drive him home in the family Cadillac.

My father used to insist that Dick really began drinking later, when he married, but I continue to suspect the turning point in his life came when his father Richard died.

Near the end of my visit Uncle Dick had me take him next door to Sylvania, the mansion Chanler the Rain King had inherited from his parents. We found Chanler sitting out under the trees at a table with his second wife Helen and their son Victor. At one point Dick asked Chanler if he wouldn't let him have a drink. Chanler got out a full-sized tumbler and filled it two-thirds full with gin. Straight, no ice or tonic. Dick finished it off in about three minutes and I never saw him again. I wondered if that hadn't been a strong dose but Chanler recited reasons for giving it to him, almost as if he'd memorized them to spiel out to critical outsiders.

Time and again over the years I have wondered how I would have lived in that place, had circumstances forced me to stay there permanently. I concluded I would have had no recourse but to find an all-consuming enterprise, whatever that may have been, constructing fine furniture in a deep basement, developing more and more advanced breeds of cattle — anything that would have taken my mind far away from the domain around me.

If I had been one of the eight siblings but refused to yield up my share of Rokeby to Margaret, how would I have held on to that share? Insist on having one-eighth of the rooms in the mansion, five and a half out of the forty-three? Which ones? I bet I'd have been haggled into accepting the ones that were the hardest to heat.

15
The Middle East
through Our Eyes

arther on my way I passed through Istanbul,
where my father was staying with Peter, whom
he'd invited out for the summer. There I met the
great Tatar raconteur Abdullah Musa, an old friend of
my father's from China, who'd come to Turkey to live
as the country had a law encouraging the ingathering
of ethnic Turks from other lands. But Abdullah never
felt at home in his land of refuge. He told my father
at dinner one night "For one million dollars I will tell
the State Department in four words how to handle the
Turks."

When I later asked my father what those might have
been he replied "Probably something like 'spare rod,
spoil child.'" Another time our father told us to go out
pub crawling and when we returned to the Divan Oteli at
two in the morning we found him arranging inebriatedly
at the desk to take a woman up to his room. No one else

was in the lobby and we tried to save him embarrassment by pretending to be too drunk to notice.

My father bought me a ticket to Erzerum, in a first-class sleeper where I was almost asphyxiated when the coal smoke blew in through all the open windows as we roared through a tunnel. Bidding farewell in the Ankara station was my real entry into the cold world.

I found considerable criticism of America and its policies in the course of my studies in Iran and then Egypt — pervasive and sometimes vitriolic. Somewhat justifiable, I came to accept, in the long run — at least if one failed to consider much of our misconduct the consequence of a grim national necessity, fighting the Cold War. I even faced criticism from Britishers. One working-class fellow sitting next to me on a bus from Herat to Meshhed deplored our aggressive nuclear policy — and behavior toward Cuba. "We have the sort of experience you don't," he insisted, "with our massive suffering in both wars, not to speak of the near-invasion."

Of course, Middle Easterners kept saying, those countries were advanced in the technical sense, but that was largely the result of political ruthlessness — "Always remember that the British and Americans speak the same language," one fellow repeatedly told me. "They never let anyone make progress in anything. It's been that way since the Middle Ages, when they were in the Dark Ages, and they acquired the great learning that the Arabs had built up over centuries. They made a monopoly of that learning and never even let us have any back. They would let little bits of it out all right, but at a great price. Where one of them has no influence, the other rules. The British leave India, the Americans move right in behind them."

A refreshing anomaly, a contemporary who had lived a while in Britain. "I am a mutation," he declared, "the sort of person the society of the future will have to model itself after if it wants to survive. America has gained its momentary lead by becoming a land of mutations."

At one point during my stay in Iran President Eisenhower came there for a visit with the Shah, Mohammad Reza Pahlavi. Some fighters flew over the airport on his arrival, spelling out "Ike." "The taxpayers should thank God they didn't spell out 'Eisenhower,'" remarked one bitter opponent of the Republicans with the Ford Foundation.

Once on a bus trip in Central Iran from Esfahan to Zahedan, passing through Rafsanjan as I headed for the once-weekly train to Quetta in Pakistan, I saw a fat, glib young man a little older than me in a white sheet-robe of some religious significance who when the bus stopped got down and began giving a spiel by the roadside, saying among other things "I want to go to Tehran and see what its political situation is." Almost all the people on the bus surrounded this youth, totally absorbed in what he had to say. I couldn't fail to take note of him either — with reason as it turned out years later.

Another time while I was in Iran, when Tehran University was temporarily shut down in the wake of student demonstrations against the Shah, I visited my father in Greece. We went for dinner at one point with various leftish American artist-expatriates, who talked vociferously about the political changes that had been happening in the world recently with the rise of Castro, Nasser, Mao, Nkruma and Patrice Lumumba. "The great new world of love is going to come from the Congo" announced one of them, Bill.

My father replied, "I was just down there two years ago, Bill, and I'm sure if you only went down there you'd see it couldn't possibly come from a place like that." Another time we stood together on the beach, by Sounion on the Attic Peninsula, watching a firing-squad of German tourists film a spectacular cherry-red sunset behind the temple, and my father stared out lovingly at the horizon. He was always happy leaving places — fleeing places really. He lived on in nostalgia for the one place he couldn't go back to, the People's Republic of China.

Writers could be very slanted on the subject of alcohol. I remember one newspaper columnist who repeatedly discussed the subject; one of his favorite words was "decoction." If the word had dim ritualistic overtones, maybe it referred to something of a higher order than vice.

It hadn't occurred to me much before, but in "objective" or "normal" terms, my father was always in bad shape by then — when I was around him at least. I had lived most of my life around people in bad shape!

My mother claimed that he had been a furious alcoholic through college and into early marriage. When her father died in Rome, Dick went over to collect his ashes, lending my father his car before he left. My father then went on a three-day drunk on a visit to Yale and could not find the car. My mother remembers him returning home to New York, sweating, his coat over his arm, his suit pants in the back pocket of his jeans. He had let a friend borrow the car and the friend had brought it back to New York and left it in an obscure area of Harlem. Eventually my father found the car but the experience so unnerved him he went on the wagon for seven years.

(I remember reading another story, many years later, about a rich German tourist who got too drunk at the end of an evening in San Francisco to find his expensive Mercedes. Ultimately he chartered a helicopter for $300 and flew about over the city till he did spot it.)

A new element had entered my father's life: a woman named Miriam Ervin, whom I'd noticed vaguely in the recent past living with a man whose father had made his subsequently-sequestered fortune in Cairo years before, selling bread made out of plaster of Paris.

Miriam was an archaeologist with an American foundation in Athens and a divorcee (later I discovered thrice-divorced) with a daughter in her early teens. She also knew how to fly a plane. During my stay that February, my father went out to the island of Mykonos with her. He was thinking of marrying her. He didn't talk much about her, except to say that he found her attractive and wanted to settle down.

Back in Iran, during further demonstrations I heard that they had got married and at the end of the school year heading west I passed by Athens to spend a few days with them. I had a difficult time finding my father. I went around to the Greek-American 17 Club and various friends, I heard at one point that Miriam was in the hospital, did not find my father at her apartment near the Acropolis and at the end tracked him down at the Hotel Cecil in the distant suburb of Kifissia. I thought it strange for him to be staying at the hotel even if Miriam was sick. He appeared red-faced at his hotel room door when I knocked on it and told me that he was divorcing Miriam. I was astounded. They'd been married only a month — it was the first of July. She'd been at the clinic for about a week and my father had left before that, so they'd really been together only about three weeks.

In the end I stayed till the middle of the month. My father continued to be in bad shape and I heard all his grievances against Miriam. He told me, going all around Athens on foot on an extremely hot evening, struggling to find a telegraph office, "She used every trick in the book on me, and some that aren't there." One of Miriam's previous husbands, a violinist, had apparently been crazy, or so she said — "but certainly isn't anymore." His close friends from long ago, also then living in Athens, the *Life* magazine photographer Jim Burke and his wife Josephine, had been skeptical of the prospects for the marriage. "I can't even work properly" my father told me. "This has affected me deeply in the heart, and I depend on my heart in my work."

My father had always had a deep affinity for Ernest Hemingway. During this visit I saw in a newsstand that Hemingway had just committed suicide. When I passed this news on to my father he locked eyes with me and declared "No fooling." He stayed locked in place, stunned. Later up at the Burkes' place he stated that he truly felt that the bell had tolled for him too with Hemingway gone. Jim Burke responded that he'd photographed Hemingway recently in Spain and found the man had deteriorated into a spoiled brat. He had been driving around in a Lancia like a twenty-year-old and insisting the most brilliant young bullfighters pay him court, which they had no intention of doing. Jim even said he thought *The Old Man and the Sea*, Hemingway's most recent work, was overrated, somewhat phony. My father just muttered in reply that he had liked it.

James Burke once told me "You should work hard till you're forty to establish yourself — that's what I told Chris — then enjoy life after that." James died two years later in a fall in the Himalayas.

I recited talk from the older women in the family, especially my grandfather Richard's sister Amey, railing to me and my brothers and sisters, as children, against alcoholics. She would refer to drinking as "voluntary insanity." I would argue with her about the restrictions that did exist on drinking: here am I, I said in my late teens, able to go fight and die for my country but unable to walk into a bar and order a beer. "Well I'm not talking about dying for your country" she said and brusquely changed the subject. I can remember a friend of Catholic background once lashing out at what he called racist WASP culture, a cold tradition which shrank in terror from love and affection, seeking solace from it in liquor.

Amey didn't often speak about anyone in level, judicious terms. She was either lavishing unqualified praise on a person or finding fault — often tiny fault — with him most of the time. Or saying nothing, as in the case of her gay brother Chester, with whom she lived perhaps a third of her life. But essentially put up a wall of misinformation, too priggish or at least unimaginative to pass more interesting commentary on much of what went on around her. She had a powerful neurosis no doubt earned from real suffering. She may well have been abused early on in her life and if so, as a female victim from those days, had to bear an outrageous burden of guilt all her life.

Still and all, with many thanks to Chester, she had a brilliant period in life, in the 1930s, when he became president of the American Academy in Rome and she accompanied him. They lived in the academy mansion, the Villa Aurilia, whose main drawing room seems rather like those in Rokeby from photographs of the time. She became well versed in Italian art and architecture and acquainted with a broad variety of famous artists and literary figures, among them Ezra Pound and Bernard Berenson. She even learned to speak some Providence-accented Italian. She also, perforce, maintained relations with Mussolini's government. At one dinner, a friend visiting her described talking after dinner with Mussolini's propaganda minister, a man named Celasia. "He was most interesting, telling me what the Fascists were trying to accomplish," wrote Amey's friend. "The draining and reclaiming of the Pontine Marshes were spoken of. The government had built farm houses all over the reclaimed land for the ex soldiers, who after certain payments for 20 years will own their land etc. etc. He also spoke of pre-natal care of mothers, wonderful tuberculosis hospitals and many things I had not known about."

Then Chester died and Amey ran the American Academy herself until the academy's trustees could find a formally educated successor.

Chester left her most of his fortune. She spent it broadly but not lavishly. In later years she would take her grand-nieces and -nephews to Italy for a summer tour, hitting every single Renaissance high spot (and not much else). One summer she took Mary and me. In museums she often happily worked to be of use interpreting Italian for other Americans; I felt a little sad watching that. Probably the highest spot for us was a visit for lunch at Berenson's estate outside Florence, I Tatti. The fellow was a little older than Amey, around ninety then, and we found him no longer very agile, not interested in traveling, but still sharp. At one point in the lunch, on hearing of my Middle Eastern studies, he told me the coming struggle in the world would be between Russia and the United States over "Persia." He also told Amey he had had Harry Truman over for lunch not long before. When she asked him his impression of the former president he replied "I found him rather like Huck Finn, actually." Later, as we were driven back to our hotel in Florence, Amey claimed that he was a man of exceptional intelligence and perception and that remark underlined the fact.

At one point in Athens I glibly informed my father that I considered one thing to be clear about alcoholics: they hated to drink. They drank, all right, rather the way a nymphomaniac had sex or a compulsive gambler played cards — fast, precipitously, to get it over with. They didn't lovingly caress the glass and sip the fluid, sucking the taste of it dry, or reject anything of inferior taste — rotgut, Ripple, bad araq. (The other side of this was that alcoholics could stop drinking, but they had to do it cold. They had to sit around talking with other alcoholics endlessly about their obsession while slurping down torrents of coffee.)

To this my father retorted, "A lot of people much older and wiser than you have labored all their lives trying to explain why people drink and they haven't come up with any answers, so don't think you can."

Maybe I can't, but the women in the family couldn't either. They kept calling it a disease. I once heard an overweight priest who'd just completed a twenty-eight-day alcohol withdrawal program observing, "If alcoholism is a disease, why do people have to confess it? We don't make them confess cancer."

My father made up for this in another area. He told me he was irrelevant, no matter how well-meaning. Not decadent, just simplehearted.

He was beginning to turn a bit garbled in his thinking. At one point, echoing his time in Sri Lanka with news of a deep groundswell of left-wing agitation in Brazil, he became convinced that we were going to get involved in a war down there, and fast. This was in the summer. Brazil then had a socialist government intent on nationalizing foreign enterprises, under the inspiration of Castro's Cuba. "Normally countries go to war after the harvest," he remarked. "In the case of Brazil though that theory doesn't apply because they don't have harvests."

But then he went on to tell me the British kept saying America was off the main stage. Afghanistan it was that stood at the center of this century. Iran. He felt ensnared in a maze and a dull longing suffused him, a melancholia he could not extricate himself from. America. Farthest extension of the northwestern marches, they used to dismiss it, really, as a land of insipid tourists — back in the days of the gold-backed dollar, anyway, the neutral host, and he was one of the neutral manservants who populated it.

He came out to Santa Barbara in 1961. We went up to visit old Sedgwick and he archly criticized us for making fun of him on the drive home. "If you accept his hospitality, you should do so graciously and not criticize him behind his back." I pointed out that Minty used to annoy my roommates for coming up from Monterey for the weekend, when he was in the Army Language School, and eating our food and repaying us in liquor. Finally the roommates had ordered me to tell him to pay his own way if he wanted to come up in the future and of course he never came back. Dad remarked that Minty's form of repayment was standard for the class of society he came from.

I drove east with my father, Dickie and Mary. We took the southern route and made a couple of quick side trips into Mexico. We first drove between Mexicali and San Luis and as soon as we crossed into Mexico my father said "this is a real border." Then we dropped over to Ciudad Acuna, where he suggested we have a carnival and vanished for a couple of hours. He was fuzzily festive.

About four years later he went down to South America on further *New Yorker* assignments. My brothers took him down to a freighter in Newark through heavy traffic for his trip to Peru, Joe Garagiola on the cabdriver's radio, endlessly wisecracking his way through a Mets game. Down in Bolivia, he got a helicopter ride with President Rene Barrientos, who later, in October 1967, ordered the execution of the just-captured Che Guevara. Afterward, in Peru, our father committed an act of violence on himself and my brother Dickie was summoned to go down and get him out of the country. The task was tricky since there was an obscure law in Peru that people deemed psychotic were not to leave the country on tourist class by plane. Dick got a vice president with Braniff (another now defunct airline) to arrange first-class seats for the two of them. Our father would not forgive him for that, from then on relentlessly complaining that Dickie had grievously cheated him by getting the most expensive tickets. Dick felt their falling-out was final but at his wedding a year later I went up to the New York state facility in White Plains, where our father had been sent, and brought him down for the wedding.

He didn't like to talk about brushes he'd had with the CIA but one day drinking heavily he got talking about them. He admitted he had done work for the organization, briefly, mostly in India, in revulsion over the Soviet propaganda campaigns he'd had to witness against the United States. He wrote up a report on the land reform leader Vinoba Bhave for one high-ranking operative, Gene Milligan, and one on the anti-Pakistani guerrilla leader the Fakir of Ipi for Frank Kiernan, who in time rose almost to the top of the CIA. (These were distillations of articles he'd done for *The New Yorker*.)

He quickly became disgusted with the work that decision had led to. In India he had to cozy up to powerful figures he found unpleasant. It also irked him that every time he came to a new capital all the undercover people in the embassy would make a noisy and embarrassing fuss over him.

It's incompetently corrupt and miserable, he went on to say on this occasion. Corrupt miserable people can have overpowering emotions. They can panic seeing ordinary people develop ordinary relations with one another. They can also be excessively resentful, bruised by slights, putdowns, rejections real or imagined. "Goddamn it, Chris," he started insisting, "always keep yourself pure. Always be what you say you are, no more and no less. To thine own self be true, whatever that corny phrase means. Remember, for all the horrors, what you stand for, what you believe in. What we all believe in.

"Stay out of that organization wherever you go in this world and if you ever get into a jam and need money or any other kind of help, come see me about it and I will bail you out." He quickly severed all ties with the organization and, as I came to learn full well, it never forgave him for that.

16
America through
Egyptian Lenses

B y then I had gone to study Arabic in Egypt and while there I met and married a young British-educated lady, Hoda. Her education had left her with mixed feelings. This was in the time of Egypt's formidable anti-British nationalist president Gamal Abdel Nasser, who had come to power through a military takeover in July 1952 and within four years conducted a sweeping land reform and nationalized the Suez Canal — with consequences we had seen a few years earlier. To a large degree it was the force of this leader's personality and arguments that had drawn me to Egypt in the first place.

France and Britain mounted an invasion to recapture the Suez Canal but were forced to abandon the operation and withdraw under Soviet and American pressure. Israel invaded Sinai in synchronization with this action and managed to hold on to the peninsula through it. Hoda well remembered watching British aircraft dropping flares off beyond the Nile at night to illuminate targets during the 1956 war, with several girls; one of them was Jewish and, Hoda learned later, had been knitting socks for Israeli soldiers. About fifty thousand Jews left Egypt in the wake of the Suez war.

As for the United States, Secretary of State Dulles antagonized Nasser, a prickly personality anyway, through several insulting acts, and Nasser soon turned to the Soviet Union for virtually all his military and civilian aid.

A major confidant of Nasser's, the columnist and editor Muhammad Hassanein Heikal, once stated that in 1956 Nasser sent him to New York to talk to Dulles on some murky mission. He took a flight which lasted thirty-six hours each way. Heikal went on to spend only a few hours in New York, visiting Dulles at the Waldorf Astoria, and even then spent most of that time waiting for Dulles to finish watching a Washington Redskins game.

Hoda knew some activist contemporaries who had meetings in their basements, where they concocted primitive homemade bombs and ground out mimeographed tracts. Years later we met a fellow who had been shot fighting the British in Suez and had a hole deep as a thumb two inches below his heart. He described the pride and elation he felt some years later as he walked down the streets of London.

Most of my working time in Cairo I spent studying Arabic literature and grammar. For a while in 1962, though, I branched out and found work as an associate editor with Egypt's English-language news magazine The Arab Observer. Among my associates there were two militant American blacks, Dave DuBois (stepson of the famous activist W. E. B. DuBois) and Maya Make ("Mockay"), wife of a South African anti-apartheid figure.

Right then a former spy for the Soviet Union, Jack Sobel, was jailed in America for his activities. His brother, Robert Soblen, was also convicted, but, after unsuccessfully appealing the conviction before the U. S. Supreme Court and fearing he would spend the rest of his life in jail, fled to Israel, where he sought asylum as a Jew under the Law of Return. A big controversy flared up over this in Israel, where the government of David Ben Gurion decided to deport Soblen but was almost overruled in an angry parliamentary vote of no confidence. Both DuBois and Mrs. Make made a big issue of this in The Arab Observer, as it was an effective story with which to lash out at America. That would have been fine with official Egypt at that time — except that in their attack the two made the mistake of endorsing a political initiative by members of the Israeli parliament, an absolute taboo. When their stand came to the attention of the magazine's editor in chief he had them fired. Mrs. Make left her husband shortly after that, eventually returned to America and became famous as the writer and activist Maya Angelou.

Hoda and I then made our way to the States. The first thing to amaze Hoda about the US was the proliferation of signs she saw on all roadways, back streets as well as highways. Another adjustment she had to make was facing bloody meat, or even red-colored meat. In Egypt, as throughout Islam, meat was drained of blood, kosher-style, before it was sold, and in this new country she would always send her portion back to the kitchen if it was not thoroughly cooked. (In Egypt, also, people did not hide their medications in the bathroom chest; they put them in a silver bowl right in the middle of the dining table.)

On arriving we took the Taconic Parkway up to Rokeby in the driving snow. Until I married Hoda, she had never been out of Egypt except for a brief trip to Syria and not even her rigorous British education could possibly have clued her in on this. With Aunt Sue we had drinks surreptitiously down in the pantry and, Hoda shivering over lunch, Aunt Sue explained to her that she wouldn't have been saddled with the burden of looking after this household were it not for modern wonder drugs — which provoked a comment from her daughter Rosalind on her tactlessness. My grandmother sat staring ahead in her chair, glazed-eyed, chewing her food down to a fine paste, and died shortly after that, in the spring.

Going on to Boston, crossing Harvard Yard, we ran into my old Groton schoolmate Joe Fletcher. On seeing my wife he began addressing her in Persian. He had branched out, begun studying the Middle East; had had some exposure as well to Turkish and Arabic, which was actually what she could speak.

We continued our studies in Los Angeles, at UCLA. Hoda had to take the foreign students' English test when she first registered there. Seated next to her were a Britisher, angry at being made to take the test, and an Indian woman who got a perfect score. Hoda got a 98, failing to tell the difference between "pin" and "pen." Decades later in the early 2000s, she applied for citizenship. When interviewed by an immigration official, she was asked what they called the head of a city. She replied, "In the community where I live we don't have a mayor because it is unincorporated." Blowing away said official. Incidentally, while at Cal as an undergraduate, I had had access to a list of all the foreign students in the university (working as I did then as an assistant on English for foreign students). The country with the most foreign students?

Guess again. It was Canada.

Christopher T. Rand

For my part, I got a master's degree in Near Eastern studies at UCLA. In one seminar we had an old Russian-born professor of medieval Arabic history, Moshe Perlmann, who told us "Between al-Biruni and Isaac Newton, and Leonardo da Vinci in between, there was nothing but interest in gossip."

We also met a number of Egyptian students at UCLA. Their attitudes were nationalistic more than political, in general. Aside from Nasser's pan-Arabism, spearheaded by the Arab Socialist Union, the main political movement in the eastern Arab world was the Baath, but few Egyptians were interested in what they considered its small-time watered-down Greek Orthodox communism — except, briefly, one fellow Nabil who was also almost killed by the British. Just to make sure, though, there were Egyptians at some of the bigger universities who had been seconded from military duties to earn higher degrees but couldn't spare time getting the English right so had to have some of those bright young Levantine Baathists ghostwrite their term papers for them.

Among the people in the relatively sophisticated UCLA community were Gamal, an engineer, and his wife Gamila. A liberated woman years ahead of the Americans around her, named in fact after a famous advocate of woman's rights from the 1910s, Gamila Attia, she appeared at special functions in a full-length yellow, purple and pink dress covered with big lavender butterflies, numerous plastic bracelets, huge round tinted glasses and a purse cluttered with little Nefertiti heads stamped in a gold leaf never exactly centered on the leather imprints. Another student was Ali, a computer scientist and devout Moslem who collected the works of Sheik Muhammad el-Ghazzali and on one wall kept a list of the five daily prayer times for three whole years, printed out by computer to the nearest minute, using complex astronomical data. On the other side of the clique stood Hamed and Ashraf, who ran a Fuller Brush franchise in his spare time and played the stock market. A sort of easygoing, neutral outsider was Hassan, who had transferred down from Oregon, to his occasional regret. He was first seen standing on the steps of the administration building, chanting out terrible oaths in Arabic over the heads of the indifferently mulling noon throng. Hamed, appalled, went up to him and rebuked him for using such language. Hassan was overjoyed. "Thank God I've at last met an Egyptian!" he declared. "I've been here two months, and I'm desperate!" At that time he was married to an American, which added to his sense of isolation.

Yet another fellow, Rashad, called them up out of the blue one day to ask if they were Egyptian. "What did you do, get us out of the Saigon phone book?" riposted Gamila. It turned out that Rashad had been riffling through the local books, looking under the "el" listings, and finally, in the last of six volumes, found the listing "el-Kafrawi." Rashad and his wife drank at parties, except when Ali and his wife were there; then they had only 7 Up.

Gamila quickly developed an aversion to Ashraf. Once she said, clearly referring to him, "I'm getting fed up with all the Egyptians around who try making themselves seem important by exaggerating the number of feddans [acres, more or less] Nasser confiscated from their families." Ashraf didn't really come from a good family anyway, she claimed; his grandfather had just been a minor railway functionary and some of his relatives worked for Ethiopian Airlines.

One of their favorite leisure activities — almost their only one — was to go gamble in Vegas. They all went, along with virtually all the other Middle Easterners they knew in the area, and they all gambled. Some women would save up a sock full of pennies for the one-cent slot machines. Hamed would always save up a hundred dollars — sixty for blackjack, forty for craps. His recreation was to see how long he could hold onto it; once he kept playing for eighteen hours straight. Gamal, the engineer and systems analyst, won regularly. Once up at Tahoe he got $2,000 at poker and immediately put it in a cabin. He rented out the cabin all year round and got enough money from it to buy another cabin and gamble some more, making more money, which he put into yet more cabins. "That's what Egyptians are supposed to do, pyramid," he protested, pyramiding.

Shortly afterward, in 1966, Hamed received a major honor at the national convention of Egyptian students in America. The government planned to hold a major students' convention in Alexandria, Egypt's second city. Nasser himself was to attend, along with some handpicked students from abroad and some from home. A certain number were to come from America and among those invited was Hamed.

Nasser's attendance at this unusual conference lasted two days. The event was carefully structured and controlled. While a hundred students had come from abroad, the Arab Socialist Union made sure that about two hundred local students, many of whom were to go abroad if they behaved well, also attended, dominating the sessions and passing their resolutions through after lengthy, complex maneuvers and floor votes. The ASU impinged on the students back from the foreign world in other ways. Its men constantly told them that it would be best if they kept quiet and did not ask embarrassing questions; this was a special treat and if they weren't careful it might be disadvantageous for their families. They were subtly disparaged on other grounds. One girl who had come from abroad was photographed talking to her brother, who had never left Egypt but was wearing a Hawaiian shirt, which Egyptians generally hold to be in boorish taste — just the sort of thing Americans wore all the time; in a magazine, the photograph bore the caption "Some of the students back from America."

Still, the students managed to express some views. Two youths down from Paris, who earlier at the embassy there had harangued the military leader Marshall Abdelhakim Amer (later a main cause of Nasser's sufferings), asked sharp questions about army perquisites and an ongoing war in Yemen. Another student asked a government minister about the latest big rumor sweeping the country: was it true that Israel had managed to build a nuclear reactor? The minister dismissed all the representatives of the press from the auditorium then after they had gone admitted quietly that it was but claimed the Egyptian army would be able to surround it and take it over if war broke out.

When Nasser himself appeared, he agreed to answer any questions the students asked but would allow no rebuttals to his answers. In general, he comported himself skillfully. One student asked him an extremely long, complicated question on industrial policy, with numerous peripheral points; Nasser answered point by point, in exhaustive detail, even including some the student had neglected to put in the question. When objections were raised about draft exemptions, study allowances and a 300 percent duty the government charged on cars some students brought home, he made generous concessions at once. At a couple of points he reacted testily, most conspicuously when asked why the Egyptian government had let itself get involved in Yemen. "We went into Yemen because we had to get out from under our isolation in the world," Hamed remembered him retorting. Then, asked about the prospects for democracy and press freedom in Egypt, he replied archly "The process of liberty and democracy according to Western patterns won't meet our case because we wish to change the face of the old society. The process of parties wouldn't be suitable, for there can be no conflicting parties."

He went on: "Someone asks for democracy and political parties. This implies we have to allow the existence of a reactionary capitalist party. Once such a party is set up, the CIA will infiltrate it the following day. If I allow the creation of two socialist parties they'd wreck one another and reactionary elements would in the end find a way to exercise influence. Hence it is necessary to form one bloc in order to create a society in which class distinction is eliminated.

"I cannot tolerate a newspaper calling for a capitalist society," he declared, "because this would be an antirevolutionary act. Such a newspaper would be hostile to the revolution."

At a supermarket in Los Angeles I ran into my old neighbor Julia. She was now studying hospital administration and told me that Charles had become a nurse. As he lived near us, she gave us his address.

Charles had become unmistakable: he dyed his hair reddish-blond, wore taboo perfume and fingernail polish and had a place done up with sandalwood walls, little lattices, roses in the garden, hi-fi playing Johnnie Mathis and Arrivederci Roma, oversized naugahyde and formica furniture and pink bathroom rugs. He seemed constantly on the run. He had an unlisted phone number, a sign on the carport door saying "Beware of the Dog" (with two tiny dachshunds inside) and stayed strictly away from the neighbors, simple folk many of whom tried to befriend him. One succeeded, a middle-aged woman who called him up every half hour. She was probably out to reform him, find him a bride. She wouldn't leave him alone, cooked for him, had him do errands for her and give her lifts in his car, even stayed the night sometimes. Once she found the bar where he was having a drink and went down after him. God knows how she found out about that.

He was working in the Santa Monica Convalarium looking after elderly people, senile for the most part. "Oh God, sometimes I could kill them," he told us — "That's mean, I shouldn't say that." One of his charges had once been a distinguished judge.

I soon acquired a property of my own there and when I went off Charles had me rent it out to Darlene, a lady who worked with him in the Convalarium. Her patient was Louella Parsons, the famous Hearst syndicate gossip columnist. Louella came from Illinois originally, Darlene told me, and first went to work for Hearst in New York. She suffered a near-fatal case of pneumonia and moved to Arizona to recuperate. After that in the twenties Hearst sent her to Los Angeles, where she became the major source of gossip on the private lives of celebrities — and a major apologist for Hearst.

Darlene had been taking care of Louella, first at her own home then at the Convalarium. Louella was senile but indestructible, Darlene told me. She didn't like to see people because she felt she was in terrible shape but a few still came around, Irene Dunne, then Ben Lyon and Bebe Daniel, an old English couple who were famous in movies thirty or forty years earlier. Perhaps the most important single figure in her life then was Dr. Rex Kammenaar, whom she had set up when he first came to Hollywood fresh out of medical school, giving him uniforms and favorable publicity. Jack Warner the mogul also had a florist send Louella a bouquet the first of every month.

Another frequent visitor was Neil Rauh, who used to be Louella's leg man, had written a couple of books and was hoping to do a third, a biography of Louella. He'd call up periodically to ask Darlene if he could come talk to Louella and every now and then Louella would receive him. When he arrived at the Convalarium he would insist on talking to her in complete privacy. Dr. Kammenaar, who by then was often flying off to London to look after Elizabeth Taylor and Richard Burton, suggested to Darlene that she go listen in on it all behind the bathroom door; presumably Neil was pumping her.

Louella still had plenty of money to take care of all her expenses. She had learned so much over the years that the Hearst syndicate had had to give her a generous pension. Darlene's husband told me that that was because in the early twenties she hushed up the Fatty Arbuckle incident which took place at the house of Hearst's mistress Marion Davies — Arbuckle had raped a girl and she'd bled to death. Darlene corroborated this and spoke of another episode where Hearst was cruising in his yacht with Marion Davies and several other people off the California coast and one of them, a director named Ince, was taken off and buried at one port after dying of food poisoning they said, though no coroner examined his corpse. It was later rumored that the man had been playing around with Marion Davies and that Hearst had shot him and paid everyone on board a million dollars to keep quiet. Another rumor was that Hearst's real target had been Charlie Chaplin, also on the boat then, because he had been having an affair with Marion. (Chaplin's wife Lita later claimed she caught Charlie in bed with Marion.) Apparently Louella Parsons was the only witness to all that still living, hence the only one who could still divulge the full story.

Among her positive acts in service of Hearst was her humiliation of Orson Welles, who had produced *Citizen Kane*, a masterful satiric portrayal of Hearst's private life. She got the scoop on the collapse of Orson Welles' marriage to Rita Hayworth and her upcoming marriage to Aly Khan; when she first heard rumor of it she ordered Rita to invite her to the wedding.

When Louella's great rival Hedda Hopper died in 1966, Darlene informed Louella, despite Rex's orders that she was not to. When Louella heard that she immediately snapped "Good." The next day someone called up and asked her if she would care to contribute anything to Hedda's favorite charity. She retorted "I wouldn't give that bitch one cent." Later, though, Darlene saw her write out a check for $500 — and spend two hours bawling shamelessly.

Periodically rumors appeared concerning Louella's death. In her early eighties then, she had been in the Convalarium for years and suffering from shingles, and perhaps even a stroke for six. Kammenaar never charged her for medical attention and made sure to treat Darlene generously as well — would give her a hundred dollars at Christmas, Mother's Day presents and so forth. Louella's daughter Henrietta was married once but not any longer and lived instead with a beautiful dancer named Eva.

I hadn't seen Minty Sedgwick for several years by then, though I'd last heard he was living in California. We'd drifted apart. As I was taking a dog out on a walk before breakfast, something reminded me of the word "atabrine" as I looked at little runner-shoots springing up from the base of a tree in the sidewalk. The word reminded me of Minty, as someone in his family took it. Then the phone rang and that was when I heard of his death.

I didn't know what to make of it. As I went to breakfast, I thought, he wasn't gristle-brained enough. He wasn't too mean to die. I thought, later, his death left a clear message to the rest of us, which we will now emboss in reverse on our retinas: don't expect things to get better because they won't, necessarily. You may not hope for them to get better, you may not pray for them to get better. You may keep on trucking. You may sustain yourself by remembering that though there are no free lunches, there is every once in a while such a thing as a free drink.

Later I heard that Minty's father, the older Duke, had strewn his ashes over the ranch and that one of Minty's sisters stayed away from the ranch in protest against this for more than fifteen years. Duke the elder died late October 1967 at age sixty-three. He left behind a body of sculptures which included a bronze cowboy on horseback at the Earl Warren Showgrounds near our old Santa Barbara house and a pioneer monument in Cypress Lawn Cemetery near San Francisco.

By that time my master's degree led to some job experience in the Middle East, followed by substantial exposure to the international oil industry. At the outset my wife and I went to live in New York City, where I found work with an oil industry newsletter.

17

The Hudson and Its Connecticut Hinterland: Father's End

From there, my wife and I went back to Rokeby from time to time.

Rokeby, as we have seen, had became a part of a massive area Robert Livingston was granted in 1685. The territory of this grant extended to Connecticut and Massachusetts on and around the Taconic Range where my father grew up. Robert and his son Philip were said to have made life hard for people in that area — forcibly collecting rents from them or, failing that, burning them out and driving off their cattle. Bloodshed and death were common in these disputes. As late as the twentieth century, my father recounted, the borderland township of Ancram, then in New York, was said to be haunted in retaliation against the Livingstons by ghosts called the Ancram Screechers, a belief well established in the folklore of the old Raggies, people who lived on Mount Riga, the highest ground around Salisbury.

By the end of the nineteenth century as we have also seen Robert Livingston's progeny, with their various branches, owned most of the Catskills and everything in a band twenty or thirty miles wide stretching from the east bank of the Hudson to the Massachusetts and Connecticut state lines. That included the Chatham Hunt grounds, Bashbish Fall, the property now occupied by Stissing's bar in Pine Plains, MacArthur's Smokehouse in Millerton and even more. On top of that, they owned some escarpments and palisades. I have known only one other person, from a wholly different background two thousand miles or so to the west, who was wealthy enough to own an escarpment.

My father's world was rather rough compared to this. Litchfield County was hard not very hospitable terrain. It consisted of stubborn stony outcroppings ranging from the high point, Mount Riga, on down. My father remembered that in his boyhood most large, woodland stretches were visited at times by traveling sawmills. The operators of these mills would come with a couple of pairs of horses, put up a rough timber shack, spend the winter there cutting timber and sawing it then withdraw, leaving great mounds of sawdust in the wilds.

He remembered one father and daughter walking up Mount Riga every day of the summer season, a three-mile climb, then returning with two twelve- or fourteen-quart pails of berries each. Berries were so cheap that while they lasted my father and his brothers each had a soup-plate of them every morning for breakfast, with pilot biscuit broken over them and milk and sugar poured on. He'd see slag on the Housatonic when he went down there swimming or fishing for trout. It came from the old Salisbury iron furnaces up on Mount Riga. The Housatonic was not bridged in the early eighteenth century — therefore much of Salisbury's commerce with the outside world came from the Hudson Valley, only twenty miles away and already well developed. Salisbury was just an extension of the world of Rokeby and this close connection remains.

The Salisbury ironworks produced kettles used by whalers setting out to sea from Poughkeepsie, to render whale blubber out in the deep.

Salisbury ore was used in an iron chain known as *chevaux de frise*, studded with iron-tipped spikes fixed in submerged frames. The revolutionaries stretched this across the Hudson at an island as a defense against British ships, to frustrate the central British strategy, which was to seize control of the Hudson and cut off New England from the south. Washington then established his headquarters at Newburgh and prevented General Bourgoyne, who was coming down from Montreal, from linking up with an army advancing north from New York. "The British seized the chain and later took it to Gibraltar, where they used it for protecting the moles," my father wrote in his book on that world, *The Changing Landscape*.

Of course my father's circumstances were not rough either. His grandfather George Curtis Rand (1848–1907) was a very prosperous printer in Boston. He produced railway tickets, among other things — almost developed a monopoly in that craft. His brother, William Henry Rand, worked awhile in his press then went to Los Angeles, where he set up and briefly ran a newspaper, the *Star*, then ventured on to Chicago, where he established and ran a railroad ticket press with the expertise he'd acquired. He and his foreman McNally branched out to offer another service to railroads, printing maps. In the Great Chicago Fire of 1890, William buried two irreplaceable presses in sand and saved them and after that went on to run a world-famous business.

None of the fortune from this trickled down to my father though his father William B., "the Beagle," did inherit wealth, established a farm in Salisbury, Hamlet Hill, and shared in the dazzling world of growing anomalies in that era through his deep involvement with fox hunting — as indeed had Winty Chanler. My father used to say that the Beagle had fine, delicate bones which gave him an elegant appearance on horseback and he was a formidable horseman. As a master of hounds, he even knew and hunted with (in those days) Colonel George Patton, also a man of hounds. My father went so far as to say that as children, he and his brothers could find common ground with their father only in his equestrian world. But even fox hunting's great attraction came to fade in the nation as a whole and in the end the Beagle was almost wiped out in the 1929 crash.

My mother's whole family, in all its length and breadth, had come up against a dilemma: having to choose between staying on these ancestral lands or keeping up with the times in the nation about them and integrating themselves into the American mainstream. With each generation, pressure became more and more intense on the individual to choose between immersion in the society or escape from it — at considerable cost either way.

By the late twentieth century, according to Winty, in the twenty- to thirty-mile stretch of the Hudson north of Poughkeepsie there were five estates that had become state or federal monuments, including of course Hyde Park, the Vanderbilt place and Clermont (a state historic park), and five that should at least have become state parks, including Rokeby and Steen Valetje, the southern parenthesis to Rokeby, mirroring Sylvania.

(Edmund Wilson, in his notebooks *The Thirties*, did pay a visit to Steen Valetje, Dutch for "the little stone villa." He declared it looked like an institution — brownish-yellow brick, with scores of narrow windows in close rows, ornamental squares of dark green inlaid among the yellow bricks toward the top of the square tower and fancy wrought-iron work over front steps that seemed to descend by a series of landings so that the hood had to follow it crookedly — a satyr's head incongruously over a side door.

(Franklin Delano, FDR's uncle, married Laura Astor (my mother's great aunt, grandmother's aunt) and they acquired Steen Valetje. However, they had no children. Then Warren Delano, uncle of FDR and brother of Sara/ Sally, came up and took over the place. He ran the Atlantic Coast Line Railroad, was allegedly an alcoholic and had several children, including my mother's friend Leila, then Jane who married Bernie Ridder, the scion of the Knight-Ridder newspaper empire.)

As for the Livingston family, only four estates remained out of the three-quarter-million acres its descendants had once owned between the Catskills and Connecticut. There were reasons for the loss of their empire. As Karen Velty wrote in *The Livingstons of New York*, this came in the wake of the transport revolution they themselves had inaugurated in the Hudson with their steamboat and trains and the opening of the Erie Canal, which brought in crops from the Midwest breadbasket. The Livingstons' meager soil could not compete with those. Then Henry Beekman Livingston (1750–1830) "cut a swath through the female population of Dutchess County, fathering a staggering number of bastard Livingstons of assorted colors, religions and social strata," financing all this by selling off land, "a practice deeply resented by his brothers." By the late nineteenth century "the most resplendent Livingston establishments along the Hudson had little to do with the manorial system."

One surviving property was the Davis place, another was an estate owned by some people named Hawkins then there was Oak Hill near the river, which the owner, Henry Livingston, had very beautifully redone. Rokeby was the fourth. These properties covered a few hundred acres each. A cousin of ours, Janet Livingston, who occupied a tiny apartment in New York City where she worked in a bank during the week — she had a tiny washing machine which plugged into her kitchen faucet — had a mansion nearby as well but gave that up in the end. (Trees lined the main drive and she claimed their predecessors had all blown down in the September 21, 1938, hurricane.)

In New York City the mansions of Mrs. William Astor and Henry Brevoort had long been razed and the Aldrich house on West Seventy-fourth evolved after my mother sold it into a twenty-studio apartment building. William and Aunt Lina Astor's mansion at the corner of Fifth and Thirty-Fourth was also demolished, to be replaced by the Temple Emanu-El. Of course the old Waldorf-Astoria was razed in 1929 and replaced by the Empire State Building, in which my grandmother's relatives all had shares.

I could imagine Aunt Sue's despair under my grandmother. She was partly to blame for remaining at Rokeby: she was passive in temperament and had a certain feeling of possessiveness toward that domain. However, her possessiveness may have emerged as a defense, a means of keeping sane in a desperate situation; she perhaps thought Well, the second twenty-five years of my life have been a terrible waste, but I did bring up three children who have turned out well and I'll become the lady of Rokeby someday. She wasn't always good to poor Uncle Dick but my grandmother was often dreadful to her — she even squashed the idea of a divorce when Sue's mother brought it up. As we have seen Aunt Sue waited on Grandmother hand and foot in surroundings of utter bleakness until my grandmother was ninety-two. My mother never understood Sue's agony — she just got out of the way.

During the winter Aunt Sue became somewhat lonely and wrapped herself up in the family as thoroughly as she could. She was largely ignored by her own children in those days. Her older son Rickie had gone out to Yugoslavia and for a long time seemed disinclined to come back. Eventually he went to Poland where he met and married a young lady, Ania, and came back to Rokeby with her. Susan took on a job screening applicants for high-level social dances, vaguely tripped around to art exhibits, read aloud to the blind, scrimped in some ways (taking on a boarder, parking on the street) and spent heavily in others (buying a pedigreed dog, sending her daughter Rosalind to the best school, preparing Rosalind's coming-out party, stocking her larder with gourmet S. S. Pierce canned foods). She had thorough knowledge of social interrelationships, photographs of all sizes and shapes everywhere in her apartment, membership in the New York Society Library, great concern to have all the young relatives over for cocktails — relatives I didn't know and sometimes hadn't even heard of. Transported with joy at arranging cocktail parties, drawing up guest lists, thumbing through the social register and unearthing ponderous addresses.

In the summer, though, a new regime took hold up in Rokeby. When it turned warm, Aunt Sue started to throw a permanent open house there. She developed the property and began to entertain exuberantly on the front lawn, with liquor. She flung open the French doors in the living room and breezes blew up from the Hudson and all over the house. She even fired Harold Day — it turned out he had made a lot of money on the side selling flowers from the greenhouse in Red Hook. Ricky and Winty had begun noticing that he was driving better cars then that he used to tool down the Hudson in his powerboat to go for "piza" in one of the gully-towns, because he had had intestinal problems and his wife forbade him to eat pizza.

Aunt Sue also had the garage up at Rokeby made into a three-bedroom house and furnished with a full range of modern appliances. Though she said she was going to rent it out to someone from the large IBM complex across the river, she spent all her weekends planting flowers around it once the weather began to lighten up slightly. Perhaps that was her way of emerging from the big house, anyway.

We'd go up regularly for the wining and dining of the cognoscenti in the area — the Dupees, the Shafers, the Gummeres, of Bard College, then the Roveres. Well-known New Yorkers made appearances, Alfred Kazin, the once-blackballed Gore Vidal, the rehabilitated Dwight McDonald. Paul Newman's name was even dropped in there somewhere. Summer always came suddenly to the estate. Looking out over it from the top of the rear sixty-foot tower, abreast of all the treetops, one felt as if on a swelling sea of green, an endless, horizonless carpet pouring down to the vast Hudson. It became new country with all the wintertime landmarks gone, drowned in the blazing green. Parks all over — one pond even had armchairs abruptly ringing it. Very warm, up in the eighties, air still, heavy, with sounds of birds and lizards all through the bursting green, yet a soft grayish-hazed light in the air from a thin layer of clouds building up way overhead, so that after a long evening on the green there would come a rumbling and crackling in the sky and the rain would tap and sprinkle and patter over the million leaves outside. One would lie in bed in the middle of the night hearing the solid wall of thunderstorms and a rumbling and crackling and splattering on and on and on. When the thunder turned especially severe old-timers quoted local legend and the Hudson Valley writer Washington Irving saying that was Rip Van Winkle bowling.

One of our visits coincided with the 150th anniversary of the mansion, for which long-exiled Chanler relatives came from all quarters. One daughter of a sister, Alida, emerged from her Long Island fastness, painted a portrait of Rokeby and composed a madrigal in celebration of my departed grandmother. One of the stanzas to that ended "Was Aunt Margaret sweet and kind." My mother, on hearing that, turned to me and declared "That's an absolute lie."

For variety, we would go visit Alida's estate, Box Hill, out on Long Island. We would pass by an endless string of bays, perhaps two miles wide, with narrow mouths, along the still purplish-brown coast, bays and sand-lines of Manhasset, Glen Cove and Huntington, and an occasional water tower over scattered houses. The early spring water was calm, a little brown, and some boats went out near the point to race and were becalmed. Old stone walls lined the bay with bright green lawns behind them and large houses — mostly rather decrepit, brown, cracked, not very stylish, still grand, some four stories high with enormous trees.

Though some years before Aunt Sue's son Winty had gone off to serve as an army officer in Vietnam, in Phu Cuong, the capital of a province forty-five minutes outside of Saigon, Aunt Sue was bitterly opposed to the war in Vietnam. She kept talking about a tenant in Harold Day's old house, who was missing a hand — "I'm surprised he hasn't gotten an artificial one by now. We've been involved in so many wars over the last half century we've become good at replacing limbs." In time this war, which Winty almost alone in the family had supported (though this writer never really managed to develop a sense of outrage over it), turned out to be a virtually unmitigated disaster though perhaps not on the order of the 2003 venture into Iraq.

The year before Lyndon Johnson precipitated the major escalation of that war my wife and I had gone to a traditional event, the Ojai tennis tournament, with my mother, Byron and Haley the old regular at Byron's courts. After the tournament we had dinner together and Byron turned to my wife, stroked her cheek and told her how beautiful she was. We went back down to Los Angeles.

Two days later my mother and Byron, after a long day of tennis, ordered a serving of fried chicken to be delivered to their place for them and their crowd. Byron always ate and drank heavily, played tennis eight hours a day and was found lying by his car at the end of the afternoon, felled at age fifty by a massive coronary. The takeout food arrived an hour later.

Bronson "Bim" Chanler — a cousin, Lewis' grandson and Styve's son, who in fact had a former Astor property of his own, the estate Orlot down the River Road from Rokeby — later declared to me that my mother had sustained very cruel blows in those times. I had never really appreciated that till he pointed it out to me. I had merely taken it for granted that she was just a victim of a haphazard violent streak that ran through the world we had always lived in but then I saw that his point was obvious: hard as it was to imagine fate dealing my mother a hard blow, here she had lost her mother as well as her husband (and indeed her brother, who'd also just died) in a period of about two years. This colored the next twenty years of her life.*

Before the end of the decade, one more event further shook my mother's ties to the world of the past.

In 1965 when we were staying in New York my father, starting on Good Friday, went on a drunk that really carried into August. He'd stagger into traffic on Bleecker Street and after we moved to East Eighty-ninth be so drunk when we had him over for dinner that he would have the plate almost vertical on his lap, spilling peas onto the floor and drooling. Helen Chapman, Chanler's defensive and maternal second wife, was once disgraced by his behavior at a lunch she gave him at their home near Rokeby and said she didn't really think he'd get

_____

* Bim incidentally had gone as a teenager to Le Rosey School in Switzerland. There he became acquainted with Mohammad Reza Pahlavi, who shortly after became the Shah of Iran, already as we've seen the target of major opposition in the country he ruled. In the sixties when the writer Reza Baraheni, one of the Shah's most articulately acerbic critics, guest lecturing at Bard, heard this, he went over to visit Bim and seek further dirt on the Shah but all Bim had to say was "He was a perfectly regular fellow, fit in quite well, don't you know." Bim had gone on during the war to hold a high position as liaison with the Free French forces in England, then France.

through that summer. Not long before, she and Chanler had got into a violent scrap with my father over a vaguely slighting reference to Egypt which Chanler had put in his newsletter, the Barrytown *Explorer*.

I read the obvious in a magazine article: among older white American men, the loss of status appears to be a major cause of suicide. A couple of family friends, Jim Burke's daughter Mae-Mae and Wendy Foster, saw my father in the Hotel Geneve in Mexico City in mid-September 1968 and found him in a state of complete euphoria. Right afterward he defenestrated himself, plunging from the window of his third-story room in that hotel. Helen Chapman looked crushed at his funeral.

18
War of Attrition

After the 1967 Arab-Israeli war, Hoda started to hear of sudden food shortages back home, such as three meatless days a week and other forms of deprivation. Once she dreamed that her family was starving and in rags. Another time she dreamed that she went back home and opened her suitcase and all the good clothes she had brought for her family turned to rags, old tights with holes in them and unraveled sweaters when she pulled them out. The entire family came over for a big banquet, she dreamt, but no one could prepare for it. Her mother in the kitchen with Omm Salim the servant kept trimming a huge grape leaf which she was preparing to stuff with rice, ground beef and onion — patiently cut it up into smaller and smaller portions, but not managing to stop until Hoda woke up. Hoda felt that if she did not go back soon she never would.

She found signs of unremitting, interminable war everywhere. Purple paint was smeared on automobile headlights and government office windows; up before the doorways there were more narrow brick wall-slabs to absorb the impact of bombs exploding in the streets than there used to be, left over from 1956. Overhead a sudden rumble, as of enormous wooden crates shunted harshly and hurriedly across the ribbed metal floors of empty freight trucks. Down by the Bent Pyramid, a crumpling of artillery.

She spent much of her time by the big family villa just down from a gas station and mosque. Entering the villa by the old loosely-chiseled iron gate she saw Amm Ibrahim the old Nubian doorkeeper napping on a wooden cot. When they were children, they used to call him Ubruhem, mimicking his Upper Egyptian accent. Amm Ibrahim shook himself up from his sleep, came over and took her hand in both of his. She saw how gray and blotched the walls of the villa had suddenly become from the leaking tangles of ceramic pipe that veined them. Inside, in one of the toilets, a heavy tear-shaped porcelain weight hanging from a chain had etched an arc into the wall through two layers of plaster, deep into the brick underneath. She looked out one of the twin louvered front windows and saw cars parked two abreast right up to the dirt sidewalk; apprentices were welding and painting one of them, a mere shell lying on its side. (I remember once running into an American who indignantly demanded to know, "What kind of a country is it where they park the cars on the sidewalks?") She wondered at all these little details of the house that had irked her or even caused her to feel resentment in the past with profound affection, gratitude even now. She regarded as miraculous each of those shells of cars, the grease on the dirt sidewalk, the shopkeeper stepping out all during the day to slosh water on it in the hope it would create a breeze, to soften the leaden heat.

An old friend Mirvat would come over from time to time. In Egypt a person owning land must either work the land himself or be on good terms with the nazer, or superintendent, paying him well and visiting him often (and perhaps also drinking with him), to derive maximum benefit from the land. Mirvat had been sent up to visit her family's nazer and raise the sticky subject of a delinquent rent payment, but she had no stomach for the business, neglecting even to order him to sit on the floor when she addressed him; her mission collapsed and she was not sent back on any further tasks.

One evening over at the big house Mirvat said quietly, when no one else was within earshot, "I think the Israelis have all the land they want, at least for now."

Amina, wife of the old family cook Mahgoub, kept coming by the big house. This was because Mahgoub, who was now in Libya, failed to send money back regularly with a relative, who went there often on conferences. Amina was an enormous woman in black shroud who was always holding her squalling baby up against her left shoulder and absently patting him. She would sit for hours in the middle of the day in the pantry, a dark chamber reeking of kerosene, with faint sunlight slowly revolving in the shaft beyond and the regular shikk, sharp as granite edges, of chiseling into stone as it echoed through the building. Above, what Mirvat called the first two bars from "My Mama Done Told Me," in reality a rooster from a nearby rooftop. The sinks were of slate, sloping to a basin with brass fixtures, the walls were covered to eye level with white tile and there was a big frosted-glass window high up the wall between the kitchen and the hallway where the refrigerator stood.

(There were conflicting explanations why the refrigerator was where it was. Some said it was to serve as decoration, even to demonstrate that their aunt could afford such an appliance, while others claimed it was so that the men could use it without having to visit the kitchen. Yet others claimed the real reason was to keep it a safe distance away from the back door around which neighborhood servants congregated: there were locks on all the cupboards in the kitchen and pantry but no one had yet succeeded in welding a hasp to the refrigerator door.)

Amina would loiter about for days and finally Hoda's aunt, or the old lady, would lend her a few pounds. Other venerable servants, now retired, would come by too and the aunt would give them rice or cans of cooking butter; Hoda let them have many of the tights, sweaters and other old clothes she'd brought back by the suitcase from Goodwill and St. Vincent de Paul. Old Amm Selim said that they could no longer afford to buy more than one cup's worth of tea at a time and the sugar to go with it. They even had to bring their own paper to wrap it in because the shops' coarse paper added too much weight to the purchase. One time, when Amina received five pounds after waiting all day, she returned them in anger and swept out, cursing Mirvat too as she departed. Mirvat, she said, who had grown up on the roofs same as them, had gone off, turned rich and didn't remember the people from her own childhood any longer.

Another day Amina came back and begged forgiveness for the things she'd said. Hoda offered her a pound. Amina, her face streaked with tears, kissed her hand and kept saying "May God never deprive us of you."

As in many communities throughout the world, the poor found access to some of the best real estate in Cairo, the burial tracts on high desert ground up against and behind the Citadel. There in the Araafa, the City of the Dead, the dead are buried in family clusters, in houses without roofs, their graves raised above the tile floors, but hundreds of thousands of squatters — no one really knows how many — inhabit these houses and courtyards, in their utmost penury, since the section is open, its air fresh and dry.

Out of the rubble on the way to the Araafa rise some splendid conical minarets out of the Middle Ages, heavily plastered with handbills. On the domes by the minarets, big miters and bread loaves and distended ovals, patterns of swirling ceramic lines, herringbone Vs, tubes tapering to a point, explosions of interlocking flower-hexagons, sinuous intertwined clubs, clovers and spades.

They frequently went up to an uncle's grave in one corner of the Araafa. To go there, it was necessary to send advance notice to the clan squatting in the structure and to get into that they had to dispatch one of the squatter's neighbors to fetch them the appropriate doorknob. Sometimes they'd end up with the wrong one.

19
Nixon's Quick Early Moves

nother leftish observation, passed on by my mother in those days: If the man in the street can't figure out what's going on in a major industry, we are in trouble. Food purveyors don't threaten to run out of grain if they aren't getting a good price. In the late sixties though some major oil companies started making just that threat about their products and the man in the street did not know how to deal with it.

Within a year it had become the strategy of the incoming president, Richard Nixon, to force a drastic rise in the world oil price. This would shift the Near Eastern balance of power toward the conservative oil states and away from the interests and forces of the Soviet Union and its secular vanguard in the Arab world (Nasser, the Syrian leaders, the Iraqis, though the latter also had great oil resources behind them).

To this end among many others the CIA under Nixon came to function as a private police force for the president. (Unlike the FBI, unaccountable to the Justice Department — the same policy Rajk had fought in Hungary a generation earlier, at the cost of his life.) One operative Nixon had at his disposal was Armand Hammer, who had long before become embedded by the CIA in the oil industry and came to acquire major operations in Libya. Russian born, familiar with the Soviet Union, he even had an autographed photo of Lenin on his desk. He committed destructive acts in his Libyan concessions, where over a long time he produced oil at an excessively high rate, bringing great harm on major oil fields which he'd paid a 3 percent commission, or "overriding royalty," to develop and exploit. I was in Libya at the time and saw evidence of this firsthand.

In 1970 Hammer came out of his closet and did Nixon's bidding on a major stroke of Near Eastern oil policy. In price negotiations with the Libyan government he took dramatic action to help Nixon's strategy by agreeing to a major rise in the prices of the oil he sold and the rates at which the Libyan government taxed the sales. It has to be said that the other oil companies operating in that country did what they could to hold the line, to preserve the standing prices and rates, which had held firm for a long time, but had no choice but to accede to the Libyan demands once Hammer had given in to them. The changes the Libyans had wrought immediately spread throughout most other oil-exporting states in the world.

20
Powerball in Oil, California and the Middle East

I had already gained some jolting exposure to this world by editing the oil-industry newsletter, which I had translated into Arabic then sent to opinion leaders in the Arab world. At one point in my quest for a translator I talked with a news expert who claimed he had worked for the Americans and owned a black book listing the name of every journalist from Gibraltar to Rawalpindi, with the price he'd paid each one. The expert claimed to have penetrated almost every newspaper in the Arab world (except perhaps Egypt's *al-Ahram*, run by Nasser's confidant Haikal; this did not call for a capitalist society).

Running a newsletter like mine, he asserted, was a hard-money proposition. "You have to make every word count" he said. "Every word that does not convey your message is a waste of money." Sometimes, he said, it was hard to work a story into a paper — he did get a five-part series on Red China into an Iraqi daily run by a very anti-American editor, but it took him two or three months to "get to" the man, who in any case would accept only dollars deposited in a European bank. The expert inserted an article on the Soviet spy network in Syria into that country's press, friendly though it was with the Soviets.

This expert shunned the conservative Beirut paper *al-Hayat* "because no one on it trusts anyone else" (in any case its editor, Kamel Muruwwa, was shot at and finally stabbed to death). However, he considered Syria and Lebanon model targets in this struggle to spread doubts on which was the "right" side in the Middle East, because they were predominantly middle class — "and any psychologist will tell you the more middle class a country is the more vulnerable it is, because the middle class has all the information but no means of coping with it." Indeed, he claimed, out of each ten-man US Army Special Forces team, two or three were psychologists.

Our audience was somewhat more sophisticated and powerful than this helpless bourgeoisie and eventually the newsletter was moved to Beirut and I moved on, to the headquarters of Chevron Oil Corporation in San Francisco.

Chevron was an organization deliberately drab in appearance. For a couple of decades after World War Two, after Aramco, Chevron's great bonanza in Saudi Arabia, hit stride, Chevron was largely under the writ of R. Gwin Follis. In a funny way, Follis' story embraced the saga of Chevron's development since World War Two. He was not well liked within the company — people described him as a man of no discernible character, imagination or innovative power. Born of a patrician family which owned a large share of Chevron's stock and grandson of a

Civil War-era senator, Follis was by all descriptions coldly snobbishly aloof. Chevron employees used to say that on his first important assignment with the firm as a young man, managing a small refinery in the southern Central Valley "oil patch" hub of Bakersfield, Follis tended to take four-day weekends up in San Francisco. His management style was reputed to be humorlessly picky. Even well before he became chairman, he expressed his power in the company — again as word had it — by selling Exxon and Mobil their large share of Aramco for a sum much lower than that some Chevron officials insisted they could get. Follis was widely rumored within Chevron to have owned a lot of Exxon stock — perhaps even 2 or 3 percent of the grand total. Another story about Chevron was that Exxon also compelled Follis to avoid setting up a corporation in Pennsylvania, which would have enabled Chevron to save on Pennsylvania property taxes, as it had some interests there.

In the past, Chevron employees had competed fiercely to impart the most affluent appearance to their offices. Their wives would outdo each other in putting up drapes, carpets and dramatically expensive furniture. This competition got out of hand so the company under Follis imposed a rigid code of stratification to suppress it and the code endured. It governed the amount of floor space an individual was entitled to, the kind of pen he could have on his desk, whether or not he could have a clock, whether or not he was entitled to walnut furniture or had to put up with ordinary yellow. When an executive was promoted his office had to be expanded by a certain number of square feet. Even if the person didn't want the extra space, workmen would come anyway and spend an entire week moving one of his steel partition-walls two feet out, disrupting everything in that area for the whole period. One department manager in the firm used to say "I can tell you what a man is making within a thousand dollars a year just by looking at his office."

Another rule about the company was that one did not mention the first names of employees in internal correspondence: one addressed them by their initials only. That went for R. G. Follis and his successor O. N. Miller as for almost everyone else. There were very few exceptions, one of them vice president for exploration named Gage "Bud" Lund: he had left Chevron at one point in midcareer and registered a brilliant string of discoveries on his own in salt domes offshore Louisiana. Then he came back, on terms very beneficial to himself. The right to use his first name in company correspondence was one of them.

In the sixties, as Follis was due to retire, Chevron found itself on the brink of bitter negotiations with Texaco over the divestiture of holdings they shared in Caltex. They had to divide these up to accede to a ruling in a major government anti-cartel case. At this point Otto Miller, another high-ranking executive, with a reputation for extreme tenacity if not ferocity in his business dealings, rose to the fore in the company. Word within Chevron, again, had it that Follis ordered his directors to appoint Miller as his successor because he believed that only Miller would be able to protect their company's interests properly against the top men in Texaco, Gus Long and Howard Rambin, whom people feared even more than Miller.

No one in the industry feared Miller more than the employees of Chevron themselves. By the dictates of his position, Miller was supposed to be a policy-making arbiter, but he soon showed no inclination to act as one. He monitored the company's entire business personally.

He followed price restoration activity in California (station by station if need be) and everyplace else in America — by himself. In his time an outsider could not even drive his own truck through Chevron property if he had to get oil out of his own lease; one operator cited that experience in Kettleman Hills. Miller kept right on top of every serious disturbance in the market. It was said that he even insisted on rescheduling the movements of the company's tanker fleet during the 1967 Arab-Israeli war, when some countries mounted a partial oil embargo of America. When one of his department heads complained that that was a job he had been hired to do and could perfectly well do himself, Miller told him to shut up.

Not that Miller was right all or even most of the time. Most spectacularly, he refused to obtain acreage in northern Alaska in the midsixties, when geologists were beginning to awaken to the chance there might be gargantuan accumulations of oil right up by the Arctic Sea. There were people in Chevron who swore that was because Miller didn't want there to be any oil up there. If northern Alaska proved prolific in reserves, that'd pose a threat to the order of the industry on the West Coast, which was already getting all the oil it needed; more would pose a problem. At a June 1969 luncheon between Miller and Steve Bechtel Jr., head of the construction giant, Bechtel wrote, in a memo from that time which this writer has seen, "[Miller] went on to say that building the Trans-Alaska-to North Slope-to-Pacific line would be a tragic mistake from the viewpoint of the oil industry." He preferred a line from the North Slope to Edmonton, Canada. Miller told Bechtel that he thought British Petroleum and Arco, the big Alaska holders, were very naive about Alaska pipelining and were off by about 50 percent in their price calculations. "Nothing was said about the potential Halifax or Montreal refineries," concluded the memo, "or about any of the several jobs we are doing for SoCal in the states, or about Indonesia. I have always been reluctant to bring up any subjects with Otto unless they came up completely naturally."

Development of the North Slope would even force cutbacks in Saudi Arabia, Miller's prize. Miller's obsession with the Saudi bonanza locked him in — and even Chevron, it seemed — for life, scrambling to meet any demand they would have to meet to be able to stay in Saudi Arabia while doing everything possible to work against oil development anyplace else. Miller did all he could to keep North Slope oil from coming down the coast and lobbied hard to have it diverted to Japan or the Midwest instead, by a trans-Canadian pipeline. None of that worked either. He might have been right about the economics, though (except that the cost overruns turned out mostly to be the result of graft).

Texaco gradually deteriorated as a functioning enterprise, losing around $3 billion in a big lawsuit Pennzoil had successfully pressed on it for raiding properties Pennzoil charged it had acquired from Getty. However, Texaco had great crude oil resources and Chevron bought the firm out in 2001. In the long run though Texaco came to haunt Chevron. From 1964 to 1992, that firm had maintained a big presence in Ecuador, exploring and producing in an area around the northern town of Lago Agrio, which had become oil-rich millions of years ago when the Amazon flowed west. (Some Texaco geologists well versed in this area's geology abandoned ship and went to work for Occidental with their knowledge of this, leading to a lawsuit which ultimately failed to yield fruit.) With the state firm Petroecuador, Texaco ran a very sloppy operation which badly polluted much residential and agricultural land in the Lago Agrio area. It pulled out of Ecuador in 1992 and residents of and around Lago Agrio sued it in 1993 for this pollution. When Chevron acquired Texaco it inherited the lawsuit. Plainly the pollution charge wasn't the fruit of Chevron's actions but it got stuck with a seemingly unending $9.5 billion suit over it anyway. Early on Chevron successfully blocked enforcement of a cleanup charge in a federal district court, but then on September 19, 2011, the Second Circuit Court of Appeals put that case on hold and lifted the district court injunction. Still, at this writing, the appeals process is ongoing in Ecuador, so Chevron will not have to pay for a while, if ever.

I worked in Chevron's economics department for about a year in the 1960s. In appearance it was most prosaic, one of the drabbest environments imaginable. The air got denser and denser as one progressed down a linoleum hall into the department, for the pipe and cigarette smoke held behind the pebbled-glass doors, all closed. The sounds were all of churning calculators, coughing and quiet, muffled indolent conversation, except when a coffee-pot plug would be jerked out of one of the metal walls — a dull but abrupt terking which occurred every workday at nine thirty and two thirty. Even a person who had worked in the department for a while and knew full well where his office was, knew, say, that his door was directly across the hall from the Xerox machine, always looked up at his number anyway, on the transom-sill, to make sure he was not going into the wrong room.

One contemporary who worked there a while was transferred over to the big refinery in Richmond across the bay. On returning he said that Del Webb used to work there as a carpenter but was fired — too lazy, not motivated enough. Webb of course in time became a real estate super-tycoon, with a drive in the Palm Springs area bearing his name, the equal of fellow boulevardiers Frank Sinatra and Gerald Ford.

While at Chevron I had, oddly, a peripheral view of what turned out in time to be major historical developments. I learned years later, as we shall see, that Chevron maintained a massive secret price-fixing brain trust in the economics department when I was there. In a case I became familiar with and will touch upon later a man who claimed he had worked in that department made a telephone call one day in the mid-seventies to the California attorney general's office and described this economics department price-fixing brain trust. Ordinary economics department employees were usually rotated out every two years or kept on late in life then retired. However, the caller contended, the members of the brain trust were sequestered away from traffic off in a corner that was largely unknown to the regular members of this dull prosperous world, who did not want to know it existed. I certainly didn't then.

In a few years I proceeded to write a book about oil in the Middle East. I didn't fully understand Nixon's conduct and strategy at the time but I did include what I had learned about the oil operator Hammer. I told my mother my oil book had got a number of favorable reviews but not one of them mentioned my description of Hammer. Later I came to learn that nobody in the media or even Congress dared single out Hammer for criticism in any of his areas of activity.

After working with Chevron I did also work briefly with Bechtel. With them, I went on an assignment to Algiers and at one point stopped by the offices of the national oil company Sonatrach. Also in the reception room there was a major American arms merchant, Henry Kuss, about whom I had just read an article in the *New York Times*. Kuss, a huge fellow with pronounced Slavic features, was unmistakable in any setting and I introduced myself and told him I had just read about him in the *Times* article. This was one of the bigger blunders of my life; I was quickly released from Bechtel, probably for doing that. Still and all, the question remains: what was that American arms merchant doing in the offices of this national oil company? Undoubtedly selling Algeria arms, if it'd let Occidental have big volumes of crude to make up for the Libyan cutbacks.

My mother snorted over it all. By then the detested war in Vietnam had come to absorb much of the attention of progressives and leftists. In fact Nixon was slowly getting us out of that imbroglio.

Some years after we left Vietnam I came upon my old friend and form mate Jan Van Roijen at a Groton reunion. For auld lang syne, we spent about an hour one afternoon walking through what had been rather grim, depressing old dormitories and basements with his teenage son and he talked about the hard times he'd had his first two years in the school, adjusting to American English and American ways, enduring classmates' obsession with football, being away from home the first time.

I told Jan "This was probably the most intense experience of your life, being here."

He told me, "No, I had one other experience which was more intense." That was living through the fall of Saigon in spring 1975.

He had been there with the Dutch diplomatic service and his foreign ministry had instructed him to stay in Saigon until it was about to fall, then be evacuated by the Americans. America's Ambassador Martin, Jan said,

absolutely refused to believe that Saigon would fall —
had utter faith in the army of the Republic of Vietnam's
power to hold onto the city, for good. Jan sent his wife
and three children out anyway and three weeks later
Saigon did fall. He went to the American embassy but
couldn't get in. It was too crowded, the desperate mobs
in front of it were impenetrable. So he joined a United
Nations convoy out to Thansonnhut Airport, which was
secured by a two-and-a-half-mile perimeter of marines.
However, Vietnamese troops, seeing the convoy, broke
down in resentment and started firing — shot up and
annihilated a UN jeep ahead of Jan full of Vietnamese
children who were supposed not to have been allowed
out. At the airport he had to lie flat on his belly for two
and a half hours under the crossfire. Finally a helicopter
removed him, to the carrier *Midway*, where he spent three
days incommunicado.

He found it very boring there — he had nothing to
do but sit in the hold, with nothing to read. At one point a
Vietnamese came by in a Cessna whose radio could only
receive messages and signaled to the carrier, by dropping
a steel case with a message inside, that he wanted to land.
The ship radioed back that he could not land because he
did not have a hook. However, they offered to make a ring
of ships to calm the water and suggested he land inside
the ring. Dropping a further case, he said he couldn't do
that because he had six children between one and eight
years old on the plane with him, as well as his mother,
and they couldn't swim. Finally the admiral gave him
permission to try a landing and ordered all personnel off
the deck. Everyone on ship watched from the closed-circuit
TV system as he came in. He landed, skidded, coasted,
screamed along -- and just made it, with five feet to spare.
The whole ship broke out in a roar of delirious exuberance.

By that time several of our classmates had also embarked on interesting careers. One, Ken Auchincloss, had become an executive editor with *Newsweek*. Among other things, he informed me he had supported research on presidential memoirs and learned that historians claimed that those of Taft were the most substantial. He also closely followed public attitudes toward the news. He discovered that the public was (at that time anyway) highly disillusioned with all the news media: they had foretold or even promised crises in various areas of society and politics but those had never come about. Incidentally, he viewed the three major television broadcasting companies as his greatest competition (aside from *Time* anyway) and at the 1984 Democratic convention announced his pleasure at learning that *Newsweek* had covered it better than any of them.

Another classmate, Gerry Studds, became a Massachusetts congressman and proceeded to devote twelve terms, from 1972 to 1997, serving Cape Cod, New Bedford and "the barnacled old fishing towns near the coast," to cite his eventual New York *Times* obituary. There was a lot about Congress reminiscent of Groton, notably the bells ringing down long halls throughout the day, summoning members to a seemingly interminable series of sessions. Occupying the central point in the anteroom to Studds' Washington office was a big cooler filled with cranberry juice. Many of his constituents were Portuguese and he proceeded to become fluent in their language. His was a maritime district and perhaps his greatest achievement as its representative was to coauthor the Fisheries Conservation and Management Act, which extended the fisheries jurisdiction of nations out two hundred miles from their seacoast. This was not an easy cause to advance. One recalls Carlos Arosamena making the same effort as president of Ecuador in 1964: after a few drinks at a banquet, he assailed the American ambassador for failing to support the limit and was immediately removed from office for that. After Gerry died his Massachusetts contemporary, Senator Ted Kennedy, stated "He was a steward of the oceans."

By then I had also resumed contact with George Gund, our wealthy onetime classmate. After leaving Groton prematurely, he worked on an ore boat as a deck hand for a while then under his father's orders joined the marines when the rest of us were going to college. He spent much of his time on the aircraft carrier *Ticonderoga* just off the islands of Quemoy and Matsu, focus of America's struggle with Communist China at that time. His main function then was to track a fellow marine and make sure he did not carry out his threat to jump off the ship. He became acquainted with San Francisco when the carrier docked there for maintenance. He then spent some months in Cuba right after Castro's rise to power, scuba diving, hanging around, doubtlessly enjoying cigars (which he did for decades to come) and hoping the country would prosper and develop a human face. He believed Castro wasn't really a communist but had been suborned by his brother Raul and Che Guevara. He took up residence in San Francisco when I was living there.

He acquired a Mitsubishi Fanjet, paying nothing down on a loan from General Electric, and took it on trips all over. At one point he invited me to a weekend at his ranch near Elko in northeastern Nevada and we flew up there in the jet with his two sons, George IV and Greg, who spent most of the flight wrestling in the aisle. His wife Teddy, later Theo, declined to join us, having found the ranch rather boring. (She would walk seven miles from the ranch house and back just to check the mailbox.) It was an enormous, striking property, complete with snow-covered mountains even in June, and an escarpment. (As I've said, George was perhaps the only person I knew actually to own one of those, though Livingston ancestors also did, but far in the past.) We went out hunting and George showed his sons how to clean their shotguns. High point of the weekend was a barbecue in which we consumed a large part of a salmon he had flown down from a recent fishing trip to Alaska.

By then George had become a serious devotee of the cinema, especially through the San Francisco Film Festival, which he established. He circulated among major cinematic figures and invested in numerous works. Among those eventually were films by Francis Ford Coppola — "until the numbers got too big," as he put it some years later. (Coppola moved on to run a Napa winery.) He was also a founding trustee of the Cleveland International Film Festival and trustee of the Cleveland Museum of Art and the Cleveland Orchestra: years later a filmmaker said that thanks to his foundation "I received my start in filmmaking in the early seventies. It kept me off the streets as a teen, and from being a juvenile delinquent."

George was especially devoted to movies from Central Europe — indeed, he maintained an apartment in Prague and often flew his plane there, where he would pick up films. The *San Francisco Chronicle* had him describing his favorite work, *Marketa Lazarova*, adaptation of a novel by Vladislav Vancura which "revolves around the son of a family of outlaws who controls a section of southern Bohemia [in the thirteenth century]." The *Chronicle* called this work "a tale of violence, savagery, incest, love, war and madness -- a tapestry of infinite complexity made more obtuse by its disjointed narration."

George also concentrated on the film industry in the Soviet Union, then Russia, and in time acquired an apartment in Moscow as well. ("It's cheaper than a hotel," he explained — $1,300 a year.) I attended a presentation at one of his San Francisco festivals in the Custer Street Stage near China Basin, featuring two bands and a broad variety of tables giving out sushi, fine cheeses, little ortolan-like chicken bits on long toothpicks and Mediterranean salads. One band threw out Cuban music with a flamboyant pianist, Sosa, and the other played cool jazz. The crowd before the former danced like mad, that before the latter stood staring silently, engrossed though. This festival centered on the great Soviet director Sergei Paradjanov and embraced numerous filmmakers from the former Soviet Union — including Kazakhstan — who'd studied at Paradjanov's feet. Paradjanov in 1969 had made one of the great films of the century, *The Color of Pomegranates*, "a ninety-minute hallucination" as one review in *The New Yorker* labeled it, "a cross between a children's theatrical and a Byzantine mosaic" where pomegranates bled, a ram was sacrificed and a thousand sheep streamed into a church to attend a burial — an opus which earned Paradjanov a four-year sentence in the Gulag. In the end he died in an automobile accident probably rigged by Soviet intelligence.

George's financial independence gave him a freedom from harassment some of the rest of us envied. For instance when he hosted the great Soviet director Sergei Bondarchuk, the FBI and CIA could not monitor him — after all, they could not gain admission to his Mitsubishi — and were reduced to going up to him long afterward to try grilling him about the director.

One leitmotif all the years at Groton had been the mythology about the Brilliance of McGeorge Bundy, who had attended the school back in the thirties. People had him reading off term papers from empty pages at lecterns, when he wasn't outdebating his classmates in Classical Greek — or indeed writing an exam on Thucydides in Greek, as Richard Irons once claimed he did. Not all the best and the brightest went to Groton though. There was David Halberstam the journalist and historian, who chronicled them (and their blunderings in Vietnam) in a book by that name. (Graduates of this institution could have answered his question on why we became obsessed with Vietnam in one sentence, probably in Latin.) Ultimately he sent his daughter to the school (Julia, class of 1998). He was about to get working on another opus in a brilliant career, grounded in part on an interview in California with the quarterback and insurance executive Y. A. Tittle, when a journalism student driving him off Willow Road from the Dumbarton Bridge to Menlo Park near Stanford was rammed by an oncoming Infiniti, killing Halberstam instantly.

When Reagan came to power he picked up Nixon's procedures focused on the CIA. Through the wanton use of executive orders, Reagan quickly unleashed wholesale espionage and harassment campaigns against domestic dissidents, a pattern which manifested itself all over the United States, in various areas.

This espionage and harassment was especially virulent among groups involved with Central America. Reagan saw to it that the Marxist regime in Nicaragua, the Sandinistas, were bedeviled by his own anti-regime military force, the Contras. He (and Bush) diverted a Senate subcommittee from its investigations into drug smuggling which their Contra allies were pursuing to raise money for the Contras to the persecution of a CIA renegade, Manuel Noriega. House Committee hearings in late 1986 revealed over forty instances of breakins where papers but nothing of commercial value were stolen from the premises of a broad range of civil rights organizations and church and political groups that protested the government's support of the Contras and provided sanctuary for refugees from pro-administration governments in El Salvador, Honduras and Guatemala. Among these were the Center for Constitutional Rights in New York, the San Francisco branch office of the American Civil Liberties Union, the San Francisco Women's Center, a Baptist church in Seattle, a Lutheran church in Berkeley, even the office of a lawyer in San Jose who represented Albert Hakim, a figure later prominent in the sales of arms to Iran that helped finance the Contras' operations. One investigative reporter of my acquaintance related an episode on CIA penetration of an organization with the bulky name CISPES (Committee for Solidarity with the People of El Salvador). A couple came into the group in Washington and quickly became dominant in it, heading up a number of committees. The reporter conducted an investigation into them and traced them back to Texas, only to find that the records on them went back just four or five years, then disappeared. So he had uncovered the fact of their treachery, if not the nature of it. (He then told the people for whom he'd conducted the investigation that their best strategy would be simply to leave the couple where they were — further investigation could be very costly and take years. After all, their identity was known and if they were blown someone else would come right in and take their place.)

The CIA even persecuted the rock impresario and holocaust survivor Bill Graham for protesting a trip Reagan was about to make in 1985 to a cemetery in Bitburg, Germany, where two SS officers were buried.

Graham placed a full-page advertisement in the *New York Times* protesting the visit just before Reagan made it and the next day his San Francisco office was firebombed. He could do nothing to track down the perpetrators of this act of violence. (This writer as well experienced the theft of a broad range of papers and computer discs, knowing exactly who stole them and under what circumstances, while, again, being unable to prove what he knew or obtain redress of any kind for the thefts.)

Around then I went by the Lutheran chapel in Berkeley to talk at modest length with its minister, Reverend Gustav Schultz, who had appeared in the *Chronicle* discussing breakins at his church and others that were involved in the Central American sanctuary movement. He told me he had got a thick file from the FBI in the wake of a Freedom of Information Act request but it was largely worthless — most everything had been "whited out" except for logs of phone calls he'd had back in 1971 with Angela Davis, a woman involved in the draft resistance movement. Going into his chapel, which was mostly a large, dark, bare church with yellow light slanting in through vertical angular windows, I saw two really downtrodden young bums sleeping on the cement. Reverend Schultz told me they were waiting to eat — he had a food program that handled 150 people an evening. On the way out, there were seven people waiting, including a young woman holding two oranges. Schultz had informed me that he couldn't afford to spend much time investigating the harassment and surveillance he was subjected to and trying to get to the bottom of it; the time and energy he would have to put into that would interfere with what he considered his real job, ministering to the needy and addressing the major moral issues of the day.

This campaign became even more intense under Bush, when his term came. He was essentially the president of the CIA. One can cite as one example of this his treatment of a Polish intelligence officer who in August 1990 sneaked six American CIA agents out of Iraq after they'd sought refuge in a Polish construction camp under a White House/CIA request. This officer managed to drive the six CIA agents through the border into Turkey by distracting a Polish-speaking officer at the checkpoint. At that Bush had William Webster, director of the CIA at that time, hand deliver a letter to Poland saying he would urge other governments to forgive half of Poland's foreign debt in gratitude for that. That amount was $16.5 billion, or about $1.375 billion per spy. Bush was starting to turn the nation into a giant Ponzi scheme.

On reading of this my mother came around, however reluctantly, to believing what I had had to say.

21
Von Hoehnel and the
Rhinoceros: Refuge in Africa

A family as enormous and as powerful as my mother's develops deep tensions and antagonisms. It then turns to some outside force or arbitrator to minister to these, as well as the various complexities of its financial affairs. In the case of Astor's descendants this task about the time of the Civil War fell upon a New York cousin named William Morris, whose practice later expanded to the law firm of Morris and McVeigh. By then each of the surviving children had a trust fund of about $800,000. On top of that the childless Laura Delano left each of them a large fund when she died, as did their great uncle Henry Astor, who left money to the survivors or their children. Rokeby and those directly connected to it fell around World War Two within the purview of a hawkeyed bookkeeper, Marion Goff, who handled the Rokeby accounts most of her life and when finally brought up to the mansion proved able to identify every object at hand as if she had lived there all her life — and could find her way around uninstructed.

Once talking to one of Bob Chanler's grandchildren, my cousin Pauline, about a dream in which a convoy of trust-fund forklift trucks were driving around a concrete floor — each one serving one of us — I mentioned that my mother and all the other Chanlers used to scoff at the Chanler men. Pauline remarked that the Chanler women were strong because they were all backed by the trust funds handled through Morris and McVeigh. Later her sister Monica got in her word against that firm. When their mother Julia died, she and Pauline discovered, just by chance, that she had had a trust fund worth $285,100. Morris and McVeigh didn't tell them about it till compelled to. Then the two daughters found out that their mother had been getting an annual income of $3,500 from it — about $8,000, really, but Morris and McVeigh took out their usual hefty commissions.

My siblings and I had had the same experience, and my mother absolutely refused to complain about the skimpy income from those funds. Indeed once when I began talking critically about the Morass of McVeighs she leapt up from dinner and ran screaming to her room. (She could be harsh with people in that firm, though — another time, I heard, she shrieked at Mrs. Lafferty, a secretary there, over a minor oversight, though later Mrs. Lafferty gushed to me with praise over her.) Monica said that my mother's attitude toward the firm was common among the people of her generation.

In 1989 we learned that through various closed trusts our mother earned an income of $85,800. She had also had rights to 50 percent of the contents of Rokeby, including much antique furniture and several fine works of art. These included a painting by the nineteenth-century artist Charles Deas, who went insane and died at twenty-nine; now, a major work of his would easily go for millions of dollars at auction. Our mother relinquished her share of those contents some years back to her nephew Wintie for one dollar. Ultimately we discovered that Morris and McVeigh, instead of giving us regular returns from a trust fund when we turned twenty-one, as stipulated, gave us a monthly allowance (which did not rise with inflation), retaining an excess of $33,000 in undistributed income — and never informed us of the fees we were paying them as tax preparers and trustees (which were revealed ultimately to be exorbitant), nor acknowledged our right to make decisions on how these funds were to be invested.

My mother often quoted another of her mother's aphorisms: "The good thing about never having been a great beauty is that you don't have to worry about turning old." My mother however had been rather a beauty. With Byron gone she discovered that she was no longer viewed as she had been even rather recently — no longer welcomed as part of a broad, glamorous social swirl.

Her ample financial resources enabled her to live more or less as she wished, but that was largely alone, from the very start, from just two days after Byron died, when a figure in the Santa Barbara tennis neighborhood, Ed Doty (considered crazy by most and avoided by virtually all), took over one of Byron's biggest clients, the Marymount Girls' School.

For a while she stayed in her house. Generally that was an empty experience. She struggled hard to develop an attachment with a mediocre local lawyer who had flashy LA connections. She'd sit waiting for the phone to ring — jump up nervously every time it did ring, furious when someone else picked it up first — but still got nowhere and refused to bend to the extent necessary to become less alone. She had a tropical fish to keep her company, and a cat at one point, but the cat swallowed gravel one day and died. Another time she befriended a spider outside her kitchen window. She became randomly stingy about her possessions. The most striking examples were the electricity, the food in the house and her car. She would rarely let anyone heat the house. When others came to visit her, she kept the refrigerator bare (or the icebox, as everyone my age and older called it) and wouldn't let people prepare coffee. When Dickie and his wife Betsy were out once, she hid the orange squeezer; Peter finally managed to get it, but she pretended to have hidden it for fear it would be broken (it was unbreakable). She labored under penury, squirreled away Blue Chip stamps, ate almost nothing — but when pressed could give out a lot of money. Later when staying with her I asked if she'd help look after my young daughter and she abruptly and curtly stated, "No, that's one thing I made up my mind that I was not going to do." One night she gave no indication, on hearing that we were going out, that she would be staying at home and Mrs. Thompson the babysitter came and sat while she was in the house.

She continued to be so strongly against the Vietnam War that she started saying she would go live abroad just to be away from all signs of it. Indeed, after the traumatic events of the sixties she could not keep going as she had. She found it necessary to reinvent herself, and that was what she did. She began traveling, with friends. Once she toured outlying areas of the Holy Land with old Santa Barbara associates, Jim and Almira Struthers. (Byron had always resented Almira for her mannish nature, and fear she'd seduce my mother.) They however failed to complete their tour as they had planned as they did not know that

Antioch, contrary to claims of the Syrian government, had been taken from Syria and given to Turkey decades before, and didn't realize that their Lebanese driver hadn't learned he'd need a Turkish visa to go there.

Later my mother went with another friend to India, where they rode elephants. She looked into the possibility of finding work in Nepal with a philanthropic organization but a woman there suggested she instead investigate an interesting prospect, the Flying Doctors in Nairobi, Kenya, a group affiliated with the African Medical Research Foundation (AMREF).

My mother had already ventured to Africa, too, largely to follow the tracks her uncle Willie "Blue Willie" Chanler had laid there. Starting in 1889 he had gone on a couple of major expeditions in what is now Kenya, bringing with him *Plutarch's Lives* and two volumes of Browning and finding a reed buck, later named Chanler capricornus, of which a stuffed version ended up in the New York Natural History Museum.

On the first expedition Blue Willie took along a young assistant, George Galvin, who was the son of the gardener at Steen Valetje, the mansion just south of Rokeby. Galvin was fifteen or maybe barely sixteen at the time and Willie twenty-two and a Harvard dropout. They marched from Mombasa up to Lake Chala then to the old slave-trading town of Tavita, south of Mount Kilimanjaro, then west, near Mount Miru, then in time back again (covering Tavita to Mombasa, a march of over 230 miles, in eight days).

Willie did not write about this expedition but Galvin kept a journal of it. Mostly it involved the movement of food and water and bedding, and hunting, by Galvin's description. He talked of their main problems — insubordination among porters and Willie's terrible foot blisters. He also wrote of killing and in general eating guinea fowl, partridge, wart hog, antelope, eland, hartebeest, wildebeest, giraffe, ostrich, hippopotamus, grantii bull (one of those was enough to feed Galvin for a week), rhinoceros, Gunguni, buffaloes "thick as mosquitoes," Thomsoni bull, oryx, zebra, elephant, lesser koodo, hyena, waterbuck, blackbuck, reedbuck, thar, jackal, axis deer, impala and walleri. Lions even got into the act; Galvin shot at some, often with his Paradox.

After that expedition, Willie saw to it that Galvin prospered. He became a travel agent in the Vanderbilt Hotel, owned in part by Willie, and in time an executive in the hotel's administration.

Then two years later, in 1892–94, Willie led a much more ambitious expedition up the Tana River, again in Kenya, with an officer in the Imperial and Royal Austro-Hungarian Navy, Lieutenant Ludwig von Hoehnel. In 1888, with a Hungarian aristocrat, Count Teleki, von Hoehnel had "discovered" Lake Rudolph and Lake Stefanie (now Lakes Turkana and Chew Bahir]. His map of the region was "one of the finest pieces of scientific achievement within our half-century," stated a geographer of the time.

It was Chanler's objective to get as far north as the southern end of Lake Rudolph and proceed east through utter wasteland to Somalia. Starting out from Lamu, the porters and animal keepers saw a very large, attractive medicine chest and proceeded to plead all sorts of ailments and fill themselves with the contents, until the heads of the journey passed out the most nauseous drugs, saving the stock. Food was sent ahead. Willie deemed the Winchester rifle good for thin-skinned animals, the Mannlicher for stopping big game. The expedition proceeded along the Lykipia Escarpment, then east down the Ewaso Ng'iro River valley past a cascade they named

Chanler Falls and on to the massive Lorian Swamp which myth had told them was a great lake (like Iran's Hamun-e Jaz Murian, where the Helmand ends up, or the Burning Man country of northwest Nevada). At that point they had reached a true dead end and could only turn back.

This was a grueling eighteen-month tour de force. A porter did try to desert early on, got caught then shot "according to the rules of caravan discipline then in place," as reported in *The Astor Orphans*. Earlier, when attacked by several hundred warriors, Willie had collapsed in feverish delirium before an interpreter called those off. They caught fish only to discover they were full of worms. Mosquitoes and flies bedeviled them mercilessly. Red ants swarmed all over their route — natives called them "boiling water." The horse belonging to Lieutenant Von Hoehnel died. They kept on through repeated attacks by rhinoceros. A tent boy was gored, a bearer died of dysentery, they took forced marches to a source of food once their supplies ran out, sustained another attack by several hundred fighting men, with three porters killed and twelve wounded, some by poisoned arrows. They progressed farther, at times pinned down by rains, messengers drowned or eaten by crocodiles. As the expedition turned south, Von Hohnel was struck by the nose and horn of a rhinoceros, his thigh badly wounded and a bit of the thigh bone chipped off. He was sent off to camp, spent months in hospital then went home. Chanler's expedition lasted six weeks less than two years, starting from the time he set off for Europe.

A story had been current in the family ever since, that Willie had shot his bearer in the course of this ordeal. Like everyone else in the family, I had heard that story before vaguely but paid no attention to it, thinking Willie mad, like some of his siblings. However, my mother dissented.

She made a trip to Africa and on investigating found that the evidence was strongly against that story. She concluded from all this that Willie had been framed. Two of his bearers had gone down to the entrepot of Dar es Salaam in the middle of the expedition and complained about him to the British authorities, who acted on their charges, but he was ultimately exonerated.

Chanler Falls, in the dead center of Kenya, still was appearing by that name on maps in 1970, most strikingly in the *National Atlas of Kenya* (Government of Kenya, 1970). This has a map titled "Approximate Routes of 19th Century Travelers," showing twenty-eight routes in different colors and markings. Among them are the Chanler and Teleki/Von Hoehnel expeditions. Following that page are reproductions of maps of east Africa going back to 1564, all brilliantly inaccurate.

Willie went on to Cuba in the Spanish-American War. He was close to Teddy Roosevelt. In 1898 with the explosion of the battleship *Maine* in Havana harbor during the Cuban uprising against the Spanish Empire, he became very anxious to intervene against Spain in what became one more jingoistic American venture — a "war of choice" rather than response to an attack on the nation. (To be sure the culprits behind the *Maine* explosion have never been identified, though some have surmised it was an accident.) The Spanish American War badly shook an already weak Spanish government which one finds it hard to believe could have been seeking further entanglement in armed conflict. Indeed, the war may have exacerbated the conflicts within Spain which led to the outbreak of violent civil war there forty years later. Willie sent out a call for able-bodied volunteers to enroll in an infantry regiment in preparation for a landing on the island of Cuba. This initiative failed and of course his friend Theodore Roosevelt became the major figure in the invasion.

Willie did subsequently receive a commission as captain and participated with Roosevelt in the charge up San Juan Hill, which led the Spanish government to sue for peace. He returned a war hero, ran for Congress as a Democrat in Manhattan, won one term by a landslide. Later, on a moderately lucrative business tour of Chile, he performed one further inestimable service to the American public, picking up on a local rum concoction and bringing the recipe for it back to New York. He labeled it the daiquiri.

Chanler Chapman, the son of John Jay and Elizabeth, recalled an occasion just before World War One when Blue Willie sought to rally desert tribes in Libya to fight alongside forces from the Ottoman Empire against the specter of Italian invasion and requested arms from the notorious dealer Basil Zaharoff, whom he had encountered in Austria with Colonel Von Hoehnel.

Zaharoff, Chanler said on another occasion, happened to be driving back to Paris after witnessing Charles Lindberg's historic arrival at Le Bourget airport and gave a ride to a young *Chicago Tribune* journalist named Wales, enabling Wales to establish his career for life by getting into Paris at record speed and sending the story of Lindberg's arrival line by line over Western Union and scooping the world. Willie even knew Butch Cassidy and was partner with several friends in a stable of New York prizefighters.

In 1914 he had to have a leg amputated as a consequence of a serious fracture. After that, he abandoned his life of adventure and turned curmudgeonly and reactionary.

The Flying Doctors were a group of plastic surgeons, mostly from Britain, who could fly small passenger aircraft (fourteen-seater Cessna 404s for the most part) to remote villages, where they would operate on residents who had been mauled by local animals — lions in particular. They would also distribute food to famine victims in drought-wracked areas like Kbwezi and Marsabit and evacuate victims of serious violence who needed hospital care, mostly from Kenya and Tanzania though at times they brought emergency aid as far north as Addis Ababa, Ethiopia. Sometimes these evacuations would run to thirty or forty a month and they were usually successful. AMREF newsletters talk about a boy bitten on the neck by a tiger and flown to Nairobi, a Masai man airlifted after being stepped on by an elephant, an eighteen-year-old Masai herdsboy shot by an arrow in a cattle raid (with a six-inch blade in his skull), a man in Northern Tanzania also shot in the head with an arrow. On one mission to rescue a man with a fractured ankle the pilot had to have someone drive up and down an airstrip near the Samburu Game Preserve to clear it of giraffes.

My mother began making an appearance in the Flying Doctors' offices, offering to volunteer for various tasks. In time, after she had acquitted herself of those competently, the group took her on as an administrator.

The head of the Flying Doctors was Michael Wood, who had mastered his profession during the Battle of Britain remaking pilots' faces as a protégé of the renowned Sir Alexander Mackindoe, the RAF's lead plastic surgeon. Wood would fly all over Kenya, operating all day, sometimes till two in the morning. He developed a very loyal following in the country. My mother once got through immigration at the Nairobi airport though her visa'd expired because the officer who checked her passport claimed Wood had saved his life. Another time a gifted woman tennis player we knew was playing at an

English tournament and a bad line call threw her into a fit, precipitating interminable, costly telephone calls to her husband back in California, and he had my mother take a trip up from Nairobi to calm her down. On the way she threw her back out so badly she could barely move. Lady Mackindoe arranged for her to see a renowned back specialist on Harley Street who normally had a six-month backup of appointments. He worked her back into shape, telling her however that she'd have to sleep on a hard floor from then on.

With AMREF in Nairobi, my mother functioned most efficiently as an administrator and was also a crack fundraiser. In fact in 1970 she established an organization, the Flying Doctors Society. She ran the society with a Kenyan colleague, Grace Syamba. This organization required well over a million dollars a year and my mother raised quite a bit of this. One American doctor who had worked out there with her awhile stated in only partial jest that when she heard a wealthy tourist was coming in from America she would go out to the Nairobi airport, greet him and turn him upside down until there was nothing left to spill out of his pockets. Her success rate was high but not total. Katherine Crosby, widow of Bing, came out on a visit once and though my mother received her generously donated nothing to AMREF. On being asked where Mrs. Crosby made her contributions, my mother snapped "Some nasty group of nuns down the San Francisco Peninsula. If she wants to come back for a safari, I'll arrange one for her, but it'll cost ten thousand dollars. That's all right. Revenge is a dish that can be eaten cold."

She said that Michael Wood though quieter than her was a superb fundraiser, on the order of Johnny Holmes from the old *Coast* magazine days. He performed plastic surgery on wealthy tourists, mostly older American women, who would come out in groups of six or seven from New York, have their operations then spend the mandatory three-week recuperation period traveling about incognito on wildlife-viewing safaris.

On one of her visits she engaged in a lot of talk about plastic surgery with her friend from childhood, the movie actress Jane Wyatt. Jane went into a lengthy description of the work a person had to keep doing to keep the original surgical work effective. Indeed, after they'd reached a certain age, Jane, while still close to my mother, didn't want to be seen with her in public. That would age-date her.

An old Santa Barbara friend of my mother's, Rhoda Prud'homme, had come to inhabit a priceless house on the slopes of Mount Kenya in exchange for going back to Marseille, getting the cremated remains of the lover of the woman who had owned it previously and scattering the remains over the mountain. "When they cremate somebody, you know, it's not a neat little sack of ashes the way they always say it is," Rhoda insisted. "It's a lot of gristle and bone. There we were, over Mount Kenya, and I had to throw his jawbone out of the plane."

On another of my mother's brief visits, I showed her an article I'd read recently in *Esquire* on African safaris. She abruptly dismissed that as shallow tourist hype — "That's the sort of thing they put out on Kenya that I don't like" — then contributed a couple of vignettes that had moved her deeply. One concerned a man who looked after old zoo animals that were sent down to a South African farm once they'd been retired, including an old female elephant he'd looked after for years. He went off unexpectedly, perhaps to a job in Kenya. When he returned to the farm many years later the old elephant came up to him, put a foot up on a stool and gave him a circus-curtsy. Then a fellow who'd looked after animals in a London zoo for years went off then, again, returned, and a giraffe came up to him and laid a fetlock on his shoulder as her eyes puddled over.

Though my mother spent most of her time in Africa those years, she didn't talk much about it on her visits home. Nairobi with its very large British population was actually a sophisticated city; in a way, my mother's community there was more British than Kenyan. Nairobi was after all a large hub, a center for international organizations working in Africa — it has been said that about a quarter of a million Westerners live there. It had, among other elegant institutions, the Muthaiga Country Club, where my mother played tennis, and the Donovan Maule Theatre with its repertory stage, cinema and restaurant, lounge and cocktail bar where numerous residents (mostly British) performed. My mother had artists donate work for free for Christmas cards sold to raise money and put on a Flying Doctors Ball at Giraffe Manor. She also maintained close relations with the safari and tour companies around.

Nairobi was also a major gathering point for international conferences. One such event was a meeting of an international organization for betterment of the lot of prostitutes. One Dutch delegate to this conference was asked to give a report on it at the royal palace on her return home. She began her address by stating, "O Queen: It uplifts my spirits greatly to attend this meeting in your presence, having received the great honor of being ushered into this palace by the front entrance for the first time."

An old friend from the days of the *Coast* magazine, Bruce Porter, once told my mother a story of psychic influence brought to bear on him by Francis Bacon, when he was going over a Shakespeare folio. As he went over the lines with his pencil, words kept getting underlined in a form of subtle pressure. Together, the words formed a message that it was Bacon, not Shakespeare, who had written that folio. In Nairobi my mother told Bruce Porter's story to one of the actors she consorted with, a Britisher later living much of the year in Lake Tahoe. His next performance onstage he spoke of taking a time capsule back to Shakespeare's England and proceeding to the Globe Theater. Once there though he decided not to meet Shakespeare. It struck him that if he did, told Shakespeare that he came from a distant land four hundred years in the future and threw in enough historical description to sound believable (hydrogen bombs, traffic jams, computerized airline scheduling blunders), Shakespeare would be swept up by the revelation and squander the rest of his life writing science fiction, working to recreate the world of twentieth-century America from the description then filling it in with imagined detail he couldn't really have got from this quick visit.

My mother spent about twenty years with the Flying Doctors.

In the course of that, she became once again in her life deeply attached to a domineering masculine woman who, through her own markedly unpleasant character, could handle other difficult unpleasant people and give her support in major struggles she had to confront. This was Anne Spoerre, a doctor from Cannes, France, and survivor of the Nazi occupation. She had worked in Kenya since 1961 and flew her own Cherokee 5Y AZT, or a Cessna 206 on occasion. Younger female relatives of my mother's quietly derogated her in terms they had been liberated to use with impunity. Diana went to Kenya at one point and flew with our mother and Anne

Spoerre in one of the small planes at hand. Anne was flying, our mother was in the back seat and Diana, sitting beside Anne, got into a terrific argument with her. As she talked back to Anne she looked back to see our mother frantically shaking her head and waving her hands back and forth to get her to shut up.

My daughter Leila went with a school friend to visit my mother in Kenya in 1982. One day they flew out into the outback with Ms. Spoerre, who let them have a large sum of money to entertain themselves with. They thought she had given it to them so they rented a Land Rover for the day — only to find her exploding in the end when they told her they had spent it all.

Anne Spoerre once admitted to my mother that during the war she had collaborated with the Nazis, as a doctor. They had her in Ravensbruck, assisting a doctor who was conducting experiments on prisoners. She collaborated in the killing of some. Afterward she was so filled with self-hatred and loathing over that that she resolved to devote the rest of her life to giving people medical care for free. That was what drove her to Kenya and her work as a flying doctor. It has to be acknowledged that ultimately when Dr. Spoerre died my mother attended as many of the four services they held for her throughout Kenya as she could, then came back gushing about her majestic sendoff. At the AMREF hangar they put her coffin in a plane and flew it around. At Lamu, a horde of Arab women in veils mobbed her coffin and demanded that she be buried there (she was sent back to France to her family gravesite).

As a child I had vaguely known a gifted Santa Barbara writer, Raoul Schumacher — remembered him as a fat fellow who would hang around the Miramar Hotel bar much of the time, starting perhaps around noon. Now, on another of my mother's visits, over dinner at the Claremont in the Berkeley hills — the sun rolling along the window sill so that they had to lower all the blinds to the bottom almost till dusk before the spectacular palm-fringed view of the gunmetal gray-mauve San Francisco Bay and bridge and the city beyond — she talked from her experience about the famous writer on Africa Beryl Markham who it turned out had lived with Raoul in Santa Barbara. My mother quietly stated that it was Raoul, and not Beryl, who'd written *West with the Night.* Character though she was, Beryl just did not have a gift for writing, my mother insisted. She quoted a number of sophisticated Santa Barbarans from the past who had always known that, known that Raoul was ghost-writing her beautiful magazine pieces for her. She claimed Ernest Hemingway once said about *West with the Night* "It's a wonderful book and one only wishes she could write another one." But Raoul had never been in Africa and there was evidence of this in the book, to someone like my mother who had spent much time in east Africa herself and knew it well — description and writing in general that was not firsthand. Then Raoul died and Beryl Markham never published another good piece.

In the course of my daughter Leila's visit, air force officers attempted to overthrow the president, Daniel arap Moi. The whole city was silenced by curfew and she and her friend had to lie low in my mother's small house; my mother gave them gin and tonics to calm their teenage nerves. The coup then failed. My mother went downtown while the curfew was still in effect and got them tickets on the first plane up to Cairo.

In those days I went through personal struggles, mostly to do with the realization of my deeper inner self. I kept saying, Next week is going to be tough. After that it got tougher, so I resorted to saying, The next month or two will be tough. Still no relief, so I began saying, Well, I can look down the road six months or so. I got through those somehow but the situation hadn't really improved, but still, I was able to tell myself, proudly, Now if I can only get through the next year.... Depressed while shaving, my attention moved over to my aftershave lotion, an Avon bottle in the shape of a rhinoceros. I recalled old Uncle Willy Chanler then his fellow explorer Von Hoehnel, the one who was so badly gored by a rhinoceros that he had to spend months at a missionary post in the outback, probably under morphine most of the time. I thought, well, those guys had *cojones*. They wouldn't let petty problems like mine upset them. At that I felt better, for a while.

22
The World Changes in Egypt

One evening at eleven on another visit to Cairo, still wracked with poverty after an unremitting war of attrition with Israel and war just to the east between the Jordanian government and the Palestine Liberation Organization, Hoda saw that the television program was interrupted by lengthy recitations from the Koran, presaging unusual news. Viewers in Cairo were sure that King Hussein of Jordan had just been assassinated at the hands of Palestinians or Syrians. He had not. Vice President Anwar Sadat appeared on the screen to announce that it was Nasser who had just died.

During this period, the cities of the Arab world reverberated with an awesome buzzing and whining. The outpouring of public grief at the funeral itself was overwhelming. Attending the funeral were indeed many important world figures such as Haile Selassie of Ethiopia, Sir Alec Douglas-Home of England and Elliot Richardson, representing President Nixon. Nasser's old nemesis, King

Faisal of Saudi Arabia, did not attend; grudgingly and belatedly, he sent a telegram of condolence.

As it had been planned, the cortege started beyond Tahrir Square, at the far end of Kasr el-Nil Bridge (later famed, at this writing, as the focus of the popular uprising that overthrew President Husni Mubarak in 2011). It proceeded over to the Corniche along the Nile then up by the Nile Hilton to the adjacent Arab Socialist Union headquarters, then inland and around to the Republican Palace at Abdin.

Policemen formed cordons down the Corniche into Garden City and tried beating encroaching crowds back with their belts. Press helicopters zipped along the riverbank twenty feet above the water, greedily churning out TV footage. Mobs overwhelmed the casket almost as soon as the procession began to move. Few believed that the casket actually contained Nasser's body; many of those who did insisted, as did Mirvat, that it was replaced by another one filled with rocks once it reached the ASU headquarters and a helicopter whisked the real one away. Or maybe there were three coffins; Mirvat heard a friend swear he drove the truck which removed the real coffin, driving desperately out to Nasser's home in Mansheyat el-Bakri (and running over some of the people in the mob) while the second false coffin was trundled along to Abdin.

Mirvat said she had gone with friends up to a third-story doctor's office overlooking the route before the cortege passed and they were spotted by people down on the street who charged up, threatening them and telling them they had no right to be there because the funeral was not for anyone from their family. Then came back later with knives, forcing Mirvat's friends to barricade themselves.

Then the second false coffin had to be whisked away from Abdin by helicopter — though Mirvat insisted that the mobs went wild every time they saw a helicopter. She believed that Cairo was on the brink of social revolution, mindless mob anarchy; for once, Hamdeyya a pro-Nasser friend agreed with her. (Indeed the day after Nasser died they both went down to a Heliopolis boulevard in slacks and blouses only to hear a cab driver stop beside them to yell, "What is this you sluts! The man hasn't even been buried!") Mirvat snorted that Nasser used to brag how he had defeated Anthony Eden, whom he branded a *khira'*, a decadent old man, but here Eden was, still alive. Hamdeyya retorted that his survivor Sadat, whom she labeled a "shoe," was barely alive either, having had a heart attack at the funeral, which Nasser's confidant Heikal had reported (thus being placed under house arrest, as punishment) — though she couldn't understand why even Heikal could be excited over the "silly death" of him, or the few other shoes Nasser had somehow allowed to stay on in the government.

Tante Aziza at the big house said "We lived on our nerves all those years under Abdel Nasser" and reminded them all of Hassan Mahmoud (who was brought up with eleven thousand feddans) and how the secret police came to his house one day, confiscated everything and, insisting he had hidden all his wealth away in furniture, tore every single piece of furniture apart.

A member of a prominent old family Hoda knew claimed that one year when Nasser failed to obtain financing for the cotton crop, his relative the National Bank Governor proceeded to raise sixty million pounds from capital sources in Saudi Arabia, Kuwait and Lebanon. This so enraged Nasser, the relative went on, that he had the banker arrested and refused to release him until he agreed to relinquish all his positions of power and directorships, except that of the National Bank. In early 1960 the government nationalized the National Bank and Bank Misr anyway.

Another fellow used to be a prosperous entrepreneur owning a packaging business as well as a battery-casing enterprise. These were nationalized and paid for by government bonds. "Someday we can stop worrying about Greece and we'll be free to compete with Yemen" he said. He did acknowledge that he shouldn't speak ill of the government he was subsidizing. "They pay me a full 4 percent on those bonds!" he trumpeted. "They even asked me to help them run the plant. After they came to see what it was they'd taken over."

Once in an argument years later with the eminent journalist Harrison Salisbury I worked to describe some powerful features of Nasser's character but he just derided that, describing Nasser as a mediocre amateur boxer from the Minneapolis YMCA contrasted with China's Mao Zedong, who had killed tens of millions. Nasser did run some nasty prison camps, but killing was not his style.

Mirvat swore that five hundred people had died in that outpouring, stampeded or crushed to death by collapsing balconies. In fact, three may have died, and within a day after the funeral an all-inclusive calm reigned over Cairo. The city stayed in mourning for forty days, the movie theaters closed down and public places refused to serve alcohol. The visual evidence that Nasser was gone centered around his mosque, which was ringed by white-uniformed policemen, standing elbow to elbow, and in the festoons of black and silver street banners — "In God's care, Gamal," they read, "May you rest in the garden of eternal paradise," "Good-bye,

Gamal, who forged a generation of heroes." Banners were hung mostly on or about government buildings and were cut of uniform cloth, but not all of them were. Someone crudely inscribed on a wall, in black paint, "The hero Gamal Abdel Nasser died on 28/9/70."

Another, repeated often in many different script styles, "Abdel Nasser Lam Yamut," Nasser has not died.

23
New Democracy in the Old Mansion

Over the decades on occasion while visiting Rokeby I'd drop by Hyde Park and look out over the sharply dropping lawn and trees across a slice of the Hudson to the religious figure Father Divine's old estate beyond. In FDR's mansion I noticed among other things his wheelchairs, each one with a little ashtray-ledge. I left the mansion imagining that FDR was essentially a simple-spirited patrician with a conventional education and a gregariousness that amounted to charisma, in the context of the thirties, where a lot of dispossessed, unassimilated and rebellious people wanted to believe in a white Anglo-Saxon Protestant leader who stood for the common man, the minorities, the oppressed. For instance there is a bust of him in the Hyde Park garden, donated by the International Ladies Garment Workers' Union. (Also a note by Roosevelt to local politicos to contribute more money to the party, and his campaigns, than they had been yielding up so far.)

Certainly he was the straight man to Winston Churchill's overpowering personality all during the war, especially at Tehran and Yalta (most strikingly then, on the verge of death). But it has to be said that his achievement in bringing America out of the Depression was great. Herb Caen, the San Francisco humorist and columnist, once stated only partly in jest "On the occasion of the fiftieth anniversary of FDR's death, the Senate has moved to observe two minutes of competence." John Kenneth Galbraith, for his part, considered Roosevelt far and away the greatest leader of the twentieth century — declared that no one else came close.

(Conversely President Truman's secretary of state, Dean Acheson, could not abide him. My father's mother Bay, a portrait painter, did two portraits of FDR, one of which hung for years in Hyde Park till it was put in storage then disappeared. These portraits were not highly regarded, by people I know anyway. My mother used to say that was because Bay didn't really like Roosevelt either.)

I saw my mother's old Vassar sidekick Martha McGahan decades later. She had well before married a fellow named Adam Green, an insurance adjuster. Some years after their wedding, on New Year's Day, he announced to her that he was leaving her for another woman — "Dumping her because now that he'd discovered he'd become more of a man, he didn't need a mother anymore," as my mother brusquely put it.

Some time after that I joined Martha for lunch along with another old figure, Sully, who like Martha had Irish roots. The two embarked on a long discussion of the cruel things that used to be said about Eleanor Roosevelt, as were being said right then about President Lyndon Johnson and his wife Lady Bird. Sully reminisced about the time she was out in California while her son Elliot was reported to be getting a divorce and how she lied to a couple of young journalists who caught her going out a back way on the road to Sacramento and prevented them from scooping the divorce.

"Oh, but that wasn't a lie," said Martha, "that was her private life."

"But don't you remember St. Thomas Aquinas' definition of lying as keeping the truth from one who has a right to know?" riposted Sully.

"From the priest at confession, yes."

Sully went on to talk about original sin.

"Yes, but hand in hand with that we were always taught about original grace," said Martha.

"Baloney. Mankind is evil, twisted and malicious. Who do you think were more significant, the twenty thousand who went out to destroy the Sioux, or the two missionaries who went along hoping to heal them?"

"That was just a bunch of American frontiersmen."

"Oh, the Irish were in on that too. And there were some blacks. Still, Irish families used to talk the same way about the British occupation."

"Oh, come now," said Martha, "they didn't have it *that* bad."

"They starved to death, you can't get much worse than that. Well, anyway," concluded Sully, "we made it to the White House."

Around that time my father and I visited Martha Green at her Sausalito apartment. She offered him a drink in the middle of the day, then told him to pour himself another one. "Might as well be hanged for a sheep as for a lamb," he stated, as he downed that.

After Adam left Martha I ran into him in downtown San Francisco practically before the Shell Building where she worked, in the *Time* office. The moment I told him I was working right around there, he asked apprehensively "The Shell Building?" He was very anxious to have Hoda and me over for drinks and pressed his card on me, promising he wouldn't even argue about Egypt and talking about an evening they'd had with the head of the Black Studies Program at San Francisco State. He insisted we get together for lunch and wondered if I'd approach Peter — a fellow almost twenty years his junior — to see if Peter would see him when he and his wife went to New York in the next few weeks. He must've been very effectively ostracized by his old friends — almost all their old friends were Martha's.

"That's another thing about those woman-chasers," my mother kept saying. "They have no friends of their own."

Martha died in August 1976. A memorial service of impeccable taste was held for her in the courtyard of the Episcopal church in Sausalito — marred only by a heavy fog and chill. A few people read little pieces they thought Martha would have enjoyed, a young fellow strummed a guitar between readings and we then went up to the balcony for an exquisite lunch which Martha might well have prepared herself: several bowls of just the right salads, wine, plates of pate, sliced and unsliced cheeses, salmon in oval slices, several types of bread and crackers. I just barely recognized Adam Green, but not Tom Williams, who later declared "I saw Martha three weeks ago and she was great." Later, Grace Macouillard, an interesting older lady and novelist, declared, "Well I had lunch with her three weeks ago and she was not great." Even the plates, and the blue and white tapestry of a dove, almost in the form of yin and yang, could have been furnished by Martha.

I had the occasion in those days to resume contact with various figures from the near and remote past.

At one point I came upon Joseph F. Fletcher IV in the lobby of the Nile Hilton. He'd been a couple of classes ahead of me at Groton, went on to become a high-powered Asian scholar and had now gained a major following at Harvard through his apparent skill with languages. He started out as a student of Chinese then on mastering that language moved on to Central Asia. That led him, as he progressed westward, into Turkish, Persian then Arabic, which he was pursuing now at this critical point in Egypt's history.

Then there was George Gund. His involvement with the world of the cinema had deepened. He and Teddy divorced and he married a prominent young filmmaker from Brazil, Iara Lee. Among the films she produced was *Synthetic Pleasures*, which received good reviews in the *New York Times* and elsewhere. One sat back and watched her show smart-bomb cameras whizzing at high speed down areas of central Tokyo and New York about a hundred feet off the ground in the dark, interspersed with shows at Vegas, a fax-chapel, Paradise Beach in southern Japan, cryogenics, bizarre animation (pliable Lego-boxes bashing each other in), various people talking about the philosophical and social implications of the Internet, Timothy Leary, cybersex and simulated skiing.

At an annual school reception in San Francisco's University Club, I encountered George and told him I'd seen *Central Station*, the Brazilian movie, and he related a story he'd heard from his wife Iara, that Walter Salles, the man who made that movie, was the son of a very famous, powerful banker who gave him almost no support at all and the story of the boy rejected by his father and searching him out had a poignant, autobiographical twist.

George also had a place up near Seattle on Stuart Island, one of the northernmost American islands in San Juan Strait. His property had a well but he had to get almost everything else from a nearby island. He would fly up to Port Angeles on the Olympic Peninsula then take a small plane out, buzzing the dirt landing strip for deer before landing.

By then he had also become a major figure in American entertainment in a broader world beyond the cinema. In fact his whole life had come to dwell on entertainment. He had become especially prominent as an investor in professional sports — basketball for one, with his acquisition of the Cleveland Cavaliers in 1983 (and the early LeBron James). When I told him at a Cavaliers game that he was in the entertainment business par excellence he said "Boy don't I know it."

Perhaps the most inspired manifestation of his enterprise was his creation, with his younger brother Gordon, of the National Hockey League's San Jose Sharks, an expansion team for which he earned the rights after giving up ownership in the Minnesota North Stars in the early nineties. Indeed the shark became the most powerful and pervasive symbol of the Bay Area's largest city, which until then (before the takeoff of the computer industry) had labored as a cultural and economic backwater where the population remained almost stagnant and the post office was the largest single employer — "a low-level equilibrium trap," economists used to call it. For this he earned the profound gratitude of the powers and even the general public in San Jose.

At the game inaugurating the Sharks' tenure, the San Jose arena was a dark, sold-out mutedly raucous structure with grayish-silver ice and chrome all about. Taking up the walls overhead were logos comprehensible only to those versed in the world of high tech — Viewsonic, Symantec, Lotus, IKON, Infineon, InterSil, PMC-Sierra. Over the scoreboard Altera and on the ice-freshening vehicle the legend Compaq — after all, it was the Compaq Arena then. (To be fair, there were ads about for Bud and other low-tech products, too.)

At the reception before the game, we circled around eating enormous shrimps, sausages draped in various sautéed chilis, sour cream cheese and lox canapés, buns with roast beef and horseradish, plenty of white wine and éclairs. At that point for the only time in my life I found myself actually talking to a person while he was being asked for an autograph, as a line of people stood waiting for George to sign their programs.

At the end of that game the Sharks' goalie, Arturs Irbe (whom George had acquired from Kansas City), was swamped by journalists from as far afield as Radio Latvia. Indeed the Sharks opened a store in Latvia's capital Riga, its inauguration attended by Prime Minister Valdis Birkavs. On George's film-gathering trips to central Europe and Russia, he quietly went about snapping up other hockey players, with names like Makarov and Larionov.

3C Math notwithstanding, George did manage to keep from being conned by Peter Ueberroth into buying the Cleveland Indians and he and his brother Gordon made hundreds of millions of dollars selling control of the Cavaliers in 2005.

The Sharks were often making playoffs by then. Overwhelming glitz, the overpowering use of teal and black (the team colors), the logo of a manic black shark chewing a hockey stick, balloons of sharks floating overhead before the games then players skating through smoke out of an enormous shark's head on the ice. I asked George if they were about to put the shark up in some attic after the season, and he laughed. Iara was there too, for once, and we talked a lot; she hadn't been doing much filming but had been educating herself at length about the Taliban, spending time at refugee camps in Pakistan then going to the Tehran Film Festival — using her Brazilian passport. She found the atmosphere in Tehran and Esfahan very congenial, laid back.

I attended another Sharks game as the sky slowly turned Chinese-lacquer turquoise, at a suite where there were sushi, munchables, beer, great wine, fine cheeses, slices of fruit in fans. Nancy Pelosi was in attendance, still only Congresswoman Pelosi. When George made a late appearance she jumped up, embraced him excitedly and not long after became House Speaker Pelosi.

Later George complained that he was losing a lot of money even though the team had sold out almost every game (more spare time for dot-commers, in Silicon Valley's recession of the time?). He even thought he might have to sell. The team had got off to a blazing start that year but a series of injuries then the suspension of a key player slowed it down.

My mother preferred to visit Rokeby in the late spring or fall. Just as she loved the summer, she felt sad with the advent of Indian summer. What she found most depressing about it was the appearance of warmth in the midst of falling yellow leaves rather than steamy green jungle. At least it was deer hunting season, so one still had cause to go out into the countryside. She'd heard her nephew-in-law Curtis over in Connecticut state (as he was about to go off hunting one weekend) that it was all right to have one deer per forty acres but when you got up to one per thirty it was not so good for the underbrush, in dry years anyway.

It seemed to my mother that there were more and more Poles about Rokeby each time she returned. Ricky kept pointing to the use of such words as traktor, truk operator, farm, dairy among the Poles there. The Poles were originally connected with Ania and branched out from there. One habitué was Konrad, who had worked in Iraq till they expelled him for attempting to establish a Solidarity Union branch in Saddam's Baghdad, then Stan (Staneeswoff) and Jersey the remodeler. Along with assorted official and unofficial relatives. Theirs, like the Russians', was very much a kitchen culture. They spent much of their days sitting around what used to be the pantry behind the main dining room, by the dumbwaiter, warmest place in the mansion in both senses. With the passage of time that high-ceilinged chamber with its glass-doored cabinets that reached almost to the ceiling had become the social meeting place of the mansion, summer evenings anyway, informal, spacious enough to seat half a dozen people or so and right by the food and drink.

They labeled Jersey the remodeler the last of the great Polish drinkers. At a wedding in a tent he climbed to the top of the central pole, bowler on head and vodka bottle in hand. The previous Christmas Eve he had had so much to drink he couldn't get up till four the next afternoon and even then just sat about weakly sipping cranberry juice.

In those days they seemed to spend most of their time speculating on the future of the Soviet Union, still extant and militarily occupying their homeland. There were in fact dogs on the premises they'd named after communist leaders — Chairman Chernyenko and the Labrador Andropov, accompanied by the terrier Jaruzelski.

The Rokeby crowd's contempt for Russians in general included the estranged, such as the late great pianist Vladimir Horowitz. Stan insisted Horowitz had given at most one serious piano lesson in his life and here in a roadside tavern just outside New York he saw a good-looking young highway patrolman — playing a tune with one finger on an upright and declaring "I picked this up from some guy named Vlad." Stan's favorite composer was Aram Khachaturian, who'd enraged Stalin back around 1946 when his Saber Dance got on the old Hit Parade.

There was seemingly endless argument in the midst of it all over when the Berlin Wall would come down. 2034, said Leonard, a tenant down the drive. Konrad shook his head. "It's been moved down to 1987. We were always saying 1981."

The good thing about America is its Bobby Fischers withdraw into chess, one of them observed once, the bad thing about the Soviet Union is its Spasskys withdraw into chess.

At another point, hearing the Poles describe Soviet losses in the space program, my mother scoffed further: their figures were ridiculous. "I read in *Newsweek* that they lost only one man on that shot" she declared. "Everyone knows that."

"Yes, that's the official propaganda," Konrad agreed, making a yakking gesture with one hand. "But the unofficial propaganda says a hundred and fifty" (a yakking gesture with the other hand) "and that's what everyone believes."

On the subject of the backwardness of the Soviet Bloc, someone snorted that they were a generation behind in computers. "Computers!" Stan railed. "What about dental equipment. The dentist drills back there you have to pump with your foot."

In mid-1979 there appeared in the *New York Times* a photo of the Soviet leader Leonid Brezhnev in a tie, white straw hat and suit with three-balled medal on his right chest, holding a teddy bear. He was about to give the bear to a group of children in a Hungarian kindergarten and had a somewhat tensely wistful expression on his face, which immediately plunged my mother into a mood of sorrow, nostalgia and remorse. Amid all the sarcasm and derision heaped on the man she claimed that here he was, his system — which we had been fighting for over thirty years — reduced to giving a gift to small children in a satellite whose adults had long gone beyond the point where they hated the Soviet Union or had any feelings toward it more powerfully negative than part-time contempt. "That man can't even walk" she snapped.

Another manifestation of the liberal streak to the place touched on earlier lay in politics. One of my grandmother's brothers was Lewis Chanler, closest sibling to her in age. A Democrat, he had been a dashing figure and there are photographs of him on the Rokeby front lawn discussing political strategy in his thirties, as he embarked on what seemed a promising political career.

Initially, Lewis became a Dutchess County supervisor. From that position he was nominated lieutenant governor, in 1906; William Randolph Hearst was nominated governor. The lieutenant governor was elected separate from the governor. Charles Evans Hughes defeated Hearst and became governor, while Lewis won the lieutenant governor's race — carrying New York City by 150,000 votes. In that era he and his family would go up to Albany for the winter, recalled his younger son Brown Willie, eight or ten at the time. (Willie further recalled that as a child he would go to England every summer with his parents, his older brother Styve and a horse. The horse always knew they were going to England because it automatically shifted to the left on disembarking from the boat over there.)

At the end of his two-year term, in 1908, Lewis was nominated for governor against Hughes, who was running for reelection. At that time there was a great to-do about racetrack gambling — the question was, would it continue to be illegal? The Democrats were in favor of the gambling because members of Tammany Hall, based in the city with a branch up in Buffalo, made a lot of money out of it. There was a great outcry among the Democrats over this issue. Lewis was against it and when there was a tie vote in the state senate he, as lieutenant governor, voted against it, breaking the tie against the Democrats. Hughes the Republican attacked Lewis, though he'd voted on Hughes' side — accused Lewis of doing the opposite! Lewis never really answered Hughes — wanted to answer "No, no, no," but couldn't. In the election, the returns came in to Rokeby by phone. Willie recalls that his father was running extremely well upstate but with New York City (and Buffalo) under the thumb of Tammany Hall he carried the city by only fifty thousand votes and Hughes ended up beating him by fifty thousand.

Lewis ran for State Assembly the next year, 1909, while compelling his contemporary Franklin Roosevelt to run for State Senate, rather against his wishes. They both won but Lewis then came down with double pneumonia and lost the energy to continue in politics.

My cousin Winty, a formidable family historian, insisted that Lewis' 1908 gubernatorial election defeat indirectly cleared the way for FDR to progress politically: it removed one senior figure in his way from the state Democratic Party hierarchy.

By Brown Willie's description, his father Lewis used to go to Rokeby two or three weeks a year, riding and walking around. Then, Willie stated, Lewis and his mother broke up; she wanted only to garden "and he just liked politics, probably."

As Willie further put it, my grandmother was "a violent Protestant, puritan, anti-Catholic, anti-everything. She got more and more sour as things went on." She did not mind Lewis' divorce but when he remarried she said "No man with two wives can go to Rokeby." He stayed down the road in Sylvania on his visits and would slip over to Rokeby after dark, walking about the grounds in pale moonlight. One night when he wandered onto the grounds my grandmother glared at him and told him "Get off Rokeby land." In conclusion Willie said "We were all pretty mad at Aunt Margaret and everyone walked out on her."

Then in 1968 the son of the reactionary Hamilton Fish, also Hamilton Fish, campaigned for the congressional seat his father had held till the war. He came to hold the seat for thirteen terms. By Ricky's description, in his small-town congressional campaign there were endless barbecues and clambakes with the Veterans of Foreign Wars, Knights of Columbus and Kingston power-boat owners' association, whose members would sit clustered around the yacht basin drinking beer, watching television and sallying forth only to get pizza at a riverfront restaurant. Ethnic organizations full of people speaking their original languages badly, women in pink tights and curlers. The war in Vietnam was getting underway. The VFW showed its muscle in a parade in New York City, where there had been a peace march a few months before — drum majorettes, brass, bagpipes, busloads from New Jersey, Illinois, California, Juneau even — potbellied men and bosomy matrons, rows of rifle-bearers, a convention at the Hilton addressed by Defense Secretary McNamara.

At one point in one reelection campaign Gerald Ford, then a congressman, came up to Rokeby as part of a tour to give Fish support. Fish complained to Ford that the county's assistant district attorney, G. Gordon Liddy, was going to run against him on the American Independent Party ticket if he lost in the Republican primary, so could the Republican party find some activity for Liddy to pursue in Washington, and get the man out of his hair? The party did — helping to bring real scandal to the Republicans and Richard Nixon several years later, when Liddy crafted the Watergate scandal.

24
The Thirties Are Dead
by the Eighties

I n Cairo I again came upon Joe Fletcher. He was now
focused on the study of Islamic religious movements
and had just come back from Yemen, where he'd
copied a major manuscript from the Arabic because there
were no Xerox machines down there yet. We arranged to
have dinner.

It turned out I had to change our dinner engagement
and went by a downtown Cairo pension where he had been
staying to leave him word of that. A note by the registration
desk stated that he would not be staying there after the end
of July. However, it was already early August. After I came
upon him in the pension anyway and expressed confusion
about his note, he tensed up and quickly told me that he
didn't want anyone to know he was still there. As it turned
out we did meet later for dinner anyway.

He was very interested to learn what little I knew
of the Shiite minority in the oil-rich Eastern Province

of Saudi Arabia. It was already known, as early as the seventies, that he was active, sometimes very quietly, interviewing and cultivating important Islamic militants, especially leaders of the Cyprus-based Naqshbandiya sect. It turns out that this sect was dominant in some regions (soon to become independent) that bordered the Caspian Sea. The tireless support he and numerous American and other Western colleagues gave members of this sect in its struggle against the Soviets, and the threat that its struggle might spread farther north, helped drive the Soviets to start seeking an accommodation with the United States in the mid-eighties. Joe never had the reward of seeing his work reach its completion. It was the last time I saw him — he died of cancer in the mid-eighties, at age forty-nine.

This was at the onset of hard violent times in the Middle East, concentrated in Saudi Arabia.

Almost every map of Arabia I'd been seeing, from Herodotus' time up through Lawrence of Arabia, showed the corner of the Great Nefudh, a mammoth sand sea, as the apex of a triangle which all the great empires of the area surrounded but did not cross (except to be sure for the early Islamic leaders, who emerged from Arabia). That included the Persian empires, the Romans and Byzantines, and of course the Ottomans. Even Lawrence could not get into the Nefudh, though he came close, as he wrote in his *Seven Pillars of Wisdom*. When he saw a "distant corner" of it whilst riding a camel on his march to Arfaja, a base from which he planned to attack the Ottoman Turks, and asked his guide, Auda Abu Tayy, if they could visit it, he related that Auda "growled that men went to the Nefudh only of necessity, when raiding, and that the son of his father did not raid on a tottering, mangy camel. Our business was to reach Arfaja alive." Arabia was the hard core no outside empire ever assimilated. Except tentatively, temporarily, in an odd way, the America of Reagan and Bush.

I heard stories about the land from Egyptians I had known in my married years well in the past. Many perhaps most of them had returned to the Middle East now, tired of the dull livelihoods they had been making in America. Suddenly the work opportunities had become much greater there, especially in Saudi Arabia and the Gulf.

The siege of the Grand Mosque in Mecca ushered in this era. One of the Egyptians we knew in the United States, Hamed, had a brother who happened to be in the mosque right then, performing the 'umra or off-season pilgrimage while looking for undocumented but high-paying labor. The siege occurred while he was in the mosque and he spent over a week there weathering it. It turned out very difficult indeed to get the interlopers out of the Grand Mosque. They had well in advance stashed arms, food and water in the miles of tunnels under the mosque. The Saudi troops were not up to the task. On being shot at they would strip off their uniforms, sometimes buy civilian clothes from hostages and go incognito. Or they would go about in underwear. The occupying zealots would shoot at them anyway.

Meantime, casting about for an exit, our friend's brother found that the place was almost impossible to patrol thoroughly. The outer second-story parapet was almost unguarded. Every day he and others would go out on it and try to work up the courage to jump down to the street below, but the drop was a little too great to be safe. People on the outside would call and whistle for them to jump anyway and that would in time draw the attention of an armed guerrilla, who would drift over and shoo them off. Finally, on the eighth day, people set a stack of mattresses out on the street below and he did jump down safely (but when the police took him in for questioning they saw he had no papers and sent him to Jidda airport, where it took him two days to get a seat to Cairo).

He claimed the people who took over the Grand Mosque had a real grievance, sacrilegious as their act was, even if they had received help from Soviets, directly or indirectly (which it turned out of course they hadn't). They came from a tribe in southwestern Arabia, near Yemen, which had supported the founder of the modern state of Saudi Arabia, Abdel Aziz, in the twenties, at a time when he needed all the support he could get. As the years passed though the royal family seemed to forget the tribe and other old allies. The people who took over the mosque proclaimed their grievances on loudspeakers, making specific charges against individual members of the royal family, mostly to do with too much money going for too many corrupt pursuits, and the charges slowly seeped into Saudi society, where in time they became ensconced as open secrets — indeed were put on tapes that kept on circulating long afterward.

Just a year after the siege of the Grand Mosque Reagan and Bush came to power. A harsh campaign they pursued was to bring about a shift in the focus of America's alliance in the Arab world from Egypt, on which Carter had centered his initiatives, to Saudi Arabia. Reagan and Bush considered, for one thing, that alliance with Saudi Arabia offered a cheap, easy strategy for controlling the other major participants in the struggles shaking and wracking the Middle East, at least over the medium range.

As time went by Reagan and Bush gave in to many of the demands of the Saudi government (or perhaps more accurately its royal family) and acquiesced in dependence on it, whether cynically or through failure of will, in order to maintain this tight alliance. The Saudi royal family imposed very strict terms on its Western ally: there was to be no criticism of Saudi culture, policy, or government in the United States. Reagan and Bush policed all potential sources of criticism of the Saudis, ruthlessly, imposing stringent surveillance, and more, on any American who criticized their ally.

Hand in hand with the extreme discipline Reagan and Bush imposed on their own operatives, there naturally occurred a pattern of wholesale policing of individuals and groups outside the direct control of their system.

The comic strip *Doonesbury*, produced by Gary Trudeau, posed one blatant example of this. In early 1991, as America was pressing an air war on Iraq using Saudi Arabia as its major springboard of attack, *Doonesbury* had several nasty, perhaps even scurrilous panels against Saudi Arabia. The week after, newspapers carrying *Doonesbury* claimed that Trudeau had come down with the flu and could not produce work that week, so they were running strips from the past.

("But don't they always have a big backlog?" my mother asked me when she saw this. "That's what your father said they always do, in newspapers." I nodded.)

The Iraq air war was on by then. And Trudeau did resume his strip the following week but rarely if ever passed comment on Saudi Arabia again. He did, though, remark on the flu, almost three years later, talking about a character named Duke who planted false information about John Kennedy's assassination among conspiracy theorists then fell silent as he was on the verge of revealing some hard details. The commentator stated,

"That was the last panel this feature's creator drew before he fell 'ill' with the 'flu'."*

Time and again the Saudis financed ventures which received American support. This could assume bizarre manifestations, as when the Saudis purchased (or at least sought to purchase) not really critically important weaponry, such as seventy-two F-16 airplanes the government would probably not let its pilots use much or four high-technology AWACS planes they may not have been able to use at all.

During the Iran-Iraq war, which lasted from 1980 to 1988, Saudi Arabia (and its northeastern neighbor Kuwait, also oil rich) gave tens of billions of dollars in aid to the government of Iraq, with which it had been in a state of cold war. The Saudis' purpose in these loans, which it was doubtful would ever be repaid, was not so much to weaken America's client state Iran (which was slowly winning the war) as to keep Iraq fighting, bleeding — and directing its military forces to the east rather than the south.

In the midst of this war, in 1986 a few hours after the Democrats regained a majority in the Senate, a scandal erupted over Reagan's shipments of spare parts and military equipment to Iran in exchange for good offices in the release of Americans held hostage in Lebanon, under Iranian auspices (and transfer of the profits from these shipments to the Contras, a group fighting the legitimate Marxist government in Nicaragua). A senior figure in the Iranian government, Ali Akbar Hashemi-Rafsanjani,

---

* Trudeau remarked further "Pretty bad timing, wouldn't you say? Just as he was about to blow the whistle on the JFK nut cases, the 'flu' nails him! A 'coincidence,' you say? Well, excuse me, but... I don't think so!"

then speaker of Iran's parliament, gave the revelation that Reagan's national security advisor Robert McFarlane, who had been involved in a secret mission to sell TOW missiles to Iran, had taken an overdose of drugs when this became exposed.*

I was amazed at the sight of Rafsanjani's photograph: he was the glib young man in white robe I had seen on the bus in Iran back in 1960. There was no way one could confuse his pudgy, hairless face with anyone else's. Shortly afterward he became president of Iran for a term and virtually the richest man in the country.

Reagan and Bush and their men harshly circumscribed people who had been critical of American oil company practices and policies over the years and their own policies and actions in the Middle East.

Their efforts focused on government bodies pursuing anti-trust actions against the international operations of major oil companies. Two such key actions were a major Federal Trade Commission anti-cartel case and Multi District Litigation 150 (or MDL-150 for short), an anti-trust action I have mentioned which several states, headed by California, had mounted in the seventies.

Among other things, these plaintiffs had come up with touchy material governing oil industry activities in Saudi Arabia as they had been pressing government lawsuits against the parents of the Saudi giant Aramco. Into the eighties, the Saudi government continued to give the four American oil companies which ran Aramco financial benefits other companies could not receive from the nations that hosted their former or reduced concessions. These parents lifted oil for about twenty-eight dollars a barrel when market prices ranged from thirty-four to forty

---

* San Francisco <u>Chronicle</u>, 5 November 1986

dollars. Just before the Reagan era, in August 1980, the lead attorney on the FTC case told me that he had recently attended National Security Council briefings where the sensitivity of pursuing an inquiry into this discrepancy was pointed out to him: the Saudi royal family, he said, was very afraid that a scandal would erupt which would force it to yield control over oil revenues and earnings to the Saudi Bureau of Finance. He also pointed out that when Exxon and Chevron, two of the Aramco Four, had complied with an August 1978 Senate subcommittee subpoena on Aramco engineering problems, the Saudi government cut their liftings back 10 percent.

In MDL-150, where seven states joined forces to sue the major oil companies for fixing oil and gasoline prices and sharing information on pricing strategies in the United States, a marketing professor at Northwestern University, Fred Allvine, had surveyed the movements of retail gasoline prices all over the United States a few years before the 1973 oil price hike cataclysm. He noticed that they looked alarmingly consistent. When he plotted those movements out on graphs he found that they all formed the same curve, a sawtooth pattern. Prices would move up suddenly in each gasoline market once every five to six weeks, then, in a few days, slowly start to decline.

What this suggested was that gasoline prices over the entire nation were regularly jacked up every five or six weeks under tight control, to an artificially high, preset figure. Their slow decline after that represented an erosion resulting from competition, ultimately irrepressible. Each set of diminishing teeth represented a price war every five or six weeks — until the major companies took notice again of the price erosion and once again jacked the price up, overnight, in a vertical line representing no gradually ascending prices.

For a while the case languished. Then the man referred to in an earlier chapter (and never identified) made a surreptitious phone call to the office of the California Justice Department and told an assistant attorney general about the secret Chevron economics department price-fixing brain trust I'd worked near but had never known about.

The trust, the caller said, was under the management of an executive, Theodore Wellman, who supervised Agnar Nerheim, a man overseeing Chevron's biggest market, the Los Angeles Basin. Nerheim's job was to learn all competitors' exact discounts. He had an unwritten special expense account, which he used partly for calling Wellman up after five in the afternoon and passing this information on to him. At Chevron meanwhile the staff in charge of monitoring competitors' prices attended numerous conventions, meetings and luncheons, though they kept the names of persons they met with out of the expense account records they submitted on these lunches — noting only the occasional laconic reference "special account."

Wellman's system within Chevron, the cryptic caller claimed, was a central information-gathering nexus for telephone calls coming from all over the Western region, reporting on the retail prices Chevron's dealers and all its competitors charged and disseminating orders on the levels of retail prices all the companies were to charge.

The conspiracy was hardly restricted to Chevron, the caller went on to state — every major oil company had a system parallel to Chevron's. In the early sixties, at the time of the big changeover from aviation gasoline to jet fuel and, in the railroads, from coal to diesel, Wellman, with Nerheim, also had meetings with representatives from competing firms. Then he would go to his vice president in Chevron's Western Operations subsidiary and dope out policy for carving up the market with those so-called competitors.

A medium-high executive with American Oil in the south, Kenyon Anderson, confirmed this in a lengthy interview he held with the MDL-150 staff. He talked about Allvine's saw-tooth curve. When asked how prices were restored after a price war he replied

Almost all at once. You would get a phone call either from the regional office pricing department or from your district office that prices were being restored in Eldon, Missouri, and surrounding markets, where the price was depressed at a certain time on a certain date. Normally the pattern was tomorrow — tomorrow morning, and this really caused you a lot of work. There were occasions where you might have a latitude of two or three days, but most of the time they would call you two, three or four o'clock in the afternoon and you had to get the word out to everybody that same day and that night, so tomorrow morning when you opened up it was restored.

A major miscreant in Anderson's recollection was Roger Glasgow, who went from American Oil headquarters in Chicago to Atlanta as a pricing manager in 1966. Anderson recalled:

They'd always work this way, always work through Glasgow. I heard it happen ten or twelve times. When there was notification of a market being restored, and all price supports were pulled and here was this thing in the mail, Glasgow would say, "Did anybody talk to anybody in Chicago about this market being restored and didn't tell me about it? Has the district been notified? No. Nobody called us. We got to call those people in Chicago and tell them to communicate better, because right now we are a day late." He would be upset.

Anderson concluded:

With the vast amount of geography involved and the extremely large number of companies, both major and independent competitors, there ain't no way, Baby, that they could have all happened at the same time without this conspiracy. If restorations were not discussed internally, between all the oil companies in the petroleum business, the market would have stayed down forever. I believe that. You'd have never had a price restored in Tampa-Clearwater-St. Pete, if somebody had not gotten together to bring that price back up to where it was before. It would have stayed down forever — Seven or eight cents.

Allvine the marketing professor went on to show that the sawtooth pattern, in evidence for a decade and pronounced for three years or so, then vanished in mid-August 1972. The price curve leveled out and the fluctuations disappeared for good. There were no more gasoline price wars anywhere in America after that time. The 1973 price explosion came right afterward. Allvine's graph was an abstract portrait of an industry at war with its own homeland.

The federal judge hearing the case, William Gray, absorbed this material then turned around and decided to grant the plaintiffs in MDL-150 very broad discovery privileges. Thanks to the discovery, in the end the plaintiffs gained access to three million pages of documents and were able to paint a sufficiently vivid portrait of conspiracy to win a settlement of $150 million, plus $10 million in gasoline vouchers — fifteen years later. Most of this went to the world's biggest fund management organization, the California state employees' retirement fund CALPERS.

At least one Reagan-imposed operative was forced into MDL-150 and engaged in wholesale surveillance, tracking people who came to the attorney general's office to study oil industry documents the state had opened to public scrutiny. He made sure people did not read copies of oil company documents concerning Saudi oil policy and oil company negotiations with Saudi officials — which quite vividly portrayed the negotiating weaknesses of these officials.

One document this CIA operative was assigned to suppress was a transcript of the initial meeting which took place in Geneva in January 1972 between the oil companies and states on the latter's drive to gain a share, or "participation," of at least 20 percent in the concessions, at a very low price, around book value (for highly depreciated facilities). Someone had secretly recorded the meeting, verbatim, then had it done up in a transcript and sent to the various companies. The meeting plainly was staged. The companies had already known exactly what the chief oil state negotiator, Saudi Oil Minister Ahmed Zaki Yamani, would be proposing and had rehearsed their response. Gradually, in a sort of minuet, Exxon's Charles Hedlund brought most of the other company representatives along with him in his willingness to continue the negotiations. Again, it is hard to imagine why Reagan's personnel would have worked so hard to repress the disclosure of documents of this sort unless that was because they suggested that Yamani and his team did not prosecute these negotiations very competently. The participation talks went on slowly and stumbled and groped their way along for the balance of the year and headed toward a resolution in essence rather favorable to the companies.

As we have seen, the 1991 Gulf War, an exercise largely carried out on behalf of the Saudi regime, furnishes an even more immediate example of the Reagan-Bush policies toward its ally. The Bush administration from the beginning of the buildup of the Gulf conflict felt intense concern that American reporters covering the conflict in Saudi Arabia stay within the physical and informational limits the American military forces set out for them. They were to say nothing that questioned the Saudi military's fighting capability or indeed anything else critical of Saudi government policy. When, in the course of the war, fifty Saudi women staged a "drive-in" in the capital, Riyadh, to protest the government ban on women driving, American authorities told reporters they would be sent out of the country if they reported on it.

In a skirmish that preceded the full-fledged war on the ground, in Khafji near Kuwait, military officials waited eighteen hours before allowing a news pool into the town. Several reporters, including the *Chronicle*'s Carl Nolte, in violation of official rules, went on their own earlier and saw that the Saudi military had played a much smaller role in the fighting in Khafji (and the American forces a much greater one) than the Pentagon had claimed.[*]

---

* See also New York <u>Times</u>, July 3, 1991

Another story which did not make the American press was that at least one Saudi pilot was beheaded for returning to base with bombs still in his rack. One Egyptian friend, based in the Saudi west coast city of Jidda, talked of American C-130s so heavily loaded they could barely get off the ground taking off in the mornings from an airbase there then returning hours later, empty and bouncing briskly as they landed.

Some years before Reagan had said, at a press conference during the Vienna summit, "I told you all the truth that first day after the — everything hit the fan, that how we had opened the negotiations that led to the things that were going on then having nothing to do with the Contras, the freedom fighters, in Nicaragua, and that word had come to me that I had not been kept informed.... We were not dealing with the government of Iran."[*]

In 1992, to drive a stake into that era, William Clinton defeated George Bush (the first) and became president. Clinton (as my mother put it anyway) didn't know his place, which was to get Bush out of the White House. However, almost immediately the Israelis, who had been fighting a cold war with the Bush CIA, resumed talking to Palestinian leaders. Perhaps the Palestinians, and even Syrians, had been more eager to resolve matters with Israel than they had seemed, if it was Israeli stalling which prevented the two sides from arriving at any form of understanding as long as Bush was in power. By the end of August a breakthrough occurred in talks between the two sides. On September 13 Yasser Arafat the Palestinian leader and Israel's Prime Minister Yitzhak Rabin signed a framework agreement for peace at the White House. There was an enormous crowd out on the

---

* New York <u>Times</u>, June 12, 1987

lawn to observe it, including eight former secretaries of state, Jimmy Carter, Anwar Sadat's widow Jihan and George Bush. Arafat reached out to shake with Rabin and Clinton had to prod Rabin to get him (stiffly) to extend his own hand. Then after they shook Arafat reached out to Rabin's foreign minister, Shamir Peres, and another high-ranking Israeli figure between the two. Bush looked downcast on this occasion. Not present at this turning point were former presidents Reagan and Nixon.

When Bush pardoned Armand Hammer just before he left office my mother, having as we saw come around, however reluctantly, to finding what I had had to say credible, passed a summary of this narrative on to our old San Francisco friend Betsy Church. She mentioned it to several wealthy conservative friends. They all disparaged it, and people (like me) who embraced it, and so, she concluded, there was truth to the narrative after all. She started to accept that now, by the mid-eighties, the thirties were dead.

25
Hard Times and into Retirement

I t came to seem extraordinary that my mother went off to Kenya and stayed there twenty years, scarcely encouraging family to visit her. Was she hiding something? Some enormous commitment of her wealth to AMREF? Or people out there whom she considered beautiful but wouldn't suffer her presence unless she gave them lavish sums of money? She almost left and returned to the States at about that time, then didn't. Were they, one speculated, about to release her from service because she had gone too old, then changed their minds and kept her on a little after she had given them such lavish sums?

On making phone calls, she did begin dialing 2464. That was our old phone number in Santa Barbara from just after the war. She was finding it harder and harder to tolerate chill.

Not long after, she contracted malarial hepatitis. This vicious disease, which took time to incubate, did not break out till she had moved on to Canada for a visit with Diana and her husband Stephen. There doctors quarantined her instantly and strictly. For nine days they kept her in a room with no access to the outer world but a window and did not even allow a television set or phone in her room for fear she would contaminate them. She was fortunate the hepatitis had struck her in Canada. Unlike an American man roughly her age who'd also contracted the disease in Kenya, she survived.

Not long after that she had a near-fatal auto accident in downtown Nairobi where a driver ran a traffic light and drove straight into the side of her Volkswagen. She survived that, too, though she spent a month in hospital, most of the time with her jaw wired shut in such a way that she could take food (including hamburger pureed with potatoes and vegetables) only through a straw. She summoned Diana to go out, look after her, bathe her and prepare her pureed meals.

The circumstances of her older daughter Mary also furnished a tormenting experience. For a long time Mary had been living on the upper West Side in New York, not far from Columbia University. She had made several attempts on her life but had always sent out signals indicating her plans. Then I began hearing that her condition had declined rapidly. People said she cut off a toe at one point, at another put most of her furniture out on the sidewalk by Broadway.

By that time I had reverted to the single life, which gave me more mobility than I'd had. I would take trips east from time to time and visit Mary when passing through New York and staying with Peter, who also lived there then. Before one trip I called to arrange to meet Mary for dinner on a Wednesday, the day after I planned to arrive, and we set a date. I told her we'd go eat at her favorite Chinese restaurant up Broadway. After arriving that Wednesday morning I called to confirm our dinner and she told me "You were mistaken, Chris. We were to meet last night." I told her I couldn't have made it the night before as I'd got in too late (I'd even written the date down on my calendar, but didn't press that point). She told me she couldn't see me; she'd made other plans. I never saw her again. Three months later she killed herself.

This time she hadn't let us know, hadn't given anyone a chance to talk her out of it or at least say good-bye to her, and now she was irrevocably gone.

It was hard to say how my mother took this. She did not seem moved after the service up in Connecticut — reacted almost blandly. I further believe though that in time she began fearing that she might lose or at least outlive another child or children as well — virtually the cruelest fate in the human condition to bear, regardless of how one feels when the child is still living.

The eventual, reluctant acceptance of the consequences not only of increasing age but also of growing vulnerability to random misfortune drove her to return to California for good. In October 1988 she bought into a unit in an elegant retirement complex in Santa Barbara, Casa Dorinda, and moved into that as her final residence.

One had to admit this retirement community was among the best of its kind. It was in a most elegant setting and was very artfully laid out. It looked magnificent and was well landscaped and manicured, its colors all soft and nicely coordinated, the backdrop of mountains often breathtaking. It consisted, in essence, of low-slung apartment buildings and bungalows among gardens and lawns, spokes radiating out from the hub of a century-old mansion of wrought-iron grills, tiles and brilliant vistas beneath a fine old Spanish bell-tower.

On passing through the lofty, curved entryway to this community, which everyone called the Casa, one saw, on a large signboard, a map of the premises. Glanced at very quickly, it looked to some like a stroke-addled brain, to others a colon as reproduced in a medical textbook. It reminded me of Dora Bradley's late husband Joe railing about his refusal to use a bedpan when thrown in a hospital almost fifty years ago. The residences in the Casa tended to be confining, the food turned more and more to stewed vegetables and boiled meats as the day wore on and the kitchens in the units themselves were almost all minute, to discourage independent cooking. Silence blanketed the place, broken only by the stuttering of lawn-sprinklers. Even the guestrooms — one resident, the famed French chef Julia Child, said they were very nice, just like hospital rooms. None of this drew visible discontent; few of the residents wished for more than they were getting. Observers repeatedly said that maybe forty of the place's 350 residents were "lucid." As one quickly learned, old people in a place such as this would rather be in a spotless environment than an entertaining one. At least one wise guy from the outside kept referring to it as a Moratorium. For my part I kept remembering an old man, hobbling behind a walker, whom my mother claimed had once been a great choreographer. One could leave one's car unlocked about the place — all the thieves around had retired.

One recent arrival in the Casa did find the place most congenial and comfortable. "It's like a permanent cruise, only on land," he said. Another resident, longer-standing, observed "He obviously hasn't been here very long."

As soon as my mother took up residence in the Casa an old friend of hers still living in her own home on the outside asked her incredulously "You like old people?"

My mother soon insisted to all the old friends she could that it was absolutely mandatory they come live in the place with her, if only for their physical well-being. Dora was one person she harangued into becoming a resident.

There were some residents she did find bright and entertaining though. One was her friend Eleanora who'd done public relations work with Conde Nast in Los Angeles. Another resident my mother knew slightly owned the Magic Mountain amusement park just north of Los Angeles, then there was a man who came from Monrovia and knew Trader Joe and a British Jew who'd been in the military in England, where at some ceremonial parade probably involving an archbishop received the order "All RCs, Parsees and Jews take one step back." One of my mother's closest acquaintances was Otto Wittman, who had been a curator in a Toledo art museum for thirty years and then a board member of the Getty Museum. One dinner he described a philosophy he'd preached to fellow board members in Toledo: "You're putting all your money in the bank and earning 2 percent on it but I can buy art with it and it'll really appreciate." He also was involved (successfully, he claimed) in tracing and returning stolen art to its owners after the defeat of Nazi Germany.

At one breakfast I heard a resident state that he used to belong to a motorcycle club in Santa Monica along with a friend who was a son of William Randolph Hearst's. Once this Casa resident, Hearst's son and a few others flew up to the Hearst Castle, back in the days when Hearst still owned it. At one point they went swimming in the pool in the round marble courtyard with its Renaissance columns and statues. Hearst the older was up there and when he spotted them ordered them off the grounds.

At another breakfast some men discussed a recent remark by the right-wing politician Newt Gingrich, who had asserted that men were different from women in that they were biologically able to stay in trenches for a month. One of the men present, a retired urologist, argued that that was true only of the circumcised: you could not stay in a trench more than five days if you weren't. Infections would get under the skin and you'd have to be sent back for treatment (perhaps to your good fortune). Another resident recalled that he had spent twenty-one days in a foxhole once in Bastogne in midwinter, during the Battle of the Bulge with the Third Armored Division. It was too cold for them to run their tank. Finally, when it warmed up enough for them to start it, they moved on. Every time they came to a new town they'd blow away the church steeples at once because those were the German snipers' main place of refuge. This old resident claimed the German Tiger tanks were superior to the American Shermans, except in one particular: they leaked gas and if you could hit the spot where gas leaked you could blow the tank up. He'd gun down Germans with his cannon as they sprang up out of their underground shelters to run for cover.

Yet another breakfast regular, Gregg, had served in the army air corps during the war. He was posted to a base in Florida at one point. In the course of his tour there Clark Gable appeared at the base, assigned to act in a film giving instructions on how to fire a tail gun in a bomber. Gregg said all the women on the base soon had memorized Gable's movements down to his last footstep but he didn't stay there long. He caught his thumb in the gun's loading mechanism and had to be sent back to California on medical leave.

As we have seen, Julia Child the masterful French chef and television hostess lived in the Casa in her last years, having food brought to her from In-and-Out Burger and the inspired Mexican taco shop La Super Rica, among other eateries. My mother took the two of us out to lunch a couple of times. Like most celebrities I'd met, Julia didn't have much to say. She did say the breakfasts at the Casa were good. That was the best time of the day around that place, really. Bustling, with bright colors, when it was sunny, and there were unlimited sausages, bacon, muffins, coffee. She did offer some speculation on a forty-acre mansion Oprah Winfrey had just bought up on East Valley Road, perhaps two miles away. Some said Oprah had been flying over Montecito, saw it and decided to buy it then. Julia said Oprah saw someone unlocking the gate, asked him what he'd take to sell it then when told it wasn't for sale but if it were would probably go for twelve, instantly whipped out a wallet, wrote him out a check for forty (or fifty) and snatched it up. She then proceeded to have dozens of trucks in from Baltimore bearing enormous terra cotta stone blocks from an old railway station, which she then had fashioned into a casting pool.

My mother spent much time talking about Rokeby, often focusing on her widowed sister-in-law, my aunt Susan. I used to find it liberating to drive with Aunt Sue over to my father's area in Connecticut. She said she always found it refreshing to pass into Connecticut from New York. She would leave the communities where patroons had lived on their vast estates, while the common people inhabited what she labeled squalid little communities like Red Hook, and pass into a series of townships which had started as egalitarian religious communities, towns where the first order of business was to provide a decent home for the pastor, after which the rest of the community would be planned outward from that.

My mother complained that Aunt Sue had been drinking, rather. Once when we went to a family wedding I escorted Aunt Sue down the aisle. She rattled like an engine on the verge of shaking itself apart. Then when we got to the reception she smoothed right out. For a while she had been down in High Watch Farm, in Connecticut, and Winty had gone over to visit her. She didn't stay long. He reported that there were various signs on the walls, enumerating steps. Winty said the third step on the list was to abandon oneself to a higher moral force, but his mother, with her skeptical rationalist spirit, couldn't submit to it.

There were the various female relatives at Rokeby, one woman with blue eyebrows, a second with fluorescent raspberry hair, a third with a ring in the middle of her tongue and almost a butch haircut. "That's what's wrong with this country" my mother kept insisting. There was a ceremony under a big tent just down from the ginkgo tree before the piazza and she complained when later Staneeswoff and his lady friend sifted through the garbage bags for cans, of which there were dozens, hundreds, worth a nickel apiece. She complained further about something on a radio in the background, jazz from an album really titled "Ooh Shoobie Doobie Shoo Oooh Oooh," a black woman singing Arabic with some competence "Ya habibi, ya ruh albi -- layla fi Tunis --" then another woman singing "Please don't suck my earlobes like that."

Rokeby, by this time, had begun falling apart — paint peeling, furniture crumbling, the piazza sinking, wood cracking from the lack of heat in wintertime. Ricky said that in the winter they burned fifty gallons of fuel oil a day heating the mansion, at a dollar a gallon. They'd use 2.4 gallons an hour. That came to $6,000 or $7,000 a season.

Ricky had been planning to go down to Pennsylvania with a friend to get a truckload of anthracite then shift the burners over to coal. I had my mother advise him against that on grounds that it would cost a couple of thousand dollars to shift the equipment over and the world oil price was due to drop drastically from its unrealistically high level of that time anyway — as indeed it did. Ricky at some point had left sixty wrecks of vehicles about the four hundred acres of the place. Later I heard my mother narrate all this in spastic phrases, so angry she could scarcely complete a sentence.

An article in the *New York Times* described the condition the mansion gravitated toward later.* Ricky's wife Ania said the tension in the place was between people needing space and the *stuff* needing space, because nothing could be thrown away. Rosalind's daughter Sophia and her partner Alex proceeded to live at Rokeby in 1998, designing the puppet pageant for the New York Halloween parade. Rosalind's other daughter, Marina, started running an organic farm on the premises in 2005. The land acquired a conservation easement: a big private donor gave money for the reconstruction of the mansion in exchange for which the Aldriches agreed to allow no new housing on the estate. Ricky went on to plan a video manual on how to care for the house, showing phone lines and stairwells. To Alexandra, his daughter, life at Rokeby as a child was lonely — "cold, dark and very isolated," except in the summer. The heat didn't work and there were no neighbors.

One mitigating feature of the mansion was work by the family artist, Uncle Robert, who had painted crows on the walls of a bedroom at Rokeby as well as screens

_____

* 22 July 2010, "The House Inherited Them."

which people would set up as partitions between living and dining areas. He was the one original personality among the eight Orphans, an overwhelming figure, six feet four in height, broad-shouldered and rather an iconoclast, with a huge head and bellowing voice to frame his artistic talent. He built a race track in Red Hook, Chanler Park, was sheriff for Dutchess County for a while, used to ride around the county with a six shooter and a ten-gallon hat and spent a great amount of money on his campaigns for local office. He gave excursions on river steamers for children and had a baseball team which used to play in Chanler Park. There he hosted a clambake, the biggest ever held in the county up to that time, and gave out around sixty-five thousand clams. He focused on painting living-room screens after his tour as sheriff and could fetch up to $5,000 for them.

As a young man, around 1910, he became enamored of a lead soprano with the Paris Opera, Lina Cavalieri. The resulting romance, if one could call it that, became at best a major source of gossip, deteriorating into scandal in view of the rather crass materialistic image this great beauty projected. The press at one point even had her stating "Mr. Chanler is very nice, very kind, very good. I like him as much as any man I know. He is very rich too, and that is a nice thing. The money a man has is a part of him, *n'est-ce pas*?... Why can he not be always glad to care for me and not for marriage? Bah! It is an ugly word! And it is so stupid to marry and spend all the time and money getting a divorce, when you need not have been married!"

When they finally did marry the union lasted two weeks. Robert handed the deed containing all his inheritance over to Lina. Within six months she took this deed south. Crossing the border into Mexico, she saw a sign that looked as if it belonged to a bootblack's store, in the words of Robert's nephew Brown Willie, but was no such thing; it read Divorce. "All you need is a marriage certificate," Willie stated. "You don't of course have to have the approval of the other side. This happened when I was practicing law [down on 40 Wall] and I got quite involved." Thanks to him Robert got most of his money back, losing eighty thousand 1912 dollars in a final settlement.

When the story broke he went down to see his brother Archie in Virginia. In the past he had helped Archie get committed for antisocial behavior. This gave Archie the opportunity to trumpet to the press "Who's loony now?" Bob admitted he had signed away most of his fortune because he had lost his wits "with those two white arms" around him. This episode got into the pop culture of the day and by the end of the century even found its way into the *National Enquirer*.

Bob went to live in France for a while in the twenties. Many people did that, my mother claimed. They insisted their purpose was to gain energy from a creative and artistic environment superior to their home world but that was in the heart of Prohibition; in reality they wanted a congenial setting in which to drink.

Bob went on to buy a house on East Nineteenth Street in the twenties and engaged in the moderate pursuit of art and the enjoyment of a lavish bohemian lifestyle. His neighbor across the street, the famous artist George Bellows, became a major participant in his soirees until Bellows' wife forbade him to attend any more of those. Bob died at age fifty-eight, not of a stroke in a bathtub caused by bad Prohibition alcohol, exactly, though that was the story that circulated in his family. When Lina Cavalieri lost her voice, finally, she proceeded to promote a cold cream, with her arms held up over the line "With these two white arms...."

Lina was the one who at age seventy was killed by a random bomb during an American air raid over Florence, as I'd first heard from my grandmother back in Miss Thomas' School during the war.

One figure who sought to keep Robert's work alive was a nephew, Alida's son Tommy Emmet, the scion of the Long Island estate Box Hill by a lavish harbor tucked away half along the North Shore of Long Island, rampant with foliage, ponds, willows, sandbars, marshes, ducks, geese, long green meadows. This was where the other Catholic wing of the family lived, Alida and many of her children. Tommy strove to have some of Robert's best works exhibited in the city — a political move to return relatives to prominence. Some of these were quite striking as I found when I went out once to visit Stony Brook.

The mansion was atop a hill overlooking the water, filled with old leather furniture and Gainesborough-like portraits of relatives long past, done by other relatives long past of some talent but now forgotten. There were shingle-like fences of old photographs in frames of all sizes strewn about at all angles on various round or square tables (one bunch around a magnificent but unexplained ostrich egg). Upstairs, there were old lion claw-mounted bathtubs, bowls and pitchers.

Parts of the Stony Brook house brought back the memories of afternoons in other such houses, like the Andersons' in Marin, with majestic trees and half-acre lawns, trellised fences, gay laughter and the voices of brothers and sisters, which dispersed in late afternoon, leaving nothing but a hollow stonily echoing silence. We would assemble in the cheery kitchen, which had a back staircase leading up from it — on the walls posters titled "Game Birds of the Maryland Coast" and "Winter Birds in Maryland," numerous faded post cards, recipes, discount-flyers and mechanics' calling cards.

Alida had married at Rokeby. They had even arranged a railway car to bring guests up from New York City for her wedding. Then my grandmother renounced Alida for turning Catholic and stopped allowing her around Rokeby as well. When Elizabeth died in 1930 all the Catholic relatives came to her funeral at Sylvania next door.

When I visited, Aunt Alida sat upstairs with a glass of water, surrounded by Catholic icons and images, embedded in the aroma of rubbing alcohol, and stared through intense-lensed glasses, one eye almost in her nose, the other staring straight out and grossly magnified. Unlike my grandmother she had been a beauty. Now she was getting into her nineties and when someone showed her her recent photograph from a magazine she thought it a portrait of the pope. Her second child, Marga Prosser, sat downstairs, deaf, taking photographs of snow patterns and trees, blowing tone deaf on her recorder. Tommy her brother would wince then declare "It's good for her morale" and applaud uproariously. Marga followed and nursed Johnnie the Swan, who was crippled by his parents for returning to their pond and suffering from asthma.

Tommy somehow preserved his sanity, an urbane, polished precious fellow, slender, balding and high-domed, with a fine nose and small mouth, who painted fairly well and sat around with the women. He had a furrowed brow and deadpan expression, broken off and on by a sly smile, and looked rather like a Renaissance man. (In fact some thought he closely resembled Robert

Emmet, in the latter's death mask anyway.) Tommy spent much time talking — parenthetically for the most part — about sin and his obligation to come to grips with it. "I worship two gods," he told me once. I had never heard anyone talk like that at Groton, or Rokeby.

Tommy went on to describe one of the Box Hill cousins, Johnny White, who had visited my mother during the war, when he was in the navy. After the war, "being one of the intermediate ones, a sort of athlete, fallen between two stools as it were, or three or four stools, and constantly dazzled by the Chanler verbosity and craving for attention," he enrolled in the Great Books course at St. John's in Baltimore, fell behind from the start then one day at the Thirtieth Street Station in Philadelphia called his family and said "I'm lost, I can't find my way. Please come and get me."

Peter White, another of the Box Hill cousins, had stagnated for three years, was barely getting by financially, then, word about the family had it, took two train rides to Long Island, in the first of which he encountered a man who wanted to sell his factory in Queens, in the second a man who wanted to buy a factory with his surplus capital. Peter merely pointed out the window to the man, got the two together and collected a $10,000 fee. That was a nice sum in those days.

Some years before, my grandmother had made up with Alida. They met at the Colony Club in New York and gossiped for several hours about the past forty years they'd spent apart from each other. Afterward, a niece asked my grandmother what her impression of Alida had been. "That hideous old woman!" she cried out. Hideous? True, Alida was no longer the beautiful lady my grandmother had last seen — and had never been herself.

26
America Squanders
Its Triumph

We finally encountered the historic irony we had lived almost half a century to see. An item from the Associated Press stated "Six months after opening, the Golden Arches" — the world's biggest McDonald's, less than a mile from the Kremlin — "have eclipsed the popularity of even Lenin's tomb, where a recent wait to see the preserved body of the Soviet founder took only 20 minutes." During the lunch hour at that McDonald's it was taking ninety minutes to get fast food. The *Times* had reported the same a few months before, so it was not a fluke.

In 1983 Soviet Marshal Nikolai Ogarkov had told the *New York Times* reporter Leslie Gelb, off the record, something all the Rokeby Poles knew though it took Gelb's story nearly a decade to come out in America. When Gelb had complained about the Soviet Union's excessive spending on defense, Ogarkov just waved him off with a sardonic smile. Then he proceeded to make the most astonishing argument Gelb had ever heard from a Soviet official: the Soviets could not equal the *quality* of American arms for a generation or two, and that was far more important than the matter of quantity, because modern military power was based on technology derived from computers. And, the marshal went on, as everyone knew, while in the United States small children played with computers even before school and computers could be found everywhere, it was "for reasons you know well" not possible for his government to allow widespread computer use in the Soviet Union. Even the Defense Ministry did not have computers at hand in every office.

After the collapse of the Soviet empire, in late 1990, Eric Honecker, previously in essence dictator of East Germany, sold an interview to a small Viennese publishing agency which ended up in a London weekly. The former Polish leader Gierek's memoirs were a bestseller, Jaruzelski was shopping for an agent in the West, the former Bulgarian chief Zhivkov was giving interviews in Bulgaria, and the Czech Dubcek had signed a contract for a book. General Nicolae Plesita, former chief of Romania's Securitate, gave numerous public statements about old tasks ordering the bombing of Radio Free Europe's offices in Munich and finding shelter for the terrorist Carlos the Jackal, as well as contriving various assassination attempts. In Hungary, someone from the *New York Times* interviewed Miklos Vasarhelyi, who'd done four years in prison after functioning as Imre Nagy's press secretary. "There are problems, but they don't worry me," that commentator asserted. "What worried me was to live under a dictatorial system and foreign domination. All other worries are peanuts compared to that."

Then August 19, 1991, grim and early, we saw the headline "Gorbachev Out. " Two, maybe three inches high. There had been a coup, all right, with a morbid Russian inevitability to it all. Tanks rolled in and around Moscow, wantonly. Military figures said they had tired of the failure to improve the system for distributing basic goods and the Group of Seven hadn't given Gorbachev money. But but but there was Yeltsin, Who Takes No Shit From Anyone. Tanks ringed him. Tuesday evening I told someone "Say goodnight, Boris." But Boris was delivering a harangue, from a tank that didn't fire on the Federal Building. And the next day, sixty hours after they started it, the people who ran the coup were routed. December 21, Yeltsin in a formal letter asked if the Russian Republic could join NATO. December 22, the Soviet Union was officially dissolved. Our cold enemy of my lifetime, that part of it since Hitler anyway, no longer existed. December 25, Gorbachev formally resigned. A year later I phoned the old Soviet Consulate on Green Street in San Francisco to learn that the nation now called itself the Russian Federation.

Even the arch-nationalist Vladimir Zhirinovsky, who bore irredentist grudges, seemed not to want to return Russia to the farthest reaches of the Cold War. A map he drew up of the new Russia included Slovakia, to be sure, all the republics of the former Soviet Union and all of Estonia, Latvia and Lithuania — except for city-states in Tallinn and Kaunas and also part of eastern Poland. Notwithstanding that, there was still a buffer zone we had lacked all during the Cold War: Poland, the Czech Republic, Hungary, Croatia, Serbia and Slovenia though Zhirinovsky would hand that over to Germany (which probably wouldn't accept it).*

---

* San Francisco <u>Chronicle</u>, 2 February 1994

Vaclav Havel, soon to be president of Czechoslovakia, said that the Communists had suspended history — antagonisms based on ethnic rather than economic grounds had been held to be irrelevant, suppressed, forcibly kept out of public discourse. But the antagonisms hadn't gone away. When the Communist writ collapsed they sprang back into life, all over eastern Europe, in Yugoslavia spectacularly but also in Czechoslovakia and Romania.

Weren't we now in a time of great anticlimax? What credible enemy remained, except rot in our own country?

Katrina Moomaw, an eleven-year-old girl from Lancaster, California, gateway to Edwards Air Force Base, paid $8,500 for a flight in a MiG-29, Russia's fastest fighter. This was through the Florida-based firm MiGs Etcetera (training perhaps included). She had a Russian test pilot perform the takeoff and landing but handled long maneuvers in a special helmet and oxygen mask. "I broke the sound barrier and it was very neat," she said. Next ambition: leading a manned mission to Mars.[*]

Finally, by around the turn of the century, there was Alaska Airlines, making it possible for one to fly from Magadan, Stalin's great Siberian concentration camp city, to the Mexican resort Mazatlan, with just one stopover in Anchorage.

In April 1993 Lt. Gen. Mallory, Commander of the Sixth Army, gave Mikhail Gorbachev a symbolic key to a house in the Presidio of San Francisco, which would function as headquarters for the Gorbachev Foundation/ USA. There was a full-color photo on the front page of the paper showing Gorbachev at a lectern before a row of flags and the Golden Gate Bridge and various notables seated

---

[*] San Francisco <u>Chronicle</u>, 15 July 1994

behind the lectern: Mayor Jordan; Walter Shorenstein a local magnate; former senator Alan Cranston and, in his Smokey the Bear hat, Recreation Superintendent O'Neill.

The era ended from another angle on Friday April 22, 1994, around nine o'clock New York time, when, after a clot in his leg moved up into his brain, Richard Nixon suffered a cerebral edema then died. At that, one dissident observed eighteen and a half minutes of silence. Someone else inquired "Will there be a used-car procession to the cemetery?"

My mother did not feel the slightest remorse. Shortly afterward Jackie Onassis died and my mother stated that the leisurely grace of her funeral was "such a relief after all that fuss over Nixon."

Still and all I felt a little sense of loss — as indeed did his adversary in the 1972 presidential elections, George McGovern. Nixon had poured out ideas and books in service of his view of the Cold War right up to a month or so earlier, when he reported his findings on his latest visit to Moscow in the *New York Times*, a fairly nice piece of writing. He was more than a mere hack, thug and jerk, he was also a fact of life — and, as one came to see within the coming decade, a professional.

27
Droves in Angloland

I came upon George Gund at the San Francisco Film Festival's opening cocktails. These had moved on to the Presidio's Building 39, which George had taken over as part of the massive privatization program the old Sixth Army headquarters was going through. The area was all solid hardwood and iron buildings with scant traffic and plenty of parking. Also in attendance were Jeanette Etheridge, the proprietor of Tosca, a tavern (and after-hours hangout) in North Beach, and co-chairman of the festival with George; Nancy Pelosi's husband, Paul; and Robert Redford (a tenant subletting a studio in the building; he informed me his father had worked thirty-nine years for Chevron, where he would get summer jobs).

That year the San Jose Sharks led their division in the National Hockey League, as they had the previous year. A *Chronicle* report predicted that "an ownership change" in the Sharks could occur shortly.

Now George told me that the NHL players' union, somewhat acrimonious in spirit, had accused him, along with all the other team owners in the league, of making money while claiming to operate at a loss. George insisted that was not so and invited the union to send accountants of its choice, at his expense, to examine his books. It did, found that George had been telling the truth and groused "Well, then, you're the only one who's being honest about it."

Later George sold most of his holdings in the Sharks but retained a minority share in the team. This gave him among other things the right to perform scouting missions for the team. His other professional sports interest, the Cleveland Cavaliers, had registered a fourfold increase in attendance with the acquisition of the previous year's top NBA draft pick, the high school phenom LeBron James. Meantime his wife Iara had been studying French, Italian and Arabic in Sidi Bou Said, Tunisia.

In early November the *Chronicle* reported that the city's Art Institute, at a Gala De Cuba benefitting its scholarship fund, honored George, a former trustee and longtime benefactor. Mojitos were served and the guests, who included Ellen Coppola and Oakland's Mayor Jerry Brown, dined on a Dan McCall dinner as a documentary on Cuba was shown on the walls.

George went on to participate in a celebrity hockey event in Las Vegas, perhaps the guest of his friend Steve Winn, the grand casino entrepreneur (and, surprisingly, rather enlightened employer), who felt an affinity with George's brother Gordon as they both suffered from retina pigmentosa, an intractable degenerative eye disease.

Not long after that I went on a visit to Santa Barbara. While shopping at a nearby supermarket I encountered a woman with a face I found faintly familiar. I asked her her name. She was Julia, the high-school medical enthusiast I'd known as a child, who'd told me Julia was not her original name.

I asked what had become of them all. She said she herself had gone into hospital administration and was on the verge of retiring. As for Charles, she shook her head and her eyes turned moist. They'd found him someplace in Europe, with no identification on him but a Liechtenstein driver's license. Well, it was the scourge, she said. A few years ago he'd stopped off in New York, met someone in a bar and the next day had him take him to the airport. As he boarded the plane, the other man handed him a box. Once on the plane he opened it. There was just a rock inside and the label Welcome to the World of AIDS.

On September 9, 1998, I got a call from my mother telling me that Aunt Sue had just died. Naturally, this saddened me, though it didn't really shock me. The last time I'd seen her she'd had to get around by walker. The next morning I talked to Ricky and Winty, who told me she'd had a stroke the week before, then another more critical one the day before she died, slipped into a coma and was dead in thirty-six hours. Almost exactly the way Hoda's father had died. As I told Rickie, I'd known her all my life.

My mother made it to the funeral. She found it rather grisly because it was attended by a leader of a sect who had obscure beliefs about killing and ritual sacrifice. The adherents went about in white robes smeared with blood and kept a fire going outside until my mother insisted to Winty that he had it put out, lest it set off a conflagration. They kept Aunt Sue's body in her bed the night after she died — before my mother got up there — then had her cremated and put her ashes in her bedroom till the funeral at St. John's. My mother slept in her house, just down the hall, but felt good about that; it was a final act of bonding, communing. She'd also spent the night in the reception room next to her mother's coffin when she died back in 1963. My mother also said that Winty Emmet was there, as part of the huge throng, one of Alida's sons, therefore a first cousin of hers. One of the very last.

By then, Winty Aldrich claimed, my mother, Brown Willie (about to celebrate his ninetieth), Ashley and Winty and Jane Emmet were the only surviving children of the Orphans, and David Aldrich was my mother's only surviving first cousin. Also still alive was Hubert Chanler's widow Beatrice. Ashley, however, died three months after our meeting.

I felt on hearing my mother mention the word "droves" that English was an archaic language with arcane medieval spelling, impossible vowels and consonant clusters and strange verb forms and plurals, while Spanish was hip, stripped down, a language of the young and efficient. Of course that illusion faded as soon as one drove away from the Casa and returned to hip enclaves of Angloland.

George Gund died some years later, in early 2013, of stomach cancer in another home he maintained, in Palm Springs (during a stretch of abnormal cold). Thanks to his major presence as a civic figure in many parts of the world he received detailed obituaries in the *Chronicle*, the Cleveland *Plain Dealer* and the San Jose *Mercury News,* as well as the *New York Times*. His memorial service was held on January 25 at San Francisco's Grace Cathedral. His wife Iara had gone on to produce *Cultures of Resistance* and most recently a documentary on Syria's uprising and strife on its border with Turkey, but she would not be able to release it until the struggle was resolved.

28
End Game:
A Century's Survivor

To the Casa staff, struggling to keep their community looking spotless and brilliant, my mother started to become an irritant. First of all, she walked around; few residents actually did. Much of the time she wore a baseball cap and rather dowdy clothes.

I saw more clearly than before that she was stuck in the Casa. For her it was a dead end (the last stop, really) and, old as she was and slowed down, she sought to get out any chance she could. She worked it so we would have lunch at a little bistro in La Cumbre Plaza, a mall on the other side of town. It was a nice place — you could just see the crest of La Cumbre Peak from the table where we were sitting out in the central esplanade. In the brilliant light through a narrow defile between the sharp stone wall of Macy's and a stand of oaks to the east, you almost felt in the presence of a lofty palisade in Yosemite looking up at that peak. Small kids were darting around, splashing water, but as my mother had gone deaf the sound of their shouts and screams no longer bothered her. She hardly went there at all, though, since she had almost no way of getting there. She insisted on dropping by See's Candies and picking up a box of honey molasses chips for a friend, also at the Casa, whom she kept almost totally to herself because she didn't want others nosing in, wondering why she liked that woman, perhaps even trying to torpedo the relationship (Eleanora especially — we had breakfast with her every day).

My mother began to turn indifferent to time and less and less comfortable with numbers. She'd also started meandering, as they put it, at rather odd hours. More than once Security found her huddled in an elevator late at night. At four one morning she told the guard on duty she was looking for warmth. She archly accused another guard of lying when saying he'd found her in the Napoleon Room at two in the morning. Then an acquaintance spotted her walking in the nearby shopping district, again at two AM. Another time she appeared in a cab, trying to pay the driver with the key to her unit.

"This place hasn't done anything since its days as a mansion except host a mediocre girls' school, and then be a place to dump old people," she told me. "I can't stand it here any longer and I'm going to leave." It took me an hour to make the case, forcefully, that she had nowhere else to go and this was the best possible place for her anyway. I almost cried as I described the library in the central mansion, where she'd always be able to go, with its broad fireplace, wide range of up-to-date books and plush leather sofa.

We descended into lower geriatric care rungs — hell rungs? At the top of course there was the Casa residential unit, a charming if cramped apartment like hers, or better, Dora Bradley's, with deck views of the main building and Medical Center towers. Then there were the rooms in the Personal Care Unit, the PCU. I went to the PCU once to visit Alexandra after she'd been found falling in her apartment and they moved her in there. I did feel after the visit that it was rather a sad place to be sent to. Secluded, but basically just a large room, thirteen feet by seventeen, with a high slanted ceiling and a little deck outside. No space for a galley or microwave. Various old people hunched forward over a cane or walker as nurses with paper cups padded up and down the halls. Then the Medical Center, a hospital room, hospital bed and swinging table, alas, but perhaps bright from two directions, as in the one Innis occupied (he too had moved into the Casa finally), and the potential for decoration, with his antique furniture and walls of fine paintings and amusing photos.

Then we descended farther, to the Alzheimer's clinics. We had Villa Alamar and the less undesirable, sepia-toned Mission Villa, but the same cast of vacant characters and the disheartening entertainment, the ubiquitous TV and oldies guitar or accordion concerts. Or, as in the Villa Alamar, religious music: When the roll is called up yonder I'll be there. Ay, men. Then the next notch down, the Buena Vista out on Patterson in Goleta, where I went with my mother and Dora in her Volvo to see the old tennis enthusiast Haley Fiske. He was lying coughing liquidly on a curtained-off bed, one of three men in a medium-sized hospital room. No space even for a TV set. He was lying on his back, *News-Press* on his lap, still sharp but basically immobile. Leila had told me not long before that people died pretty much the way they lived. The place was taking almost all Haley's income, now slightly more than $500 a month (mostly from his participation in two World War Two invasions). He would walk down three long halls to the entrance or the TV room for the exercise, faint as that was, or the meals, which were awful, he said. Terrible.

I believed him. There was no place a barely ambulatory person like him could go, off the grounds. No shopping areas or delis nearby.

What was the next rung down? The decrepit trailers over by Dwight Murphy Field across from the zoo? I'd noticed that people were no longer allowed to park there overnight.

My mother promised she would never wander again, but that was not enough to satisfy the authorities. After three months of struggle and pressure she gave in, handed them the key to her apartment and signed a release on it. She still had a duplicate key, but Peter suggested he keep that, then passed it on to me and I handed it over to the authorities as well.

At first they moved her out of her old unit into a large room in the Personal Care Unit. It became more and more starkly apparent to me that given her ego and her long history of total independence, total freedom to move just as she liked, which she'd had for almost exactly forty years, since the death of Byron, this move was tantamount to death. Her physician told me, when they tried moving her to the PCU, that part of her attitude was guilt. "I've done something wrong. I've committed a crime and have had to pay for it. But what did I do? Just try to walk down the Coast Village Road?" (In the dead of night?)

At first I rather empathized with her, felt sorrow over her plight. They moved her bed over to the temporary unit, along with a photo of Michael Wood. "That's it — I'm leaving in the morning, getting the train," she announced, and called the staff people frauds.

They still couldn't keep total watch on her movements, so they transferred her to the Medical Center. It had many doors to the outside, though, and it was not feasible for the authorities to put a keypad on each one (to prevent anyone who did not know the code from leaving). She wandered out of that fastness as well. Exasperated, out of their depth by then, the authorities told me to take her thirty-five miles down to St. John's Hospital in Oxnard, the closest place with a geriatric "acute care center," for a lengthy evaluation. They allowed me to stay in my mother's PCU room till one evening I wandered into the lobby to watch TV, only to see a couple of nurses watching soft porn with the sound off.

Driving down to the geriatric center I told my mother a soldier who'd just been killed in Iraq had come from Oxnard, but she didn't understand what I was saying. (In all fairness, one must admit that very few others around, there or anywhere else, could understand why he'd been in Iraq either, how we were losing a decade and up to four trillion dollars through the hubris of Ralph Nader, who gave the 2000 presidential election to Bush and Cheney and empowered them to invade Iraq — which Al Gore, the real winner, would never have done.)

The "acute care" center was on the fourth floor of St. John's, a large gray steel and glass battleship (with a couple of plywood-covered windows on the third floor). One could get into the center only by calling over a phone then passing through a door with keypad and alarm. As soon as it clicked open for us a man in a wheelchair yelled "Open it wide!" and tried to zip out, only to be yanked back in by a nurse. Some of the walls beyond, it turned out, were padded. A woman about my age came up to me. "Hey, I want to talk to you," she announced.

Once lodged in this center, my mother befriended a grizzled, trim silvery-haired guy. He suffered from Parkinson's, almost to the point of disorientation. The Saturday before daylight saving time I noted that they should change the time on the "dining room" clock and he said "Not that it makes much of a difference around here." Sunday I saw him walking around, endlessly squeezing a tennis ball. "When you get to where you have to end it all, you no longer can," he charged further. Then another time he came out of his room yelling "You took away my razor!" at a beautiful Asian nurse.

Someone else stated "Of course she took away your razor, else you'd slash your wrists."

"That's not funny," he snapped.

One psychologist in the wings shrugged over all this, claimed "They hardly shrink 'em anymore anyway. They've simplified it now. Psychoanalysis is a dinosaur. It worked beautifully up to about 1950, in a world that does not exist any longer. That ended with the end of the written word."

One cannot tell if a living person has Alzheimer's (unless the person is drooling helplessly, which my mother was not). However, they put her on Zyprexa, soon to become the subject of a big scandal as it was a medication for schizophrenia, not dementia. Then after a couple of weeks they sent her to the Villa Alamar, the grim Alzheimer's facility back in Santa Barbara.

At one point, sitting in one of her armchairs in her room there, she told me "I have nothing to look forward to." Sitting on her bed she said she kept thinking she'd lost part of her face and sat running her hands over her cheeks: "I've lost it — how? Have I lost these things (hearing aids)?" There were people wandering into her room, a couple of newly-admitted men especially, then Nellie, who resented having been moved out of the room so my mother could move into it. The men, she claimed, tended to get into bed with her at night — though that happened to other women as well, so the meager staff had to correct the situation, fast. "All the time I was with Byron I never saw any crooks," my mother remarked further. "They need to go to a place that's really bad. Worse than this."

Finally, her family raised stiff objections to her detention in this place, even though the Casa was paying the difference between her monthly residence fee and what the Villa charged (almost $6,000 a month, for a drab room with bath and access to a backyard with basketball hoop and overstuffed sofa). When the family brought in a lawyer to investigate the Casa's moves, they let her back to the Medical Center.

She picked back up for a while. There were Donald Patterson the doctor and wife by the elevator on the second floor as she came in and she sprang to life with recognition. "You've been searching for me and now you've found me!" she exclaimed. She had known them about sixty years, after all.

At another point she told me "I don't have very much memory. I do remember a little bit but then it disappears. I'm trying, but I do hurt a lot.... It's not easy to feel unless you're *it*."

Staring at Animal Planet, which she was doing for hours now, she declared "These animals keep doing the same thing." Then, watching tennis, she said she was just staring at a bunch of people batting a ball back and forth with sticks.

I came to know an aide, Aurora, one of the rare Mexicans there who came from the state of San Luis Potosi. She mirrored the world of the Hudson estates in the newer communities like Santa Barbara or indeed

286

Aspen, Colorado, where maids, nurses, gardeners and other service providers had to live far away from the expensive places where they worked. She had a thirty-five-mile commute every day to the Casa from her home down in Oxnard. She was not a tourist and was a good source of information on the inner workings of the place.

When I arrived in the evening and mentioned the previous visit, with my younger daughter Camilla, my mother frowned in perplexity and asked "Kahlua?" Watching Julia Child whisked off in a wheelchair she remarked "Oh that's Mrs. Cook — didn't we have lunch once?"

Julia died shortly after and I heard from Aurora that the administrative manager assembled most of the wait staff and told them they'd get into serious trouble if they let anyone in the outer world hear that Julia had just died there. Nobody dared. We didn't see any vans with telescoping antennas in the parking lots that weekend.

Even when my mother had her sophisticated hearing aids on I had to repeat almost everything. "You left it in the bag?" "I put it in *back*."

In the second-floor dining-room, two old women in wheelchairs sat staring, eyes glazed, as a tape played Indrani Bogoda singing in Sinhalese, one of the nurses' tongues. Out in the hall a man sat in a wheelchair by the nurses' station, growling "Hellooohhh" to anyone who passed by, even if the person tried to slip around him unnoticed. (He made one exception, in the case of a buxom lady whom he always addressed "Hellooohh Fatso.") It so happened the man, a professor emeritus, had been a major figure in the development of the atomic bomb, working at Los Alamos as Oppenheimer's deputy in World War Two. At one point during the war, the fellow's obituary said later, Oppenheimer lost faith in the project and in despair announced that he was going to resign. This deputy talked Oppenheimer around — indeed he was perhaps the voice who had saved the bomb, over sixty years in the past.

Though my mother'd started babbling more or less incoherently, she'd be smiling sometimes. "It's theoretical," she announced, as she kept pushing to try to work her way up off her bed and into a standing position. Time and again she insisted her mother was still alive, still lingering in a room upstairs near the swimming pool (she herself lived on the top floor).

She kept talking about her mother, more than forty years after her death. "I still think of her all the time," she repeatedly said. "I'm still looking for her approval, every time I think of something or set out to do something. She had such a strong personality."

Then my mother began desperately trying to get out. At first she tried to wriggle out of bed. She worked to propel herself out by wheelchair, once they put her in that — I saw her by the nurses' station, being attended to by a couple of aides, then when we took her back to her room she tried wheeling out again. I set the brakes on her wheelchair but that did no good — she either undid them or just shoved along with them still on. It was even worse the next day. She kept reaching out at me, telling me to take her to my car then to Rokeby, which was nearby. She hadn't talked like that in several years. Then at supper back in her room, after screaming when they changed her diaper, she grabbed the food cover and tried dashing it to the floor, then lashed out furiously when an aide tried to feed her or at least offer her food. The aide however did leave her a grilled cheese sandwich and she proceeded to devour that — something I had not seen in years either.

I couldn't cope with these outbursts any more than I ever had. I kept thinking of an outburst she had had back in the days of propellor airplane travel when you were allowed only to check twenty pounds of baggage at no charge. Traveling with my siblings it turned out we were overweight. The excess baggage fee might have come to twenty dollars all told but our mother told us, "All right, open your suitcases and remove the excess" — which we did, right on the floor by the counter, blocking off all the passengers in the line behind us. That unpleasant scene put us on the plane without paying any charges. I had no more success coping with these scenes now than the airplane personnel had in the past. I tried to make sense of them, interpret them for signs of a real driving force behind them — being demented of course she couldn't respond rationally to whatever was eating her. It was panic, I decided — maybe at the prospect of death. Diana claimed she was trying to get out of her body but didn't know how.

Then I saw her doctor. He agreed that what she was going through was very unusual for her. He offered the conjecture that she had developed a new form of pain but of course couldn't describe it. Maybe she was suffering from a growing tumor that she couldn't point to, and they could hardly investigate, as it'd probably take an MRI to do so — totally unworkable of course with anyone who couldn't lie still for an hour in a raucous cramped cylinder.

Then she'd be mentally quite alert, stating how horrible the food was, pointing to a piece of hamburger I'd just cut up for her with her fork, looking over at me and grinning sarcastically. My visits, though frequent, always ended. Almost each time she told me I was going back to Rokeby, and would I take her with me? It was too long a trip, I'd reply — a full five hours on the freeway.

She still derived one pleasure from life: she loved to be driven around. I took her to the Carpinteria Beach State Park, where we managed, barely, to find a narrow space in eighty-seven-degree weather and hobble over to the lot where our beach house had once stood — the state had condemned it long ago and now its site had become mere barren ground. A Santa Ana wind brewed up as the weekend progressed and it got warmer and warmer. But since it had been raining up till a few days before, most hills were still green — a touch dark, when the sun wasn't on them.

Her life, what remained of it, had become a long telephone line strung along a stretch of poles tapering off to the far horizon and beyond, each pole holding up the line though that often sagged almost to the ground at the midpoint between some of those poles.

In time those poles faded down into the ground. She lived almost six months beyond her hundredth birthday. It was another trip back in time going down the old 101 after she had departed. As she used to say, 101 was an efficient medium for effecting the transfer from the real world to Santa Barbara.

Along the coast the Big Basin redwoods, Big Sur, the Hearst Castle, San Simeon. They still had the old Highway 1 signs in those days, black and white with the stalking bear over the number.

It was bright even in Salinas however, windy. Within a fifty-mile radius grew 70 percent of the vegetables consumed in America: enormous steel tarantulas kneeling over the lettuce fields, the gentle green alluvial slopes of the Santa Lucia foothills in the background. Around Greenfield the stench of boiled broccoli. Yet farther down in a billboard in Spanish: Clamato y cerveza — ¿ya los mezclaste? (Clamato and beer — have you mixed them?).

Farther south it became more palatable: Have you mixed Clamato and tequila?

The centipede-shaped Atascadero, home of the state hospital for sexual deviates, probably the roughest psychiatric testing ground around. (In the middle of what used to be nowhere, an Adopt-a-Highway sign for Temple Ner Shalom.) In Atascadero I really did see a white old sedan with curb feelers. Then, as I proceeded along past the entrance to the state facility, a very long brown limousine was swinging back into traffic from the place.

San Luis Obispo, San Luis Obispo de Tolosa, named for St. Louis the bishop of Toulouse. All of California was Franciscan during its days in the Spanish empire. Los Angeles' full name was Nuestro Pueblo de Los Angeles de Porciuncola, "Our Village of the Angels of Porciuncola," St. Francis' personal chapel in Assisi.

Beyond, by the tufts of green, a wall of steel gray — perhaps the ocean, maybe the sky. On the eastern side of the road a thick, impenetrable eucalyptus forest which had gone wild for fifty years. Lodged in this forest, around a bend, was a gas station, later reconstructed into a shop where they sold olives of all flavors and avocados of all sizes for almost nothing. Then forgotten oilfields, blue and orange pumps all run by the old Union Oil — Lompoc, Guadalupe, Cat Canyon — and the essentially Mexican town of Guadalupe, just south of the Santa Maria River. Here it was hard to tell where the fertilizer ended and the broccoli and cauliflower began on the brilliant flat green fields. It hit me that someone who was kidnapped and thrown in a trunk might well be able to trace the route he was taken over by the smells: "It was onions (after a specific succession of others), so I could tell we were in the foothills just south of Bakersfield."

The town was one street of sooty brick building-facades sheltered by distant dunes starting white then gradually going vermillion. These dunes were fantastic — high, unending, the same color as the flares licking up from stacks of Union's almost perfectly hidden Arroyo Grande refinery just behind.

Then, on the outskirts of Santa Barbara, a big truck for the grocery chain Jordano's with the legend www.jordanos.com.

I could imagine in the forties, in our house across from where Jordano lived then, going over to his house and stating "Half a century from now you will have your own website."

This last visit was focused on a cemetery overlooking the ocean. There was the Pacific, shrugging away at the coastline. In the wind and heat, the air turned Middle Eastern — an overpowering hot dusty sky as the afternoon wore on, stark yellow. There was humidity in the air some places, reminiscent of the air about the Nile, or San Jose's Central Expressway among the heavy trees. It was as warm as I'd ever seen it in Pismo Beach, too; no fog till Santa Barbara, near dusk.

The most affluent tenants had plots right at the south edge of this cemetery, overlooking the ocean, so they could hear the ocean roar, perhaps. (In time it became necessary to move those in, as the surf eroded that cliff.) Our mother's site was in still farther and after a service, mantras and a few brief comments we placed her urn next to Byron's coffin.

Not long before then one Casa tenant told me "No one is born with a hundred-year warranty." She had been.

Index

Fish, Hamilton 9, 10, 240
Flam, Herb 85
Fletcher, Joseph Francis IV
    ("Joe") 159, 242
Flying Doctors Society (Flying
    Doctors, The) 210, 214,
    215, 216, 219
Follis, R. Gwin 189, 191
Ford, Gerald 195, 241
Foxen Canyon Road 42, 82
Francis, Henrietta 167
Francis, Henry 60
Fuchs, Klaus 34

G

Gable, Clark 262
Galbraith, John Kenneth 229
Galvin, George 210
Garrison, William Lloyd 29
Gelb, Leslie 271
Geneva 253
Gershwin, George 39
Gingrich, Newt 261
Girard, Private 114
Girvetz, Harry 53, 54, 140
Glasgow, Roger 251
Gonzalez, Richard ("Pancho")
    86, 87, 88
Gorbachev, Mikhail 274
Gore, Al 284
Gorham, Hal 52, 88
Graf Spee 9
Graham, Bill 203
Grand Mosque, The 244, 245
Grass, Guenter 120
Gray, Judge William 253
Great Nefudh, The 243
Green, Adam 229, 231

Green, Martha McGahan 11,
    14, 16, 52, 229
Groton School 36, 43, 60, 63,
    64, 65, 66, 74, 75, 78, 95, 97,
    98, 99, 105, 111, 126, 127,
    128, 139, 159, 196, 198, 199,
    201, 202, 232, 270
Gulf War, 1991 254
Gund, George 96, 199, 232,
    276, 279
Gund, Gordon 233, 234, 277
Gund, Iara Lee 232, 235, 277,
    279

H

Halberstam, David 202
Hammer, Armand 187, 256
Harvard University 107, 305
Hashemi-Rafsanjani, Ali
    Akbar 247
Havel, Vaclav 274
Hayes, Helen 73, 75
Hayes, Rutherford B. 10
Hearst Castle, The 261, 290
Hearst, William Randolph
    238, 261
Hedlund, Charles 253
Heikal, Muhammad
    Hassanein 157
Hemingway, Ernest 136, 138,
    149, 221
Herald Tribune, The New York
    36, 58
Herodotus 243
Hess, Dame Myra 71
Hitler, Adolf vii, 9, 10, 18, 19,
    140, 273
Holmes, Johnnie 14, 15
Homberger, Eric 7, 121

Lorentz, Elizabeth ("Bis") 38
Lorentz, Pare 38, 88
Los Alamos (New Mexico) 33, 34, 287
Los Angeles 36, 39, 40, 52, 81, 84, 86, 87, 89, 97, 101, 159, 164, 165, 171, 178, 250, 261, 291
Los Angeles Basin, The 250

M

Madison, President James 2
Maidu (Indian language) 134
Make, Maya 157
Maleter, Pal 104, 106
Marfa (town in Texas) 34
Marin County (California) vii, 5, 6, 14, 19, 20, 23, 31, 32, 38, 41, 42, 53, 58, 90, 99, 100, 101, 113, 120, 121, 133, 135, 136, 137, 139, 140, 166, 167, 188, 192, 195, 202, 216, 230, 240, 248, 250, 253, 259, 262, 274, 291, 305, 306, 307
Markham, Beryl 221
McAllister, Ward 7, 120
McCarthy, Mary 39, 131
McFarlane, Robert 248
McGahan, Martha. *See* Green, Martha McGahan
McGovern, George 275
McNamara, Defense Secretary Robert 241
Mead, Margaret 131
Mecca, Grand Mosque 244
Medical Center, The 282, 284, 286
Midway (aircraft carrier) 56, 79, 197, 199

Miller, Otto N. 191
Miramar Hotel 220
Miss Thomas' School 6, 11, 22, 32, 34, 35, 268
Mobil Oil Company 190, 306
Monache (Indian language) 134
Moore, Roger 66
Morris and McVeigh 206, 207, 208
Moss, Robert 64, 128
Mount Riga 170, 171
Multi-District Litigation 150 (MDL-150) 248, 249, 251, 253
Munroe, Louisa 74

N

Nader, Ralph 284
Nagy, Imre 104, 272
Nairobi 210, 215, 216, 218, 219, 258
Nan (governess) 27, 49, 50, 51, 52, 79, 108, 132
Napoleon 2, 281
Nasser, Gamal Abdel 103, 146, 156, 157, 160, 161, 162, 163, 186, 188, 223, 224, 225, 226, 227
National Hockey League (NHL) 233, 276, 277
National Security Council 249
Nerheim, Agnar 250
Nesbit, Evelyn 30, 31
New Mexico 33

O

P

R

About the Author

Mr. Rand graduated with honors in Middle Eastern languages and history at the University of California, Berkeley, in 1959. In 1959–61 he pursued studies in Persian language, culture and literature at the Universities of Tehran, Mashhad and Shiraz, with extensive travel through Turkey, Iran and Afghanistan on grants from the Ford Foundation and government of Iran. In 1961–62 he pursued studies in modern and classical Arabic literature and colloquial Egyptian Arabic at the American University and Cairo University, Cairo, Egypt.

He went on to acquire a master's in Islamic Studies at UCLA (1964), with a grant from the National Defense Education Act. In 1965 he became assistant editor and assistant secretary for Petroleum Information Foundation, New York City. His duties involved preparing a twice-monthly petroleum newsletter, *Anba Al-Petrol* (*Oil News*), published in Arabic and English and distributed to opinion leaders throughout the Arab world. Under the auspices of this foundation, he attended graduate seminars in Political Economy of Near Eastern Petroleum and Near Eastern Economics at Harvard University.

In late 1966 he became a government relations analyst with Standard Oil Company of California (later Chevron), San Francisco, and was attached to the Executive Office Staff, the Foreign Advisory Staff and the Public Relations Department.

In 1969 he transferred to Occidental Petroleum Corporation, Bakersfield, California, and then Bechtel Corporation, San Francisco, where he became an administrative assistant. His various assignments were in the Pipeline and Production Service Division (primarily regarding Occidental Petroleum Corporation operations in Libya), the Scientific Development Department and the International Petroleum and Chemical Division.

Since leaving Bechtel in 1971 he has worked as a freelance writer and commentator, primarily on energy and Near Eastern subjects. In this period he published a book, *Making Democracy Safe for Oil* (Atlantic/Little, Brown, 1975), and numerous articles. He made a number of radio and television appearances, gave lectures and appeared on panels.

In the meantime he worked as a consultant for various government bodies:

1. State of California, Franchise Tax Board, 1976–77 and 1985–87, investigating major oil company tax practices, focused on the relationship between Chevron Oil Company and the government of Saudi Arabia, then the study of tax problems connected to Mobil and Texaco interests in the Iranian Consortium. Assignments included a book-length study of world oil price and tax developments in the 1970s.

2. US Federal Trade Commission, 1976–80, dealing with international aspects of the FTC's investigation of the major American international oil companies.
3. State of California et al., Multidistrict Litigation Case 150, 1978–79, investigating major oil company practices in the world oil market.
4. County of Suffolk, New York, et al., 1976–77; this included expert testimony in litigation against the US Department of the Interior and another book-length study investigating the political and economic implications of the federal government's offshore oil and gas lease sales.

In the interim, from 1971 to 1989, he worked as a translator from Arabic and Persian to English, primarily for the US Department of Commerce, consistently translating a high volume of materials, averaging one hundred thousand words a month for long periods, mostly laws and economic, political and social materials.